多感觉整合加工

特征、机制与应用

顾吉有 著

中国社会科学出版社

图书在版编目（CIP）数据

多感觉整合加工：特征、机制与应用 / 顾吉有著． —北京：
中国社会科学出版社，2023.8
ISBN 978 - 7 - 5227 - 2463 - 8

Ⅰ. ①多… Ⅱ. ①顾… Ⅲ. ①教育心理学 Ⅳ. ①G44

中国国家版本馆 CIP 数据核字（2023）第 165200 号

出 版 人	赵剑英
责任编辑	许　琳　姜雅雯
责任校对	季　静
责任印制	李寡寡

出　　版	中国社会科学出版社
社　　址	北京鼓楼西大街甲 158 号
邮　　编	100720
网　　址	http://www.csspw.cn
发 行 部	010 - 84083685
门 市 部	010 - 84029450
经　　销	新华书店及其他书店
印　　刷	北京明恒达印务有限公司
装　　订	廊坊市广阳区广增装订厂
版　　次	2023 年 8 月第 1 版
印　　次	2023 年 8 月第 1 次印刷
开　　本	710×1000　1/16
印　　张	13
插　　页	2
字　　数	168 千字
定　　价	68.00 元

凡购买中国社会科学出版社图书，如有质量问题请与本社营销中心联系调换
电话：010 - 84083683
版权所有　侵权必究

前　　言

我们生活在一个充满各种刺激的环境中，来自视觉、听觉、嗅觉、味觉和触觉等多种感觉通道的信息，每时每刻都在涌入我们的大脑等待被加工。通过整合这些纷繁复杂的信息，我们感受到一个丰富多彩的世界。事实上，整合这些来自不同通道的信息，是我们进行深度加工的基础。比如，学生在课堂学习中，不仅要看书、看黑板，还要听老师的讲解，通过同时加工这些听觉和视觉信息，学生才能更好地理解所学知识。因此，有必要系统梳理与多感觉整合有关的理论和实证研究。

本书在前期大量相关研究的基础之上，从研究机制、被试群体、发展特点、理论和实证等方面对多感觉整合加工进行介绍。在内容上，本书分为五章：第一章介绍多感觉整合的概念、相关特性、神经生理基础和测量方法；第二章简要介绍多感觉整合的发展特点；第三章介绍在特殊群体中开展的多感觉整合相关研究，比如听障和视障群体、自闭症群体和发展性阅读障碍群体的多感觉整合加工；第四章介绍注意与多感觉整合加工的关系；第五章介绍探索注意影响视听整合加工的实验研究，包括行为和事件相关电位实验。

希望本书能对多感觉整合加工相关领域的发展提供一定的理论和实证支持。

顾吉有

2023 年 5 月

目 录

绪 论 ……………………………………………………………（1）

第一章 多感觉整合概述 ……………………………………（2）
 第一节 多感觉整合的概念 ………………………………（2）
 第二节 多感觉整合的空间和时间特征 …………………（3）
 第三节 不同类型研究中的多感觉整合 …………………（8）
 第四节 多感觉整合的神经相关物与神经机制 …………（19）
 第五节 多感觉整合的量化方法 …………………………（25）
 第六节 情绪信息的多感觉整合加工 ……………………（30）

第二章 多感觉整合的发展 …………………………………（36）
 第一节 新生儿的多感觉整合加工 ………………………（36）
 第二节 视听言语知觉的发展 ……………………………（39）

第三章 特殊群体的多感觉整合加工 ………………………（48）
 第一节 听障与视障群体的多感觉整合加工 ……………（48）
 第二节 自闭症群体的多感觉整合 ………………………（53）
 第三节 发展性阅读障碍群体的多感觉整合 ……………（58）

第四章 注意与多感觉整合加工的关系 ……………………（60）

第一节 早期整合模型：多感觉整合不依赖于注意 ………（61）

第二节 晚期整合模型：多感觉整合的产生依赖于注意 …（63）

第三节 注意影响多感觉整合加工的机制 ………………（65）

第五章 注意影响视听整合加工的实验研究 ……………（72）

第一节 选择性注意和分配性注意对视听整合

　　　加工的影响 …………………………………………（72）

第二节 分配性注意条件下注意负荷对视听言语

　　　整合加工的影响 ……………………………………（94）

第三节 分配性注意条件下的注意起伏对视听言语

　　　整合加工的影响及其神经机制 ……………………（107）

第四节 注意与视听整合加工的总讨论 ……………………（155）

参考文献 ………………………………………………………（171）

绪　　论

多感觉整合是指来自不同感觉通道（视觉、听觉、触觉等）的信息同时同地呈现时，被个体有效地整合为统一、连贯的知觉信息的现象。通过合并来自不同感觉通道的信息，多感觉整合能够减少知觉系统的噪声，帮助个体更好地知觉信息，在行为上表现为对同时呈现的多通道信息的判断更快更准确。已有研究将这种对双通道信息的加工优势称为冗余信号效应。

已有研究多关注多感觉整合本身的特性和加工方式。本书首先回顾了已有研究中有关视觉—听觉、视觉—触觉、听觉—触觉等通道的整合加工特性，然后针对多感觉整合加工发展过程中的年龄特征进行总结和概括，并探讨了包括视障、听障、自闭症等特殊群体的多感觉整合加工特性。

近几年，研究者们逐渐将兴趣点转向注意与视听整合加工的关系。但是，已有研究大多针对注意与非注意条件对视听整合加工的影响是否存在差异进行探讨，而忽略了注意除可以指向空间和客体之外，还可以指向感觉通道的特性。因此，本书最后部分通过行为实验和事件相关电位技术考察了注意对多感觉整合加工的影响及其机制。

第 一 章

多感觉整合概述

第一节 多感觉整合的概念

我们生活在一个充斥着各种信息的世界，这些信息通过不同感觉通道涌入我们的脑中等待被加工。比如，当你坐在嘈杂的餐馆中看报纸，很有可能被邻桌的谈话所干扰，以至于不能很好地读懂报纸的内容。这表明，听觉信息（邻桌的谈话）能影响视觉信息（报纸的内容）的加工。又如，有字幕的电视剧会比没有字幕的电视剧让你感觉听到的台词更清晰，即视觉信息（字幕）会影响听觉信息（台词）的加工。现实生活中，这种不同感觉通道的信息之间相互作用的例子比比皆是。心理学领域将这种现象称为多感觉整合（Multisensory Integration），它是指来自不同感觉通道（视觉、听觉、触觉等）的信息同时同地呈现时，被个体有效地整合为统一、连贯的知觉信息的现象。①② 通过合并来自不同感觉通道的信息以减少知觉系统的噪声，多感觉整合帮助我们更好地知觉信息，在行为上

---

① Spence C., Audiovisual Multisensory Integration, *Acoustical Science and Technology*, Vol. 28, No. 2, March 2007, pp. 61-70.

② 刘强：《多感觉整合的脑机制研究》，博士学位论文，西南大学，2010年，第1页。

表现为对同时呈现的多感觉通道信息的判断更快更准确[1][2]。

第二节　多感觉整合的空间和时间特征

一旦多通道刺激在感觉水平被编码，它们便可以被我们用来理解和知觉外部环境。由于感觉信息有时是互补的[3][4]，因此，对于个体而言，合并感觉信息便成为一种比较明智的策略。在一些情况下，尤其是当一个感觉通道的信息比较模糊时，其互补的成分能够提高对模糊性信息的注意控制[5]，甚至在整体上改变知觉。尽管我们的知觉系统看似轻松地将来自不同感觉通道的信息进行捆绑，并形成新的知觉[6]，但是，一些研究仍然发现多感觉整合的产生需要满足时间和空间上的要求[7][8]。

---

[1] 孙远路、胡中华、张瑞玲、寻茫茫、刘强、张庆林：《多感觉整合测量范式中存在的影响因素探讨》，《心理学报》2011 年第 11 期。

[2] Koelewijn T., Bronkhorst A. & Theeuwes J., Attention and the Multiple Stages of Multisensory Integration: A Review of Audiovisual Studies, *Acta Psychologica*, Vol. 134, No. 3, July 2010, pp. 372 - 384.

[3] Ernst M. O. & Bülthoff H. H., Merging the Senses into a Robust Percept, *Trends in Cognitive Sciences*, Vol. 8, No. 4, April 2004, pp. 162 - 169.

[4] Burr D. & Alais D., Combining Visual and Auditory Information, *Progress in Brain Research*, Vol. 155, 2006, pp. 243 - 258.

[5] Raymond V. E., Boxtel J. J. A. V., Parker A. L. & David A., Multisensory Congruency as a Mechanism for Attentional Control over Perceptual Selection, *Journal of Neuroscience the Official Journal of the Society for euroscience*, Vol. 29, No. 37, September 2009, pp. 11641 - 11649.

[6] Ernst M. O. & Bülthoff H. H., Merging the Senses into a Robust Percept, *Trends in Cognitive Sciences*, Vol. 8, No. 4, April 2004, pp. 162 - 169.

[7] Bolognini N., Frassinetti F., Serino A. & Ladavas E., "Acoustical Vision" of Below Threshold Stimuli: Interaction among Spatially Converging Audiovisual Inputs, *Experimental Brain Research*, Vol. 160, No. 3, January 2005, pp. 273 - 282.

[8] Frassinetti F., Bolognini N. & Ladavas E., Enhancement of Visual Perception by Crossmodal Visuo-auditory Interaction, *Experimental Brain Research*, Vol. 147, No. 3, December 2002, pp. 332 - 343.

一 多感觉整合的空间特征

知觉系统处理多通道空间冲突的一个最容易理解的例子就是腹语术效应（Ventriloquism Effect）。在此效应中，视觉和听觉刺激在时间上是同步的。[1] 在最适度的距离内放置视觉刺激将会导致听觉刺激被视觉刺激"捕获"（听觉刺激被知觉成与视觉刺激在同一位置上）。即使视觉刺激和听觉刺激的位置差异足够大，以至于不能产生完全的空间注意捕获，仍有研究发现被试将听觉刺激的位置定位于视觉刺激的方向[2][3][4]。

在空间位置上产生的多通道交互作用是自动化的。比如，向被试呈现一个同时呈现但在空间位置上分离的双通道刺激，被试的任务是定位双通道刺激中的听觉成分，此时被试的判断倾向于将听觉刺激定位于视觉刺激的位置[5]。其他采用不同技术的研究也发现了腹语术效应的自动化。[6][7] 事实上，这种空间判断上的偏差并不仅

---

[1] Slutsky D. A. & Recanzone G. H., Temporal and Spatial Dependency of the Ventriloquism Effect, *Neuroreport*, Vol. 12, No. 1, January 2001, pp. 7–10.

[2] Welch R. B. & Warren D. H., Immediate Perceptual Response to Intersensory Discrepancy, *Psychological Bulletin*, Vol. 88, No. 3, November 1980, pp. 638–667.

[3] Bertelson P. & Aschersleben G., Automatic Visual Bias of Perceived Auditory Location, *Psychonomic Bulletin & Review*, Vol. 5, No. 3, September 1998, pp. 482–489.

[4] Battaglia P. W., Jacobs R. A. & Aslin R. N., Bayesian Integration of Visual and Auditory Signals for Spatial Localization, *Journal of the Optical Society of America A Optics Image Science & Vision*, Vol. 20, No. 7, August 2003, pp. 1391–1397.

[5] Bertelson P. & Radeau M., Cross-modal Bias and Perceptual Fusion with Auditory-visual Spatial Discordance, *Percept. Psychophys*, Vol. 29, No. 6, January 1981, pp. 578–584.

[6] Bertelson P. & Aschersleben G., Automatic Visual Bias of Perceived Auditory Location, *Psychonomic Bulletin & Review* Vol. 5, No. 3, September 1998, pp. 482–489.

[7] Vroomen J., Bertelson P. & de Gelder B., Directing Spatial Attention towards the Illusory Location of a Ventriloquized Sound, *ActaPsychologica*, Vol. 108, No. 1, June 2001, pp. 21–33.

仅适用于视觉和听觉，还发生在视觉—触觉[①②③]、听觉—触觉的交互作用上[④]。

另有研究采用呈现在视野中央的接近阈限的刺激作为材料，考察了刺激呈现位置对多感觉整合是否存在影响，结果发现，听觉线索的位置并不总是与视听刺激的整合有关。[⑤⑥] Stein、London、Wilkinson 和 Price[⑦] 考察了听觉刺激对被试知觉到视觉刺激的敏感性的影响。他们的研究发现，听觉刺激能增强视觉敏感性，当视觉刺激和听觉刺激呈现在外周位置时，空间接近性对多感觉整合的产生是至关重要的。也就是说，听觉刺激对视觉探测敏感性的增强作用只发生在当视听刺激呈现在外周位置，并且二者呈现在同一位置时。而当视听刺激呈现在视野中央区域时，这种增强作用并不受视听刺激的空间接近性的影响。这个结果表明，视听整合产生的空间限制只对呈现在外周位置的刺激有效，而对呈现在中央位置的刺激无效。这个观点引起了 Odegaard、Arieh 和 Marks 的质疑。他们认为，

---

① Anne C., Salvador S. F., Alan K. & Charles S., Tactile "Capture" of Audition, *Perception & Psychophysics*, Vol. 64, No. 4, May 2002, pp. 616 – 630.

② Jean – Pierre B., Franziska D. & Ernst M. O., Vision and Touch are Automatically Integrated for the Perception of Sequences of Events, *Journal of Vision*, Vol. 6, No. 5, April 2006, pp. 554 – 564.

③ Pavani F., Spence C. & Driver J., Visual Capture of Touch: Out-of-the-body Experiences with Rubber Gloves, *Psychological Science*, Vol. 11, No. 5, September 2000, pp. 353 – 359.

④ Steve G., Caroline C., Donna L. & Charles S., Audiotactile Interactions in Roughness Perception, *Experimental Brain Research*, Vol. 146, No. 2, September 2002, pp. 161 – 171.

⑤ Lippert M., Logothetis N. K. & Kayser C., Improvement of Visual Contrast Detection by a Simultaneous Sound, *Brain Research*, No. 1173, October 2007, pp. 102 – 109.

⑥ Noesselt T., Bergmann D., Hake M., Heinze H. J. & Fendrich R., Sound Increases the Saliency of Visual Events, *Brain Research*, No. 1220, July 2008, pp. 157 – 163.

⑦ Stein B. E., London N., Wilkinson L. K. & Price D. D., Enhancement of Perceived Visual Intensity by Auditory Stimuli: A psychophysical Analysis, *Journal of Cognitive Neuroscience*, No. 8, November 1996, pp. 497 – 506.

Stein 等人的研究是基于反应偏差而非多感觉整合。① 尽管如此，仍有研究者支持 Stein 等人关于多感觉整合的空间限制具有必然性的观点。②

二　多感觉整合的时间特性

多感觉整合除了具有空间特性，还有一定的时间特性。比如，Frassinetti 等人③考察了声音对探测视觉明度敏感性的影响。结果发现，声音的确可以增强对视觉明度的探测敏感性，但这种增强作用仅发生在当实验中的视觉和听觉刺激在时间和空间上一致时，也就是说，视觉和听觉刺激必须同时同地呈现才会产生这种对明度探测敏感性的增强作用。Meredith、Nemitz 和 Stein 发现，当视觉刺激和听觉刺激开始呈现的时间差在 100ms 之内时才会产生强烈的多感觉整合效应。④ 同时，他们在实验中观察了猫的上丘细胞，发现当视觉和听觉刺激之间的时间窗口大于 100ms 时，多感觉整合效应有明显的减弱，而当两种刺激之间的时间分离逐渐增大时，可能会导致上丘细胞的抑制化（become inhibited），因而无法产生整合效应。另有研究者采用功能性磁共振技术（functional Magnetic Resonance

---

① Odegaard E. C., Arieh Y. & Marks L., Cross – modal Enhancemnt of Perceived Brightness: Sensory Interaction Versus Response Bias, *Perception & Psychophysics*, Vol. 65, No. 1, February 2003, pp. 123 – 132.

② Lippert M., Logothetis N. K. & Kayser C., Improvement of Visual Contrast Detection by a Simultaneous Sound, *Brain Research*, No. 1173, October 2007, pp. 102 – 109.

③ Frassinetti F., Bolognini N. & Ladavas E., Enhancement of Visual Perception by Crossmodal Visuo – auditory Interaction, *Experimental Brain Research*, Vol. 147, No. 3, December 2002, pp. 332 – 343.

④ Meredith M. A., Nemitz J. W. & Stein B. E., Determinants of Multisensory Integration in Superior Colliculus Neurons. I. Temporal Factors, *The Journal of neuroscience*, Vol. 7, No. 10, 1987, pp. 3215 – 3229.

Imaging，fMRI）对视听言语知觉进行了考察。[1] 在实验中，他们通过不同方式呈现某个故事。视觉呈现方式为向被试展示读这个故事的嘴唇动作，听觉呈现方式是让被试听这个故事，视听呈现方式为视觉和听觉故事都呈现。视听呈现方式分为两种条件，一是视觉故事和听觉故事为同一内容，二是视听故事涉及不同内容，从而达到时间上不同步的效果。实验发现，与单通道呈现刺激的方式（视觉呈现方式和听觉呈现方式）相比，视听呈现方式中被试的颞上沟（Superior Temporal Sulcus，STS）后部有明显的激活，并且伴有视觉枕叶区和听觉皮层的激活，但是，这种激活仅限于故事同时呈现且为同一内容（视听信号同步）的情况下。

上述研究表明，多感觉整合的产生有明显的时间特性，即视听刺激必须同步呈现才会产生多感觉整合。但是，有研究者提出了不同观点：对于视听刺激的整合来说，视觉和听觉刺激并不需要同步呈现，只要二者开始的时间差异在一个特定的时间范围之内，也有可能使被试感知为同时呈现，从而产生视听刺激的整合。[2] 这个时间窗口的大小取决于研究所采用的实验范式和刺激材料，通常为150—450ms之间。

总之，上述研究显示，视觉和听觉刺激之间的时间接近性对于中央视野产生多感觉整合是必要条件，而视觉和听觉刺激之间的空间接近性对于在外周视野产生多感觉整合是必要条件。

---

[1] Calvert G. A., Campbell R. & Brammer M. J., Evidence from Functional Magnetic Resonance Imaging of Crossmodal Binding in the Human Heteromodalcortex, *Current Biology*, Vol. 10, No. 11, June 2000, pp. 649–657.

[2] Conrey B. & Pisoni D. B., Auditory-visual Speech Perception and Synchrony Detection for Speech and Nonspeech Signals, *Journal of Acoustical Society of America*, Vol. 119, No. 6, June 2006, pp. 4065–4073.

第三节 不同类型研究中的多感觉整合

一 动物的解剖学和生理学研究

一直以来,一些研究者认为,感觉系统和相关的神经机制是相互独立的,也就是说,他们认为,一个感觉通道内的信息加工发生在通道特异性的神经结构或区域内,在这些结构或区域内信息会被传递至更高阶的加工区域,来自不同感觉通道的信息就发生在这些更高阶的加工区域中。这些加工区域(联合或多通道区域,association or multimodal areas)包含一些重要结构,比如顶叶(parietal cortex)、颞上沟以及前额皮层(prefrontal cortex)。一些研究发现,这些区域在多感觉整合中起重要作用。[1][2][3] 但也有一些研究者认为,一些在传统意义上被认为是"通道特异性"(modality-specific)的区域也涉及多感觉整合。[4]

多感觉整合在早期研究中最为代表性的一个实验来自猫的上丘(superior colliculus)研究[5]。上丘的功能是使用视觉、听觉,以及体感信息来激活和控制与注意或者朝向有关的行为。[6] 在不同的神

---

[1] Barraclough N. E., Xiao D. K., Baker C. I., Oram M. W. & Perrett D. I., Integration of Visual and Auditory Information by Superior Temporal Sulcus Neurons Responsive to the Sight of Actions, *Journal of Cognitive Neuroscience*, Vol. 17, No. 3, March 2005, pp. 377 – 391.

[2] Bernstein L. E., Auer E. T., Wagner M. & Ponton C. W., Spatiotemporal Dynamics of Audiovisual Speech Processing, *Neuroimage*, Vol. 39, No. 1, January 2008, pp. 423 – 435.

[3] Calvert G. A., Hansen P. C., Iversen S. D. & Brammer M. J., Detection of Audio-visual Integration Sites in Humans by Application of Electrophysiological Criteria to the BOLD Effect, *Neuroimage*, Vol. 14, No. 2, August 2001, pp. 427 – 438.

[4] Driver J. & Noesselt T., Multisensory Interplay Reveals Crossmodal Influences on "Sensory-Specific" Brain Regions, *Neuron*, Vol. 57, No. 1, January 2008, pp. 11 – 20.

[5] Stein B. E. & Meredith M. A., *The Merging of Thesenses*, Cambridge: MIT Press. 1993.

[6] Ortega R. & López V., *Crossmodal Attention-The Contribution of Event-Related-Potential Studies*, Springer Berlin Heidelberg. January 2009.

经层级中，一些上丘神经元只对来自一个感觉通道的信息反应，其他神经元接收来自两个感觉通道的信息，还有一些神经元接收三个感觉通道的信息，并在每个感觉通道都有一个接收区域。随后一些关于人类和非人类灵长类动物的研究表明，一个通道内的刺激能激活那些被认为是相对于其他通道来说具体或独有的感觉皮层的活性。[1][2] 比如，Schroeder 等人以恒河猴作为被试，采用密度测量（densenty measurement）和多导记录（multiunit recordings）的方式发现，同时呈现的听觉和体感刺激在初级听觉皮层（A1）后的听觉联合皮层中产生汇聚性反应（convergent response）。[3] 并且人类的神经成像研究也发现了类似的结果。[4] 最近，有研究发现，这种由体感刺激引发的汇聚性活性也能影响 A1 区域，产生 10Hz 左右的慢波震荡（slow-wave oscillation）。[5] 同样地，Kayser、Petkov 和 Logothetis 以猴子作为被试发现，视觉刺激能调节听觉皮层的神经活性。[6] 他们采用了两种类型的刺激：自然的刺激（在自然环境中动物的感觉）和人为的刺激（以噪声和闪光作为刺激），以及以单通道形式呈现的相同刺激，即噪声和闪光。实验结果发现，在视听条件（采

---

[1] Ghazanfar A. A. & Schroeder C. E., Is Neocortex Essentially Multisensory, *Trends in Cognitive Sciences*, Vol. 10, No. 6, June 2006, pp. 278–285.

[2] Kayser C. & Logothetis N. K., Do Early Sensory Cortices Integrate Cross–modal Information, *Brain Struct Funct*, September 2007, No. 212, pp. 121–132.

[3] Schroeder C. E., Lindsle R. W., Specht C., Marcovici A., Smiley J. F. & Javitt D. C., Somatosensory Input to Auditory Association Cortex in the Macaque Monkey, *Journal of Neurophysiology*, Vol. 85, No. 3, March 2001, pp. 1322–1327.

[4] Foxe J. J., Morocz I. A., Murray M. M., Higgins B. A., Javitt D. C. & Schroeder C. E., Multisensory Auditory-somatosensory Interactions in Early Cortical Processing Revealed by High-density Electrical Mapping, *Cognitive Brain Research*, Vol. 10, No. 1, September 2000, pp. 77–83.

[5] Lakatos P., Chen C. M., O'Connell M. N., Mills A. & Schroeder C. E., Neuronal Oscillations and Multisensory Interaction in Primary Auditory Cortex, *Neuron*, Vol. 53, No. 2, January 2007, pp. 279–292.

[6] Kayser C. Petkov C. I. & Logothetis N. K., Visual Modulation of Neurons in Auditory Cortex, *Cereb Cortex*, Vol. 18, No. 7, July 2008, pp. 1560–1574.

用自然的刺激和人为的刺激条件）下，初级和次级听觉皮层的激活增强，这种增强效应与单通道听觉刺激和单通道视觉刺激引发的激活效应不同。他们因此得出结论，信息从早期听觉皮层向更高级的加工阶段传递不仅反映了唤起的环境，还依赖于一个声音是否处于多通道环境之中。

Stanford 和 Stein 以及 Kayser 和 Logothetis 提出了产生与多通道相关的神经活性的三个原则：空间一致性、时间一致性，以及相反有效性（inverse effectiveness）。[1][2] 空间一致性，是指多通道神经元的接收区域重叠，并且只有那些呈现在重叠区域的刺激才会产生神经反应的增强。时间一致性，是指在时间上接近的刺激才会产生增强的神经反应。相反有效性，是指多感觉整合是由单通道刺激的神经反应的强度所调节的。当单通道刺激比较强烈时（有效地获得了关于环境的相关信息），多通道交互作用很少发生；反过来，当对单通道刺激的反应比较微弱时，如果第二个刺激遵从前面提到的两个原则之一，那么产生多通道交互作用的概率就会增大。这三个原则可以解释"超加性效应"（super-additiveeffect），即与单通道刺激相比，对多通道刺激的神经反应增强的现象。

多感觉整合的另外一个重要因素是允许这种整合产生的生理上的联结。在最近几年中，一些研究发现了属于不同感觉皮层的区域之间直接的皮层连接。比如，Falchier、Clavagnier、Barone 和 Kennedy 以猴子作为被试，发现了从初级和次级听觉皮层到初级视觉皮层之间的单向连接。[3] 在另外一项研究中，Rockland 和 Ojima 以恒

---

[1] Stanford T. R. & Stein B. E., Superadditivity in Multisensory Integration: Putting the Computation in Context, *Neuroreport*, Vol. 18, No. 8, May 2007, pp. 787–792.

[2] Kayser C. & Logothetis N. K., Do Early Sensory Cortices Integrate Cross-modal Information, *Brain Struct Funct*, September 2007, No. 212, pp. 121–132.

[3] Falchier A., Clavagnier S., Barone P. & Kennedy H., Anatomical Evidence of Multimodal Integration in Primate Striate Cortex, *Journal of Neuroscience*, Vol. 22, No. 13, July 2002, pp. 5749–5759.

河猴作为被试,发现了在听觉皮层和次级视皮层(V2)之间直接的连接,同时,预测这种连接可能能够延伸至初级视皮层(V1)。① 此外,他们还以绒猴为被试,发现了在单通道感觉皮层之间存在三种类型的连接:从视觉区域向体感皮层(1/3b 区域)的投射、从体感皮层(S2)向听觉皮层的外侧沟前部(anterior bank of the lateral sulcus)的投射,以及从视觉区域颞上沟之前的部分(anterior to superior temporal sulcus)向初级听觉皮层的投射。最近有研究用雪貂作为被试,发现了视觉和听觉皮层之间的连接,其中一部分连接了初级听皮层和初级视皮层,而大部分连接了上视觉区域和听觉皮层。②

在啮齿类动物研究中,Budinger、Heil、Hess 和 Scheich 发现了初级听皮层和体感、嗅觉皮层之间的连接,以及其他一些能够到达次级视觉皮层的部分。③ 他们还发现了大部分在丘脑的多通道区域中听觉皮层的传入连接,表明在到达皮层之前可能就有多感觉整合产生。其他一些研究在恒河猴中也发现了这种向听觉皮层的传入投射,其中听觉联合皮层似乎能接收更多来自丘脑核心而非初级听皮层的投射。④

---

① Rockland K. S. & Ojima H. , Multisensory Convergence in Calcarine Visual Areas in Macaque Monkey, *International Journal of Psychophysiology*, Vol. 50, No. 1, October 2003, pp. 19–26.

② Bizley J. K. , Nodal F. R. , Bajo V. M. , Nelken I. & King A. J. , Physiological and Anatomical Evidence for Multisensory Interactions in Auditory Cortex, *Cerebral Cortex*, Vol. 17, No. 9, September 2007, pp. 2172–2189.

③ Budinger E. , Heil P. , Hess A. & Scheich H. , Multisensory Processing Via Early Cortical Stages: Connections of the Primary Auditory Cortical Field with other Sensory Systems, *Neuroscience*, Vol. 143, No. 4, December 2006, pp. 1065–1083.

④ Teder-Salejarvi W. A. , McDonald J. J. , Di Russo F. & Hillyard S. A. , An Analysis of Audio-visual Crossmodal Integration by Means of Event-related Potential (ERP) Recordings, *Cognitive Brain Research*, Vol. 14, No. 1, June 2002, pp. 106–114.

二 人类行为研究

大量人类行为研究也考察了多感觉整合的效应,这些研究均发现知觉一个感觉通道内的刺激会影响知觉其他感觉通道内的刺激。当两个通道的刺激在相同的空间位置以及相同的时间点呈现时,其中一个通道内的刺激能促进个体对不同通道内其他刺激的知觉,表现为反应时更短,任务中的正确率更高,或者二者均出现。[1][2][3][4]一些研究者提出了不同的模型尝试解释这类现象,其中竞争模型(race model)认为,反应时降低是由于反应是被探测到的线索所激活的[5];共激活模型认为,单通道线索产生单独的激活,这些单独的激活合并成为双通道反应;交互式共激活模型认为,由双通道刺激产生的激活大于以单独的方式呈现的两个刺激所产生的激活之和[6]。因此,一个通道内的刺激加工会影响另一个不同通道内的刺激的加工。

另有一系列研究关注不同感觉通道之间的冲突信息的加工,这

---

[1] McDonald J. J., Teder-Sälejärvi W. A. & Hillyard S. A., Involuntary Orienting to Sound Improves Visual Perception, *Nature*, Vol. 407, No. 6806, October 2000, pp. 906 – 908.

[2] Teder-Salejarvi W. A., McDonald J. J., Di Russo F. & Hillyard S. A., An Analysis of Audio-visual Crossmodal Integration by Means of Event – related Potential (ERP) Recordings, *Cognitive Brain Research*, Vol. 14, No. 1, June 2002, pp. 106 – 114.

[3] Vroomen J. & de Gelder B., Sound Enhances Visual Perception: Cross – modal Effects of Auditory Organization on Vision, *Journal of Experimental Psychology: Human Perception and Performance*, Vol. 26, No. 5, October 2000, pp. 1583 – 1590.

[4] Zampini M., Guest S., Shore D. I. & Spence C., Audio-visual Simultaneity Judgments, *Perception & Psychophysics*, Vol. 67, No. 3, April 2005, pp. 531 – 544.

[5] Raab D. H., Statistical Facilitation of Simple Reaction Times, *Transactions of the New York Academy of Sciences*, Vol. 24, March 1962, pp. 574 – 590.

[6] Miller J., Divided Attention: Evidence for Coactivation with Redundant Signals, *Cognitive psychology*, Vol. 14, No. 2, April 1982, pp. 247 – 279.

种信息加工发生在当两个感觉通道接收一个单独事件的不一致信息时。① 在这种背景下，会产生一些幻觉效应。

第一个 McGurk 效应是一种视觉影响言语知觉的现象。② 比如，被试听到的是"ba"，同时向其展示一个面孔在发"ga"的音，被试通常会报告听到了"da"。早期研究者多关注 McGurk 效应本身的加工特性。最近，有研究者利用这种效应来考察那些在获得言语能力之后失聪的聋哑人群多感觉整合的恢复能力。这项研究结果显示，在这种获得言语能力之后失聪的聋哑人群的多感觉整合效应与正常被试没有显著差异，但聋哑人群对于通过视觉呈现的图片的知觉更明显，可能是由于他们在失去听觉之后读唇的能力增强导致的。③

第二个经典幻觉效应是被我们熟知的"腹语术效应"，即在不同空间位置上同时呈现的视觉和听觉刺激倾向于被知觉成来自同一处。比如，在 2014 年央视春晚的节目《空空拜年》中，腹语表演艺术家在操纵玩偶的同时，通过改变发音方式，在嘴唇闭合的情况下发声，造成玩偶"说话"的假象。在实验室条件下，一些研究者通过在不同位置上同时呈现一系列闪光和短音来诱发此效应。被试的任务是忽略闪光，同时要报告声音的位置，但他们倾向于在闪光出现的位置来定位声音。④ 当闪光和声音呈现在相同或不同的空间位置，但是，在时间上分离时，相似的效应也会发生。如果刺激在空

---

① De Gelder B. & Bertelson P., Multisensory Integration, Perception and Ecological Validity, *Trends in Cognitive Science*, Vol. 7, No. 10, October 2003, pp. 460 – 467.

② McGurk H. & MacDonald J., Hearing Lips and Seeing Voices, *Nature*, Vol. 264, No. 5588, December 1976, pp. 746 – 748.

③ Rouger J., Fraysse B., Deguine O. & Barone P., McGurk Effects in Cochlear-implanted Deaf Subjects, *Brain Research*, No. 1188, January 2008, pp. 87 – 99.

④ Spence C. & Driver J., Crossmodal Space and Crossmodal Attention, Oxford, New York, USA: Oxford University Press, 2004.

间位置上吻合,那么被试倾向于报告刺激之间的间隔较短,这种效应被命名为"时间腹语术效应"(temporal ventriloquism effect)[1][2]。另有研究发现,当与听觉刺激同时呈现的视觉刺激以相反的方向运动时,被试不能判断听觉刺激运动的方向。[3]

第三个归因于多通道整合加工的效应是"Colavita 视觉主导效应"(Colavita visual dominance effect)[4]。实验中向被试呈现听觉、视觉和视听刺激。当要求被试对视听刺激的听觉成分反应时,被试的正确率更低,尤其是在视听刺激之前呈现一个视觉刺激时。产生这个结果的可能原因是,一个刺激的视觉特征可能会比其听觉特征更多地吸引被试的注意。[5]

除上述幻觉效应以外,多感觉整合还会造成其他幻觉效应。比如,Shams 等人发现,当一个单独的闪光伴随多个短音同时出现时,被试容易将这个单独的闪光判断为多个闪光。[6] 这个研究表明,视觉刺激能影响个体对听觉信息的加工。然而,另有研究发现,听觉刺激也能促进个体对视觉信息的加工[7],表现为促进对视觉目标的探

---

[1] Aschersleben G. & Bertelson P., Temporal Ventriloquism: Crossmodal Interaction on the Time Dimension, Evidence from Sensorimotor Synchronization, *International Journal of Psychophysiology*, Vol. 50, No. 1, October 2003, pp. 157–163.

[2] Bertelson P. & Aschersleben G., Automatic Visual Bias of Perceived Auditory Location, *Psychonomic Bulletin & Review*, Vol. 5, No. 3, September 1998, pp. 482–489.

[3] Soto-Faraco S., Lyons J., Gazzaniga M., Spence C. & Kingstone A., The Ventriloquist in Motion: Illusory Capture of Dynamic Information Across Sensory Modalities, *Brain Research. Cognitive Brain Research*, Vol. 14, No. 1, June 2002, pp. 139–146.

[4] Colavita F. B. & Weisberg D., A Further Investigation of Visual Dominance, *Percept Psychophys*, Vol. 25, No. 4, April 1979, pp. 345–347.

[5] Koppen C. & Spence C., Audiovisual Asynchrony Modulates the Colavita Visual Dominance Effect, *Brain Research*, No. 1186, December 2007, pp. 224–232.

[6] Shams L., Kamitani Y. & Shimojo S., What You See is What You Hear, *Nature*, Vol. 408, No. 6814, December 2000, p. 788.

[7] Frassinetti F., Bolognini N. & Ladavas E., Enhancement of Visual Perception by Crossmodal Visuo-auditory Interaction, *Experimental Brain Research*, Vol. 147, No. 3, December 2002, pp. 332–343.

测,并且这种对视觉探测和显著性上的促进作用能够影响时间搜索[1]。比如,在 Vroomen 和 de Gelder 的研究中,被试需要在一系列快速呈现的干扰刺激中探测视觉目标。[2] 在一个实验条件中,低音仅与视觉目标的开始同时呈现;在另一个实验条件中,高音一直与视觉目标同时呈现。结果发现,在后一个实验条件中,被试对视觉探测的成绩更好。由于在实验中被试报告目标在屏幕上停留的时间长于干扰刺激停留的时间,就像目标刺激被冻住一样,因此 Vroomen 和 de Gelder 将这种效应命名为"Freezing 效应"。

Van der Burg、Olivers、Bronkhorst 和 Theeuwes 在实验中向被试呈现不同方向的线段,同时需要被试在其中搜索水平和垂直的目标线段。[3] 这些线段的颜色在红色和绿色之间随机变换。当一个短音与目标线段的颜色变换同时呈现时,被试对目标线段的搜索时间明显减少。Van der Burg 等人将这种现象叫作"凸显效应"(pip and pop effect)。这种凸显效应表明,多感觉整合能提高目标的显著性,并在其后的阶段促进其捕获注意。

在大部分我们所熟知的跨通道效应中都发现视觉影响其他感觉通道的信息加工,这符合"视觉线索对于人类来说比其他感觉通道的线索更为重要"[4] 的论断。即便如此,仍有一些研究发现听觉刺

---

[1] Vroomen J. & de Gelder B., Sound Enhances Visual Perception: Cross-modal Effects of Auditory Organization on Vision, *Journal of Experimental Psychology: Human Perception and Performance*, Vol. 26, No. 5, October 2000, pp. 1583–1590.

[2] Vroomen J. & de Gelder B., Sound Enhances Visual Perception: Cross-modal Effects of Auditory Organization on Vision, *Journal of Experimental Psychology: Human Perception and Performance*, Vol. 26, No. 5, October 2000, pp. 1583–1590.

[3] Van der Burg E., Olivers C. N., Bronkhorst A. W. & Theeuwes J., Audiovisual Events Capture Attention: Evidence from Temporal Order Judgments, *Journal of Vision*, Vol. 8, No. 5, May 2008, p. 2.

[4] Eimer M., Facilitatory and Inhibitory Effects Ofmasked Prime Stimuli on Motor Activation and Behavioral Performance, *Acta Psychologica*, Vol. 101, April 1999, p. 294.

激能调节视知觉的某些方面。比如,当一个闪光伴随着一系列短音呈现时,被试倾向于将其知觉成多重闪光。①② 其他一些研究发现,听觉和触觉刺激能影响被试解释视觉刺激的含义;③④⑤ 还有一些研究致力于考察听觉对触觉的影响。比如,当被试触摸一个具有一定结构的表面,同时呈现一个短音,这个短音的不同频率能够提供关于表面结构的信息。在 Guest、Catmur、Lloyd 和 Spence 的实验中,被试的任务是判断不同表面的粗糙程度。结果发现,被试对不同表面粗糙程度的判断受到不同声音频率的影响,即高频率的衰减导致被试将表面感知得更为柔软。⑥

随着相关领域的技术发展,多感觉整合的实验研究开始向视听整合之外的其他通道的研究发展。一些最近的研究开始考察嗅觉和味觉领域的感觉整合。事实上,这种嗅觉、味觉领域的感觉整合加工可能更具实践意义,比如,生活中我们常常需要品尝食物或者饮料,这样,嗅觉、味觉和一些体感线索对于形成单一的知觉来说是尤为重要的⑦。White 和 Prescott 采用 Stroop 效应的变式进行了一项

---

① Shams L., Kamitani Y. & Shimojo S., What You See is What You Hear, *Nature*, Vol. 408, No. 6814, December 2000, p. 788.

② Shams L., Kamitani Y., Thompson S. & Shimojo S., Sound Alters Visual Evoked Potentials in Humans, *Neuroreport*, Vol. 12, No. 17, December 2001, pp. 3849 – 3852.

③ Sekuler, R., Sekuler, A. B., & Lau, R. Sound alters visual motion perception. *Nature*, Vol. 385, No. 6614, January 1997, p. 308.

④ Watanabe K. & Shimojo S., Attentional Modulation in Perception of Visual Motion Events, *Perception*, Vol. 27, No. 9, 1998, pp. 1041 – 1054.

⑤ Watanabe K. & Shimojo S., When Sound Affects Vision: Effects of Auditory Grouping on Visual Motion Perception, *Psychological Science*, Vol. 12, No. 2, March 2001, pp. 109 – 116.

⑥ Guest S., Catmur C., Lloyd D. & Spence C., Audiotactile Interactions in Roughness Perception, *Experimental Brain Research*, Vol. 146, No. 2, September 2002, pp. 161 – 171.

⑦ Small D. M. & Prescott J., Odor/taste Integration and the Perception of Flavor, *Experimental Brain Research*, Vol. 166, No. 3, October 2005, pp. 345 – 357.

实验。① 实验中，被试需要判断是甜味还是苦味，同时向被试呈现能够和知觉的味道一致或者不一致的香味物质。结果发现，当香味与味觉相匹配时，被试在任务中的反应时更短。

味觉线索也能调节个体对于面孔吸引力的判断。Dematte、Osterbauer 和 Spence 在他们的实验中要求女性被试判断一些男性面孔的吸引力，同时向她们呈现令人愉悦和令人厌恶的味道。② 结果发现，当面孔与令人厌恶的味道同时呈现时，被试倾向于将面孔判断为更让人厌恶，且更不具有吸引力。其他一些研究还发现面孔的味道信息与字词加工之间的相关性。③

三 事件相关电位研究

由于事件相关电位（event-related potential，ERP）技术具有良好的时间分辨率，近年来，相关领域研究者开始采用此技术来考察多感觉整合的加工进程。在一项关于物体识别的视听整合研究中，Giard 和 Peronnet 采用了一项在动物模型中使用过的技术来提取只与多感觉整合有关的神经活性。④ 方法如下：从由双通道刺激诱发的神经反应（AV）中减去由单通道刺激诱发的神经反应之和（A + V），即 AV − (A + V)，其中，A 代表听觉刺激，V 代表视觉刺激，AV 代表视听刺激。通过这种方法，他们描述了由多通道信息交互作用所引发的 ERP 成分。其中，有一个非常早

---

① White T. L. & Prescott J., Chemosensory Cross-modal Stroop Effects: Congruent Odors Facilitate Taste Identification, *Chemical Senses*, Vol. 32, No. 4, May 2007, pp. 337 – 341.
② Dematte M. L., Osterbauer R. & Spence C., Olfactory Cues Modulate Facial Attractiveness, *Chemical Senses*, Vol. 32, No. 6, July 2007, pp. 603 – 610.
③ Walla P., Olfaction and Its Dynamic Influence on Word and Face Processing: Cross-modal Integration, *Progress in Neurobiology*, Vol. 84, No. 2, February 2008, pp. 192 – 209.
④ Giard M. H. & Peronnet F., Auditory – visual Integration during Multimodal Object Recognition in Humans: A Behavioral and Electrophysiological Study, *Journal of Cognitive Neuroscience*, Vol. 11, No. 5, September 1999, pp. 473 – 490.

的与跨通道交互作用相关的成分出现在刺激呈现之后 40ms。但是，有研究者对此结论提出质疑。[①] 他们认为，这种早期效应是人为因素产生的，比如减法技术或者刺激之前的那些与期待有关的慢波，均有可能是产生早期跨通道交互作用成分的原因。然而，Giard 和 Peronnet 的研究结果被同样对其提出批评的一些研究者的实验所证实[②]，并且在采用不同视听刺激的研究中也被证实[③]。

Talsma 和 Woldorff 考察了在注意和非注意条件下的视听整合加工。实验中，单通道视觉刺激由简单图形组成，单通道听觉刺激由纯音组成。[④] 实验中的刺激分为偏差刺激和标准刺激。偏差刺激与标准刺激相似，只是在强度上有所减弱。比如，标准刺激是简单图形，而偏差刺激是闪烁的简单图形；标准刺激是短纯音，偏差刺激是断断续续的短纯音。被试的任务是要选择性注意屏幕一侧，并注意所有刺激，对偏差刺激进行按键反应。同时，Talsma 和 Woldorff 记录了被试的脑电信号，发现在额区附近，注意条件下的 AV 波幅显著大于 A + V 的波幅，即空间注意能够影响视听整合加工，表现在目标刺激呈现后 100ms 左右。

最近的一些研究更关注前文中提到的幻觉效应的神经相关物。比如，Bonath 及其团队考察了腹语术效应的神经机制，他们发现两

[①] Teder-Salejarvi W. A., McDonald J. J., Di Russo F. & Hillyard S. A., An Analysis of Audio-visual Crossmodal Integration by Means of Event-related Potential (ERP) Recordings, *Cognitive Brain Research*, Vol. 14, No. 1, January 2002, pp. 106 – 114.

[②] Fort A., Delpuech C., Pernier J. & Giard M. H., Dynamics of Cortico-subcortical Crossmodal Operations Involved in Audio-visual Object Detection in Humans, *Cerebral Cortex*, Vol. 12, No. 10, October 2002, pp. 1031 – 1039.

[③] Molholm S., Ritter W., Murray M. M., Javitt D. C., Schroeder C. E. & Foxe J. J., Multisensory Auditory-visual Interactions during Early Sensory Processing in Humans: A High-density Electrical Mapping Study, *Cognitive Brain Research*, Vol. 14, No. 1, June 2002, pp. 115 – 128.

[④] Talsma D. & Woldorff M. G., Selective Attention and Multisensory Integration: Multiple Phases of Effects on the Evoked Brain Activity, *Journal of Cognitive Neuroscience*, Vol. 17, No. 7, July 2005, pp. 1098 – 1114.

个 ERP 成分与此幻觉效应有关。① 第一个成分是出现在刺激之后 180ms 左右的正波，在所有条件下它在头皮的分布均是对称的。第二个成分是在刺激之后 260ms 左右的负波，只有当被试知觉不到幻觉时它的分布才是对称的。当幻觉效应出现时，在视觉刺激对侧的视野中 N260 的波幅更大。随后，他们采用 fMRI 考察了这种神经活性的脑内源，发现其定位于听觉皮层的颞平面。Saint-Amour 等人考察了在 McGurk 效应中众所周知的听觉成分——失匹配负波（Mis Match Negativity，MMN）。② 结果发现，MMN 在 175ms 处在左侧半球有更强的偏侧化，随后表现出双侧额中区分布，峰值在 290ms 左右，接着在 350—400ms 之间其波幅分布再次出现左半球的偏侧化。溯源分析发现这种神经活性定位于左侧颞叶听觉皮层。

第四节　多感觉整合的神经相关物与神经机制

20 世纪 60 年代，以动物为被试的电生理研究在动物大脑中发现了能够对多个感觉通道反应的神经元。这些研究为以人类为被试考察多感觉整合的神经机制研究提供了丰富的技术和实证支持。这些在一系列脑区中发现的多模态脑区（heteromodal regions）③ 包括

---

① Bonath B., Noesselt T., Martinez A., Mishra J., Schwiecker K., Heinze H. J. & Hillyard S. A., Neural Basis of the Ventriloquist Illusion, *Current Biology*, Vol. 17, No. 19, October 2007, pp. 1697–1703.

② Saint-Amour D., De Sanctis P., Molholm S., Ritter W. & Foxe J. J., Seeing Voices: High-density Electrical Mapping and Source-analysis of the Multisensory Mismatch Negativity Evoked during the McGurk Illusion, *Neuropsychologia*, Vol. 45, No. 3, February 2007, pp. 587–597.

③ Calvert G. A. & Thesen T., Multisensory Integration: Methodological Approaches and Emerging Principles in the Human Brain, *Journal of Physiology Paris*, Vol. 98, No. 1–3, June 2004, pp. 191–205.

颞上沟[1][2][3]、腹侧和横向内沟区（ventral and lateral intraparietal areas）[4][5]，以及一些皮层下区域，比如上丘[6][7][8]。图1-1展示了这些区域在大脑中所处的位置。

已有研究发现，颞上沟（STS）是涉及视听整合的重要区域。[9] 比如，Barraclough等人考察了颞上沟是否能够整合目标刺激的图像和声音。结果表明，颞上沟的神经元对于整合加工具有重要作用，它们能够形成对所观察到的动作的多通道表征。[10] Ghazanfar、Maier、Hoffman和Logothetis以猴子作为被试，发现当它们看到其他猴

---

[1] Barraclough N. E., Xiao D. K., Baker C. I., Oram M. W. & Perrett D. I., Integration of Visual and Auditory Information by Superior Temporal Sulcus Neurons Responsive to the Sight of Actions, *Journal of Cognitive Neuroscience*, Vol. 17, No. 3, March 2005, pp. 377-391.

[2] Benevento L. A., Fallon J., Davis B. J. & Rezak M., Auditory-visual Interaction in Single Cells in Cortex of Superior Temporal Sulcus and Orbital Frontal Cortex of Macaque Monkey, *Experimental Neurology*, Vol. 57, No. 3, December 1977, pp. 849-872.

[3] Bruce C., Desimone R. & Gross C. G., Visual Properties of Neurons in a Polysensory Area in Superior Temporal Sulcus of the Macaque, *Journal of Neurophysiology*, Vol. 46, No. 2, August 1981, pp. 369-384.

[4] Lewis J. W. & Van Essen D. C., Corticocortical Connections of Visual, Sensorimotor, and Multimodal Processing Areas in the Parietal Lobe of the Macaque Monkey, *Journal of Comparative Neurology*, Vol. 428, No. 1, December 2000, pp. 112-137.

[5] Linden J. F., Grunewald A. & Andersen R. A., Responses to Auditory Stimuli in Macaque Lateral Intraparietal Area II, Behavioral Modulation, *Journal of Neurophysiology*, Vol. 82, No. 1, July 1999, pp. 343-358.

[6] Meredith M. A. & Stein, B. E., Spatial Determinants of Multisensory Integration in Cat Superior Colliculus Neurons. *Journal of Neurophysiology*, Vol. 75, No. 5, May1996, p. 1843-1857.

[7] Meredith M. A., Nemitz J. W. & Stein B. E., Determinants of Multisensory Integration in Superior Colliculus Neurons. I. Temporal Factors. *The Journal of Neuroscience*, Vol. 7, No. 10, 1987, pp. 3215-3229.

[8] Wallace M. T., Meredith M. A. & Stein B. E., Multisensory Integration in the Superior Colliculusof the Alert Cat, *Journal of Neurophysiology*, Vol. 80, No. 2, August 1998, pp. 1006-1010.

[9] Hein G. & Knight R. T., Superior Temporal Sulcus—It's My Area: Or is It, *Journal of Cognitive Neuroscience*, Vol. 20, No. 12, December 2008, pp. 2125-2136.

[10] Barraclough N. E., Xiao D. K., Baker C. I., Oram M. W. & Perrett D. I., Integration of Visual and Auditory Information by Superior Temporal Sulcus Neurons Responsive to the Sight of Actions, *Journal of Cognitive Neuroscience*, Vol. 17, No. 3, March 2005, pp. 377-391.

子动态的脸和声音时，在进行言语加工时颞上沟被激活。① 与这些研究结论一致的是，当加工多通道的言语信息时，人类的颞上沟也被激活。②

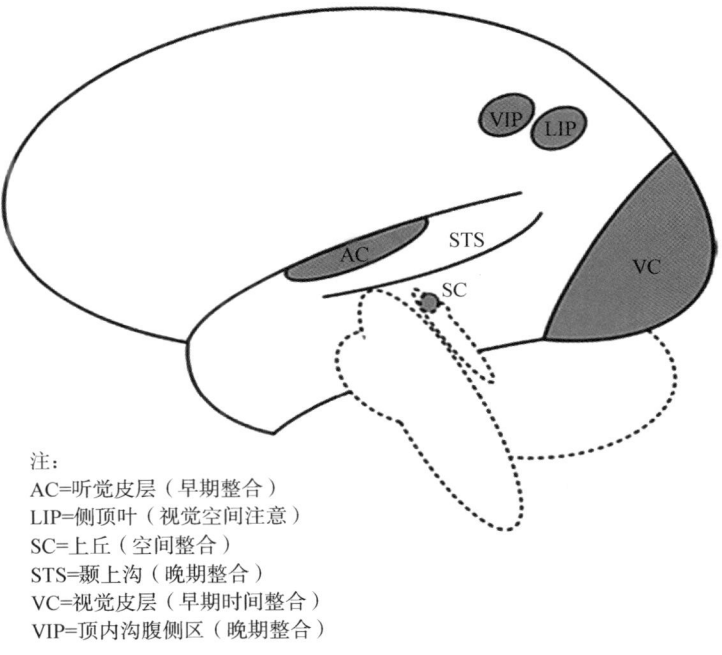

注：
AC=听觉皮层（早期整合）
LIP=侧顶叶（视觉空间注意）
SC=上丘（空间整合）
STS=颞上沟（晚期整合）
VC=视觉皮层（早期时间整合）
VIP=顶内沟腹侧区（晚期整合）

图1-1 涉及视听整合的重要脑区

上丘（SC）也是涉及视听整合的一个重要部分。虽然它接收视觉皮层和其他皮层的信息，但是，上丘神经元也能对体感刺激和

---

① Ghazanfar A. A., Maier J. X., Hoffman K. L. & Logothetis N. K., Multisensory Integration of Dynamic Faces and Voices in Rhesus Monkey Auditory Cortex, *Journal of Neuroscience*, Vol. 25, No. 20, May 2005, pp. 5004–5012.

② Senkowski D., Saint-Amour D., Gruber T. & Fox J. J., Look Who's Talking: The Deployment of Visuo-spatial Attention during Multisensory Speech Processing under Noisy Environmental Conditions, *Neuroimage*, Vol. 43, No. 2, November 2008, pp. 379–387.

听觉刺激进行反应。① 这些来自不同通道的信息的接收域重叠，使得呈现在同样位置的视觉和听觉事件将会激活相同的神经元。② 相同接收域内的双通道刺激将会导致超加性的神经元反应。③ 除空间位置以外，相同的呈现时间或时间接近性也能导致强烈的神经活性。④

上丘在朝向行为中起着重要作用，不论外显朝向（如头部或眼睛的转动）还是内隐朝向（如向兴趣区分配空间注意）。有研究者认为，上丘为多感觉整合研究提供了一个完美的模型，因为上丘是一个接收上行传导的视觉、听觉和体感信息的低水平结构。上丘中的深层细胞通常是双通道的（其表层细胞纯粹是单通道视觉，深层双通道细胞主要为视听和视觉—体感），甚至是跨通道的。⑤

如果一个神经元接收超过一个感觉通道以上的信息，那么我们将其定义为多通道神经元。事实上，这就意味着确定一个给定单元是否具有对视觉和/或听觉和/或体感刺激反应的空间接收域。当实施这种加工时，上丘中的结构有一个非常重要的原则，即多通道神经元中单独定义的接收区域是"空间寄存器"（spatial register）。这意味着一个神经元的接收区域会重叠，这样它们能对来自空间中相

---

① Meredith M. A., Nemitz J. W. & Stein B. E., Determinants of Multisensory Integration in Superior Colliculus Neurons. I. Temporal Factors, *The Journal of neuroscience*, Vol. 7, No. 10, 1987, pp. 3215 – 3229.

② Meredith M. A. & Stein B. E., Visual, Auditory, and Somatosensory Convergence on Cells in Superiorcolliculus Results in Multisensory Integration, *Journalof Neurophysiology*, Vol. 56, No. 3, September 1986, pp. 640 – 662.

③ Wallace M. T., Meredith M. A. & Stein B. E., Multisensory Integration in the Superior Colliculusof the Alert Cat, *Journal of Neurophysiology*, Vol. 80, No. 2, August 1998, pp. 1006 – 1010.

④ Meredith M. A., Nemitz J. W. & Stein B. E., Determinants of Multisensory Integration in Superior Colliculus Neurons. I. Temporal Factors, *The Journal of neuroscience*, Vol. 7, No. 10, 1987, pp. 3215 – 3229.

⑤ Alais D., Newell F. N. & Mamassian P., Multisensory Processing in Review: From Physiology to Behaviour, *Seeing & Perceiving*, Vol. 23, No. 1, 2010, pp. 3 – 38.

同方位的刺激进行反应。多通道细胞的接收区域能提供对外部空间的功能性映射。① 同时,视觉接收域依赖于眼球的位置,听觉和体感接收域倾向于向主要的空间寄存器做出补偿性位置转移。②

当多通道上丘神经元被空间上一致的刺激所激活,它们可能会显示出有趣的非线性反应。其中一个反应是多通道反应增强,即多通道反应会超过单通道反应之和,也就是"超加性"③。当所输入的成分比较微弱并且只能形成针对它们本身最为适当的反应时,常常会观察到这种多通道反应增强,这对于机体确保不会漏掉微弱的刺激来说是非常重要的。随着所输入的成分的显著性减弱,超加性会增强,这被称为"相反有效性"④。对这种效应的一个解释是:如果一个刺激事件在多感觉神经元的每一个通道都引发一个强烈的反应,那么就没有必要再去增强它,不管怎样,对于任何神经元的反应范围有一个限制。另一个值得注意的问题是,在空间上有分离位置的同时呈现的多感觉刺激,一个落入一个神经单元的接收区域,另一个与它相邻,那么将会倾向于诱发一个比任一单独成分都弱的反应,这被称为"反应抑制"(response depression)⑤。

有研究者认为,多通道刺激除需要在空间上一致之外,它们在时间上也必须接近。⑥ 有趣的是,在上丘神经元中,多通道交互作

---

① Meredith M. A. & Stein B. E., Spatial Determinants of Multisensory Integration in Cat Superior Colliculus Neurons, *Journal of Neurophysiology*, Vol. 75, No. 5, May 1996, pp. 1843–1857.

② Groh J. M. & Sparks D. L., Saccades to Somatosensory Targets. I. Behavioral Characteristics, *Journal of Neurophysiology*, Vol. 75, No. 1, January 1996, pp. 412–427.

③ Stein B. E. & Meredith M. A., *The merging of thesenses*. Cambridge: MIT Press, 1993, p. 225.

④ Stanford T. R. & Stein B. E., Superadditivity in Multisensory Integration: Putting the Computation in Context, *Neuroreport*, Vol. 18, No. 8, May 2007, pp. 787–792.

⑤ Stein B. E. & Meredith M. A., *The merging of thesenses*. Cambridge: MIT Press. 1993.

⑥ Meredith M. A., Nemitz J. W. & Stein B. E., Determinants of Multisensory Integration in Superior Colliculus Neurons. I. Temporal Factors, *The Journal of neuroscience*, Vol. 7, No. 10, 1987, pp. 3215–3229.

用发生的时间窗口相当长。[1][2] 其原因可能是，通道之间在转换时间和神经潜伏期上存在差异，在光和声音的传播速度上也存在差异。这些时间差异意味着多通道信号的感觉成分可能会不可避免地在一段时间的不同时刻到达。为使上丘满足其多通道功能，需要能容纳接收的信号中有相当大的时间变异。

总之，上丘神经元的多通道功能有空间一致和时间一致的要求。对微弱刺激反应的超加性确保机体不会丢失那些并不显著的刺激。并且，反应抑制能帮助机体减弱对看似同时但并不同时呈现的刺激的反应。另外，有研究者发现，一些长期被人们认为是单通道视觉皮层的部分，比如外侧顶内沟区（lateral intraparietal area），也能够接收听觉刺激。[3] 外侧顶内沟区的神经元在视觉或听觉刺激开始呈现时变得活跃，在延迟扫视反应中也会被激活。[4] 这些外侧顶内沟区的神经元活性并不依赖于朝向刺激方向的实际的扫视动作。[5] 也正因为此，外侧顶内沟区域被认为也是涉及视觉空间注意的区域。

除上述多模态脑区之外，有研究者认为，如初级视觉皮层这样

---

[1] Meredith M. A., Nemitz J. W. & Stein B. E., Determinants of Multisensory Integration in Superior Colliculus Neurons. I. Temporal Factors, *The Journal of neuroscience*, Vol. 7, No. 10, 1987, pp. 3215–3229.

[2] McDonald J. J., Teder-Sälejärvi W. A. & Hillyard S. A., Involuntary Orienting to Sound Improves Visual Perception, *Nature*, Vol. 407, No. 6806, October 2000, pp. 906–908.

[3] Linden J. F., Grunewald A. & Andersen R. A., Responses to Auditory Stimuli in Macaque Lateral Intraparietal Area II. Behavioral Modulation, *Journal of Neurophysiology*, Vol. 82, No. 1, July 1999, pp. 343–358.

[4] Colby C. L. & Goldberg M. E., Space and Attention in Parietal Cortex, *Annual Review of Neuroscience*, Vol. 22, No. 1, February1999, pp. 319–349.

[5] Colby C. L., Duhamel J. R. & Goldberg M. E., Visual, Presaccadic, and Cognitive Activation of Single Neurons in Monkey Lateral Intraparietal Area, *Journal of Neurophysiology*, Vol. 76, No. 5, November 1996, pp. 2841–2852.

的单通道脑区也会对来自其他感觉通道的刺激产生反应。①②③④ 比如，Shams 等人发现，幻觉闪光效应（illusory flash effect）与物理闪光引发的 ERP 相似。⑤ 这表明，视知觉机制可以被声音所影响。Shams 等人后续的研究发现，导致闪光幻觉的声音也能影响被认为是单通道视觉加工区域的枕区。⑥ 同时，有研究发现，初级听觉皮层的活性也能被视觉信息或体感信息影响。

第五节　多感觉整合的量化方法

最近几十年间，研究者们开始不断探索不同感觉通道信息加工的行为表现及其神经机制。随着研究的深入，研究者们遇到越来越多的挑战，其中一项便是多感觉整合的量化问题。从简单的行为实验到采用复杂的事件相关电位、功能性磁共振成像以及经颅磁等技术的实验，对于多感觉整合的量化并非一成不变。可以说，实验中采用的数据收集方式不同，实验所针对的被试群体不同，对于多感觉整合的量化就有所不同。本书以行为实验和采用事件相关电位技

---

① Foxe J. J., Morocz I. A., Murray M. M., Higgins B. A., Javitt D. C. & Schroeder C. E., Multisensory Auditory-somatosensory Interactions in Early Cortical Processing Revealed by High-density Electrical Mapping, *Cognitive Brain Research*, Vol. 10, No. 1, September 2000, pp. 77 – 83.

② Martuzzi R., Murray M. M., Michel C. M., Thiran J. P., Maeder P. P., Clarke S. et al., Multisensory Interactions within Human Primary Cortices Revealed by BOLD Dynamics, *Cerebral Cortex*, Vol. 17, No. 7, Aug ust 2007, pp. 1672 – 1679.

③ Romei V., Murray M. M., Merabet L. B. & Thut G., Occipital Transcranial Magnetic Stimulation Has Opposing Effects on Visual and Auditory Stimulus Detection: Implications for Multisensory Interactions, *The Journal of neuroscience*, Vol. 27, No. 43, November 2007, pp. 11465 – 11472.

④ Shams L., Iwaki S., Chawla A. & Bhattacharya J., Early Modulation of Visual Cortex by Sound: An MEG Study, *Neuroscience Letters*, Vol. 378, No. 2, April 2005, pp. 76 – 81.

⑤ Shimojo S. & Shams L., Sensory Modalities are not Separate Modalities: Plasticity and Interactions, *Current Opinion in Neurobiology*, Vol. 11, No. 4, September 2001, pp. 505 – 509.

⑥ Shams L., Iwaki S., Chawla A. & Bhattacharya J., Early Modulation of Visual Cortex by Sound: An MEG Study, *Neuroscience Letters*, Vol. 378, No. 2, April 2005, pp. 76 – 81.

术考察多感觉整合的研究为例介绍对其的量化方法。

一 行为实验中对多感觉整合的量化

在任何心理学的实验研究中,反应时都是一个普遍且简单的指标。[1] 在一个典型的心理物理学范式中,多通道刺激(如视听刺激)与其组成成分的单通道刺激(如单通道视觉和单通道听觉刺激)交织在一起反复出现。要求被试对每一个试次中的目标刺激进行探测、定位、确认或者做出判断。在这种情况下,大多数研究[2]发现,被试对双通道刺激(如视听刺激)的反应时显著小于对组成这个双通道刺激的任意单通道刺激(如单通道视觉和单通道听觉刺激)的反应时。在多通道加工领域,这种现象叫作冗余信号效应(redundant target effect)[3][4]。这种冗余信号效应的出现是否代表双通道刺激的两个单通道成分产生整合而促成了最终的反应呢?

有研究者针对这个疑问提出了不同的数学模型来进行解释。竞争模型(race model)认为,双通道刺激的两个成分分别在两个单独的感觉通道中被加工,被试最终的反应由那个最先完成加工的感觉通道触发。以掷骰子为例,当我们想得到一个6点时,掷两个骰子得到一个6点的概率要远远大于掷一个骰子得到6点的概率。因此,双通道刺激(如视听刺激)条件比单通道刺激(如视觉和听

---

[1] Stevenson R. A., Ghose D., Fister J. K., Sarko D. K., Altieri N. A., Nidiffer A. R., ⋯ & Wallace M. T., Identifying and Quantifying Multisensory Integration: A Tutorial Review, *Brain Topography*, Vol. 27, No. 6, April 2014, pp. 707–730.

[2] Frassinetti F., Bolognini N. & Ladavas E., Enhancement of Visual Perception by Crossmodal Visuo-auditory Interaction, *Experimental Brain Research*, Vol. 147, No. 3, December 2002, pp. 332–343.

[3] Miller J., Divided Attention: Evidence for Coactivation with Redundant Signals, *Cognitive Psychology*, Vol. 14, No. 2, April 1982, pp. 247–279.

[4] Miller J., Timecourse of Coactivation in Bimodal Divided Attention, *Perception & Psychophysics*, Vol. 40, No. 5, November 1986, pp. 331–343.

觉刺激）条件下被试的反应时短于给定时间 t 的概率要高，从而导致了较短的反应时。[1] 因此，竞争模型认为，冗余信号效应实质上是一种统计便利（statistical facilitation）。另有研究者提出了共激活模型（co-activation model），此模型认为，来自两个通道的信息在某个特定的加工阶段汇聚并被整合为统一的知觉信息。这种整合信息的强度及可靠度比任意一个单通道信息的强度和可靠度都高。因此，对多通道冗余刺激的加工比单一通道刺激的反应更快。[2] 为了验证竞争模型和共激活模型，Miller[3] 推导出下列竞争模型不等式：

$$P(RT_{av} < t) \leq [P(RT_a < t) + P(RT_v < t)] - [P(RT_a < t) \times P(RT_v < t)]$$

在此不等式中，P 为反应时概率的累积量分布函数（CDFs），代表在任意给定时间 t 内对目标刺激做出反应的概率。其中 A 和 V 分别代表两个感觉通道（听觉和视觉）的刺激。其中，$P(RT_{av} < t)$ 代表在给定时间 t 内被试对视听双通道目标做出反应的概率，$P(RT_a < t)$ 和 $P(RT_v < t)$ 分别代表在给定时间 t 内被试对单通道听觉目标和单通道视觉目标做出反应的概率。不等式的右边代表竞争模型预测值，即在给定时间 t 内分别对两个单通道刺激反应的概率值。这个不等式所表达的含义是，如果对双通道刺激的反应符合竞争模型，那么对于双通道刺激的反应不可能快于对两个单通道刺激的反应中最快的一个；亦即在给定的时间

---

[1] 刘强：《多感觉整合脑机制研究》，博士学位论文，西南大学，2010 年。
[2] 刘强：《多感觉整合脑机制研究》，博士学位论文，西南大学，2010 年。
[3] Miller J., Divided Attention: Evidence for Coactivation with Redundant Signals, *Cognitive Psychology*, Vol. 14, No. 2, April 1982, pp. 247–279.

范围内,对双通道刺激做出反应的概率小于或等于两个单一通道刺激条件下做出反应的概率之和。而当这一不等式不成立的时候,接受共激活模型。大部分实验结果都会出现竞争模型的背离,即都支持共激活模型假设。[1][2][3]

二 事件相关电位研究中对多感觉整合的量化

由于行为实验所依托的反应时等观测指标只能反映心理加工的综合结果,而对于高速加工的多通道信息很难进行有效预测,因而无法揭示多感觉整合加工的时间进行。事件相关电位技术具有较高的时间分辨能力,能够对认知过程的神经活动特征提供即时的评价,从加工初始就可以对单个的认知过程进行识别和分离[4],因此,一些研究者开始采用此技术探讨多感觉整合的时间进程和神经机制。

Giard 和 Peronnet 采用了与动物研究中相似的技术来提取与多感觉整合有关的神经活动。[5] 他们将双通道刺激的神经反应减去单通道刺激神经反应之和,即 AV – (A + V),其中 A 代表单通道听觉刺激的神经反应,V 代表视觉单通道刺激的神经反应,AV 代表

---

[1] Giary M. & Ulrich R., Motor Coactivation Revealed by Response Force in Divided and Focused Attention, *Journal of Experimental Psychology: Human Perception and Performance*, Vol. 19, No. 6, December 1993, pp. 1278 – 1291.

[2] Miller J., Divided Attention: Evidence for Coactivation with Redundant Signals, *Cognitive Psychology*, Vol. 14, No. 2, April 1982, pp. 247 – 279.

[3] Miller J., Timecourse of Coactivation in Bimodal Divided Attention, *Perception & Psychophysics*, Vol. 40, No. 5, November 1986, pp. 331 – 343.

[4] Rhodes S. M. & Donaldson D. I., Association and Not Semantic Relationships Elicit the N400 Effect: Electrophysiological Evidence from an Explicit Language Comprehension Task, *Psychophysiology*, Vol. 45, No. 1, Jannuary 2008, pp. 50 – 59.

[5] Giard M. H. & Peronnet F., Auditory – visual Integration during Multimodal Object Recognition in Humans: A Behavioral and Electrophysiological Study, *Journal of Cognitive Neuroscience*, Vol. 11, No. 5, September 1999, pp. 473 – 490.

视听双通道刺激的神经反应。Giard 和 Peronnet 采用这种方法描述了由多通道交互作用引发的不同的 ERP 成分。这其中有非常早的与多通道交互作用有关的成分，它出现在刺激呈现后 40ms 左右。但是，Giard 和 Peronnet 的方法受到 Teder-Salejarvi、McDonald、Di Russo 和 Hilliyard 的质疑。Teder-Salejarvi 等人认为，这种早期的效应实际上是由减法技术以及在刺激开始之前代表预期的慢波造成的。[①]

Talsma 和 Woldorff[②] 针对已有研究可能将关联性负变（Contingent Negative Variation，CNV）当作早期整合效应 ERP 成分的潜在问题，对传统实验范式做出调整。为减少预期 ERP 的形成，他们采用随机变化的 SOA（350—650ms）呈现所有刺激，这些刺激以相等的概率呈现在左侧或右侧视野，要求被试注意指定一侧的所有刺激，并对目标刺激进行按键反应，同时记录被试的脑电成分。数据分析主要关注对非目标刺激的反应。他们认为，这种呈现刺激的方式虽然能有效减少预期 ERP 的形成，但也可能会产生相邻刺激反应的 ERP 重叠的问题。因此，他们在实验中增加了无刺激的试次，即，试次中没有任何刺激，这样就有效减少了相邻刺激反应的 ERP 重叠问题。他们的研究发现，与非注意条件相比，注意条件下与多感觉整合效应有关的 ERP 波幅更大，这表明空间注意能够影响整合加工。

---

① Teder-Salejarvi W. A., McDonald J. J., Di Russo F. & Hillyard S. A., An Analysis of Audio-visual Crossmodal Integration by Means of Event-related Potential (ERP) Recordings, *Cognitive Brain Research*, Vol. 14, No. 1, Junnuary 2002, pp. 106 – 114.

② Talsma D. & Woldorff M. G., Selective Attention and Multisensory Integration: Multiple Phases of Effects on the Evoked Brain Activity, *Journal of Cognitive Neuroscience*, Vol. 17, No. 7, July 2005, pp. 1098 – 1114.

最近，有研究者考察了不同频率的声音与视觉图像同时呈现时的视听整合加工。① 视觉刺激分为标准刺激和偏差刺激，均为栅栏图形，二者只在强度上略有不同。听觉刺激为 0.5kHz、1kHz、2.5kHz、5kHz 的短音。被试的任务是忽略听觉刺激，只对视觉目标进行反应，同时记录脑电信号。根据已有研究中的方法，Yang 等人在不同频率的声音条件下将 AV 和 A + V 的 ERP 进行比较。结果发现，声音频率越高视听整合产生越早。同时，较低频率的声音（0.5kHz、1kHz、2.5kHz）在额中区与视觉图形产生整合。

Mishra、Martinez、Sejnowski 和 Hillyard 考察了当一个闪光与两个短音同时呈现时被知觉成两个闪光的幻觉效应。② 结果发现，在第二个短音呈现后 30—60ms，视觉皮层的活性有所增强，并且，来自视觉皮层的伽马波激活与听觉皮层的 ERP 调节同时呈现。这表明，第二个声音激活了视觉和听觉皮层之间快速且动态的交互作用，这可能是这种特殊幻觉的真正的神经相关物。

第六节 情绪信息的多感觉整合加工

情绪信息是我们在现实社会中的重要社交线索。在社交场合中，我们往往利用情绪提供的信息去选择适宜的社交手段。而当我们去判断他人的情绪时，来自不同通道的情绪信息会带给我们重要价值。比如当我们跟某人交谈时，通过他（她）的音调、语速（听觉通道）和说话时的表情（视觉通道），我们能对他（她）的

---

① Yang W., Yang J., Gao Y., Tang X., Ren Y., Takahashi S., et al., Effects of SoundFrequency on Audiovisual Integration: An EventRelated Potential Study. *PLoS ONE*, Vol. 10, No. 9, September 2015, e0138296.

② Mishra J., Martinez A., Sejnowski T. J. & Hillyard S. A., Early Cross-modal Interactions in Auditory and Visual Cortex Underlie a Sound-induced Visual Illusion, *Journal of Neuroscience*, Vol. 27, No. 15, April 2007, pp. 4120 – 4131.

情绪甚至意图进行一定程度的推理,以此为依据进行下一步社交方案。相关心理学研究表明,人类在对情绪信息进行加工时,并非单独依赖于听觉信息或单独依赖于视觉信息,通常是同时依赖于这两种感觉通道的信息进行加工。[1] 然而,我们却意识不到对同时同地呈现的视觉和听觉信息的整合,这种对情绪信息的无意识的整合加工是保证人际交往质量的重要心理基础。那么,这种对来自不同感觉通道的情绪信息的整合加工具有怎样的发生、发展特点以及相应的机制?

相关研究表明,在成人[2][3]、婴儿[4]、特殊人群[5][6]中均发现了对情绪信息的多通道整合加工。对于来自不同通道(尤其是面孔表情、音调情绪)的情绪信息,已有研究多关注如下两方面:首先是在双通道情绪信息的加工中是否存在情绪信息一致性效应,即与视听双通道情绪不一致的条件相比,个体对视听双通道情绪一致的信

---

[1] Spence C. & Driver J., Crossmodal Space and Crossmodal Attention. Oxford, New York, USA: OxfordUniversity Press, 2004.

[2] Collignon O., Girard S., Gosselin F., Roy S., Saint-Amour D., Lassonde M. & Lepore F., Audio-Visual Integration of Emotion Expression, *Brain Research*, Vol. 25, No. 1242, November 2008, pp. 126 – 135.

[3] de Gelder B. & Vroomen J., The Perception of Emotions by Ear and by Eye, *Cognition and Emotion*, 14, 2000, pp. 289 – 311.

[4] Grossmann T., Striano T. & Friederici A. D., Crossmodal Integration of Emotional Information Fromface and Voice in the Infant Brain, *Developmental Science*, Vol. 9, No1. 3, May 2006, pp. 309 – 315.

[5] de Gelder B., Vroomen J., de Jong S. J., Masthoff E. D., Trompenaars F. J. & Hodiamont P., Multisensory Integration of Emotional Faces and Voices in Schizophrenics, *Schizophrenia Research*, Vol. 72, No. 2, Jannuary 2005, pp. 195 – 203.

[6] Magnée M. J., de Gelder B., van Engeland H. & Kemner C., Audiovisual Speech Integration in Pervasive Developmental Disorder: Evidence from Event-related Potentials, *Journal of Child Psychology and Psychiatry*, Vol. 49, No. 9, 2008, pp. 995 – 1000.

息加工更快更准确①②③④;其次是比较单通道情绪信息和双通道情绪信息的加工效率⑤。

已有的大量研究结果对上述两个问题进行了回答。首先,在双通道情绪信息的整合加工中,的确存在情绪一致性效应,即个体面孔表情和声音情绪一致的信息加工更快、更准确⑥⑦;其次,存在双通道加工优势效应,即与视觉单通道或听觉单通道情绪信息相比,个体对视听同时呈现的双通道情绪信息的加工处理既快又准确⑧。

不论是行为研究,还是电生理研究,近年来大量研究结果提示,双通道信息整合加工存在以下特点:第一,不论是与单通道视觉还是单通道听觉相比,同时同地呈现的视听双通道的信息具有加工优势,即被试对这种信息的加工既快又准确;第二,视听双通道情绪信息的效应大于任意一个单通道信息的效应,也大于两个单通道加工效应之和,即具有超加性,这种特性在视觉信息并不清晰

---

① Klasen M., Kenworthy C. A., Mathiak K. A., Kircher T. T. J. & Mathiak K., Supramodal Representation of Emotions, *Journal of Neuroscience*, Vol. 31, No. 38, September 2011, p. 15218.

② Mileva M., Tompkinson J., Watt D. & Burton A. M., Audiovisual Integration in Social Evaluation, *Journal of Experimental Psychology: Human Perceptionand Performance*, Vol. 44, No. 1, Jannuary 2018, pp. 128 – 138.

③ Muller V. I., Cieslik E. C., Turetsky B. I. & Eickhoff S. B., Crossmodal Interactions in Audiovisual Emotion Processing, *Neuroimage*, Vol. 60, No. 1, 2012, pp. 553 – 561.

④ Pourtois G., de Gelder B., Vroomen J., Rossion B. & Crommelinck M., The Time-course of Intermodal-binding between Seeing and Hearing Affective Information, *Neuroreport*, Vol. 11, No. 6, April 2000, pp. 1329 – 1333.

⑤ Jessen S. & Kotz S. A., The Temporal Dynamics of Processing Emotions from Vocal, Facial, and Bodily Expressions, *Neuroimage*, Vol. 58, No. 2, September 2011, pp. 665 – 674.

⑥ Campanella S. & Belin P., Integrating Face Andvoice in Person Perception, *Trends in Cognitive Sciences*, Vol. 11, No. 12, December 2007, pp. 535 – 543.

⑦ Klasen M., Kreifelts B., Chen Y. H., Seubert J. & Mathiak K., Neural Processing of Emotion in Multimodal Settings, *Frontiers in Human Neuroscience*, Vol. 8, No. 8, October 2014, p. 822.

⑧ de Gelder B. & Vroomen J., The Perception of Emotions by Ear and by Eye, *Cognition and Emotion*, 14, 2000, pp. 289 – 311.

（模糊的面孔表情）时仍然存在；第三，在单通道视觉或单通道听觉信息较为模糊，或是视听双通道情绪信息较为模糊时，视听整合效应更为明显。[1][2][3]

随着研究工具和相关技术的不断发展，研究者可以通过电生理技术实现对视听双通道情绪信息整合加工的时间进程和相关脑区的探索。通过早期的行为研究可以发现，虽然视听双通道情绪信息的整合是自动化的，但是其整合的具体时间进程还要依赖于具有较高时间分辨率的事件相关电位技术（ERPs）。De Gelder B. 等人[4]通过该技术考察了视听情绪信息整合可能发生的时间节点。在这项研究中，视听双通道情绪不一致信息出现后180ms左右出现了早期的失匹配负波（Mismatch-negativity，MMN）。在 Barbara 等人[5]的研究中，视听情绪信息的整合发生在刺激呈现后的200ms左右。

另有一些研究发现，与视听情绪不一致的双通道信息相比，视听情绪一致的双通道信息诱发了波幅更大的N100[6]；与视觉单通道

---

[1] Stein B. E. & Stanford T. R., Multisensory Integration: Current Issues from the Perspective of the Single Neuron, *Nature Reviews Neuroscience*, Vol. 9, No. 4, April 2008, pp. 255 – 266.

[2] Stein B. E., Stanford T. R., Ramachandran R., Jr Perrault T. J. & Rowland B. A., Challenges in Quantifying Multisensory Integration: Alternative Criteria, Models, Andinverse Effectiveness, *Experimental Brain Research*, Vol. 198, No. 2 – 3, September 2009, pp. 113 – 126.

[3] 王苹、潘治辉、张立洁、陈煦海：《动态面孔和语音情绪信息的整合加工及神经生理机制》，《心理科学进展》2015年第7期。

[4] De Gelder B., Boecker K., Tuomainen J., Hensen M. & Vroomen J., The Combined Perception of Emotion from Voice and Face: Early Interaction Revealed by Human Electric Brain Responses, *Neuroscience Letters*, No. 260, Jannuary 1999, pp. 133 – 136.

[5] Barbara A. B., Lucy J. M., William J. G. & Patricia L. D., Multisensory Integration in Children: A Preliminary ERP Study, *Brain Research*, No. 1242, November 2008, pp. 283 – 290.

[6] Pourtois G., de Gelder B., Vroomen J., Rossion B. & Crommelinck M., The Time-course of Intermodalbinding Between Seeing and Hearing Affective Information, *Neuroreport*, Vol. 11, No. 6, April 2000, pp. 1329 – 1333.

或听觉单通道情绪信息相比,视听双通道信息所诱发的 N1 波幅更小[1][2]。这些研究结果表明,视听双通道情绪信息的整合发生在早期知觉阶段,起码在刺激呈现后 100ms 左右就已经开始了。

从情绪内容的角度考虑,在视听情绪内容不一致甚至出现冲突时,P2 的波幅会产生明显变化。比如,有研究发现,愤怒面孔与中性声音同时呈现会导致 P2 波幅减小[3],恐惧表情与笑声同时呈现诱发的 P2 波幅显著小于中性面孔与笑声同时呈现时诱发的 P2 波幅[4]。

N400 是代表语义加工的重要成分,在视听情绪整合加工中同样出现了 N400。研究者认为,在这类研究中的 N400 代表对情绪信息的分类、评估等深度加工过程。[5][6][7][8]

由于较为出色的空间分辨率,功能性核磁共振技术被用来探索

---

[1] Jessen S. & Kotz S. A., The Temporal Dynamics of Processing Emotions from Vocal, Facial, and Bodily Expressions, *Neuroimage*, Vol. 58, No. 2, September 2011, pp. 665-674.

[2] Kokinous J., Tavano A., Kotz S. A. & Schroeger E., Perceptual Integration of Faces and Voices Depends on the Interaction of Emotional Content and Spatial Frequency, *Biological Psychology*, No. 123, February 2017, pp. 155-165.

[3] Balconi M. & Carrera A., Cross-modal Integration of Emotional Face and Voice in Congruous and Incongruous Pairs: The P2 ERP Effect, *Journal of Cognitive Psychology*, Vol. 23, No. 1, 2011, pp. 132-139.

[4] Doi H. & Shinohara K., Unconscious Presentation of Fearful Face Modulates Electrophysiological Responses to Emotional Prosody, *Cerebral Cortex*, Vol. 25, No. 3, March 2015, pp. 817-832.

[5] Campanella S., Bruyer R., Froidbise S., Rossignol M., Joassin F., Kornreich C., …& Verbanck P., Is Two Better than One? A cross-modal Oddball Paradigm Reveals Greater Sensitivity of the P300 to Emotional Face-voice Associations, *Clinical Neurophysiology*, Vol. 121, No. 11, November 2010, pp. 1855-1862.

[6] Liu P., Rigoulot S. & Pell M. D., Culture Modulates the Brain Response to Human Expressions of Emotion: Electrophysiological Evidence, *Neuropsychologia*, No. 67, Janntuary 2015, pp. 1-13.

[7] Paulmann S., Jessen S. & Kotz S. A., Investigating the Multimodal Nature of Human Communication Insights from ERPs, *Journal of Psychophysiology*, Vol. 23, No. 2, 2009, pp. 63-76.

[8] Proverbio A. M. & De Benedetto F., Auditory Enhancement of Visual Memory Encoding is Driven by Emotional Content of the Auditory Material and Mediated by Superior Frontal Cortex, *Biological Psychology*, No. 132, February 2018, pp. 164-175.

视听情绪信息的整合出现在脑的哪些部位。已有大量研究表明，左侧颞叶的部分结构是视听双通道情绪信息整合的关键区域。比如，Kreifelts 等人发现，与单通道视觉和单通道听觉信息相比，视听双通道情绪信息显著激活了双侧的后颞上回（pSTG）和右侧丘脑。[1] 同时有研究表明，双通道的情绪信息还能明显激活左侧后颞上沟、双侧后颞上回等部位。[2] 此外，由于恐惧情绪与杏仁核密切相关，因此，在研究材料中，如果选用了恐惧的声音或面孔，在视听双通道情绪材料呈现后，会明显激活杏仁核周围灰质。[3][4]

---

[1] Kreifelts B., Ethofer T., Grodd W., Erb M. & Wildgruber D., Audiovisual Integration of Emotional Signals in Voice and Face: An Event-related FMRI Study, *Neuroimage*, Vol. 37, No. 4, November 2007, pp. 1445–1456.

[2] Kreifelts B., Ethofer T., Huberle E., Grodd W. & Wildgruber D., Association of Trait Emotional Intelligence and Individual FMRI-activation Patterns during the Perception of Social Signals from Voice and Face, *Human Brain Mapping*, Vol. 31, No. 7, July 2010, pp. 979–991.

[3] Park J. Y., Gu B. M., Kang D. H., Shin Y. W., Choi C. H., Lee J. M. & Kwon J. S., Integration of Cross-modal Emotional Information in the Human Brain: An fMRI Study, *Cortex*, Vol. 46, No. 2, February 2010, pp. 161–169.

[4] Epperson C. N., Amin Z., Ruparel K., Gur R. & Loughead J., Interactive Effects of Estrogen and Serotonin on Brainactivation during Working Memory and Affective Processing in Menopausal Women, *Psychoneuroendocrinology*, Vol. 37, No. 3, August 2012, pp. 372–382.

第 二 章

多感觉整合的发展

自呱呱坠地的那一刻起,我们就生活在充满各种刺激的环境中,每一种刺激都提供了有关某件事或某个物体的相关信息。比如,新生儿通过视觉信息看到闪光的玩具,通过听觉信息听到妈妈的呼唤或玩具发出的声音,通过触觉信息感受妈妈的体温或毛绒玩具的柔软,通过味觉信息感受母乳的甘甜。但是,这些信息并不是孤立存在的,或者说,新生儿在面对这些来自不同通道的信息时,并没有把这个世界感受成支离破碎的部分。通过前文可知,对来自不同感觉通道的信息进行整合加工,是个体快速、准确、经济的利用认知资源的重要途径,那么这种加工在个体发展过程中都存在哪些特性?

第一节 新生儿的多感觉整合加工

一 视听整合加工

如前所述,成人在面对来自不同感觉通道的信息时,能够将其整合成统一、连贯的知觉,这可能是成人在纷繁复杂的世界中长期学习并获得经验的结果。新生儿在出生后,第一次面对如此丰富多彩的刺激,他们是如何使这些色彩、形状、声音、味道、硬度等信息整合成一个整体的？

早在 1961 年韦特海默（Wertheimer）就采用眼动实验的方式探讨了这一问题。实验中，采用出生仅 10 分钟的新生儿作为被试，结果发现当把声音刺激呈现在新生儿左耳时，出现左眼的眼动；当把声音刺激呈现在新生儿右耳时，出现右眼的眼动。研究者认为，这种与听觉刺激同侧的眼动现象是个体发展早期就能产生视觉和听觉整合加工的证据，因此认为，视听整合加工是生来就有的。

相关研究发现，听觉刺激还能影响婴儿对于视觉刺激的唤醒度和注意偏好。比如，Lewkowicz 和 Turkewitz 发现，向新生儿呈现浅色的光点，他们倾向于注视中等强度的光。[1] 当向新生儿呈现白噪声之后再呈现不同的光点，他们则倾向于注视最低强度的光点。

知觉到一个事件中，视觉和听觉的相同属性是产生视听整合的重要证据。Lewkowicz[2] 认为，多通道时间经验有四个基本维度——时间同步性、持续时间、频率和节奏，这些特性在个体出生后的一年内以序列和层级的形式出现。Morrongiello 等人[3]发现，新生儿能在同步呈现的线索基础上将一个物体和声音联系起来，也能学会将同步呈现的简单视觉和听觉刺激（如实验中用的彩色短线和短音节）组合起来。上述结果均证明了在新生儿中已经存在视听整合加工，这种加工依赖于视听刺激的同步性，这就为后期学习词汇的发音及其含义打下了知觉基础。

---

[1] Lewkowicz D. J. & Turkewitz G., Intersensory Interaction in Newborns: Modification of Visual Preferences Following Exposure to Sound, *Child Development*, No. 52, September 1981, pp. 827–832.

[2] Lewkowicz D. J., The Development of Intersensory Temporal Perception: An Epigenetic Systems/limitations View, *Psychological Bulletin*, Vol. 126, No. 2, March 2000, pp. 281–308.

[3] Morrongiello B. A., Fenwick K. D. & Chance G., Cross-modal Learning in Newborn Infants: Inferences about Properties of Auditory-visual Events, *Infant Behavior and Development*, No. 21, 1998, pp. 543–554.

在出生后，新生儿就接触到不同的面孔，同时伴随着各种各样的语音。面孔和语音的同步呈现为新生儿至婴儿期言语的习得奠定了认知基础。Coulon 等人以视频作为实验材料，考察了新生儿在加工面孔和语音时的特性。[1] 结果发现，视频中新生儿不熟悉的、却在讲话的面孔能显著提高对面孔的识别。这表明视听整合是个体出生后面孔及其相关线索加工的重要基础。

二 触觉参与的整合加工

在和母亲的肌肤接触中，新生儿第一次感受着这个世界的温暖与美好。除视觉和听觉之外，触觉是新生儿感受世界的重要途径。很多研究者从新生儿的视觉—触觉的整合与跨通道转移中，考察了个体发展早期跨通道加工的特性。Gibson 发现在一个月大的新生儿中出现了从对物质的手感（如光滑的/颗粒状的）和"口感"（新生儿用口部感受到的软/硬）向视觉的转移。[2] Streri 也发现，两个月大的婴儿能够用眼睛识别一个曾经用右手操控过的物体的形状。[3]

Strerie 和 Gentaz 考察了新生儿从右手到眼睛的关于形状的跨通道识别特点。[4] 实验分为两组：触觉条件是给新生儿可以用手触摸却不让他们看到的物体；然后是视觉测试条件，即向新生儿呈现刚才那个触摸过的物体和一个新的物体，每个物体呈现 60 秒。被试由 24 名新生儿组成（平均年龄为出生后 62 小时）。触摸的物体是

---

[1] Coulon M., Guellai B. & Streri A., Recognition of Unfamiliar Talking Faces at Birth, *International Journal of Behavioral Development*, No. 35, April 2011, pp. 282–287.

[2] Gibson E. J., *Principles of perceptual learning and development*. New York: Appleton.

[3] Streri A., Tactile Discrimination of Shape and Intermodal Transfer in 2-to 3-month-old Infants, *British Journal of Developmental Psychology*, No. 5, 1987, pp. 213–220.

[4] Streri A. & Gentaz E., Crossmodal Recognition of Shape from Hand to Eyes in Human Newborns, *Somatosensory and Motor Research*, No. 20, 2003, pp. 11–16.

一个小圆柱体或小棱柱（直径为10mm）。向实验组（12名新生儿）呈现触觉和视觉条件的刺激，向控制组（12名新生儿）呈现视觉条件的刺激。实验结果发现，与熟悉的物体相比，实验组的新生儿注视新物体的时间更长；控制组的新生儿注视两组刺激的时长相同。而且，实验组的新生儿更倾向于将注视点转向新的物体而不是熟悉的物体，这种情况在控制组中没有出现。这些结果表明，新生儿通过触觉与视觉的对比进行熟悉物体的识别，由此说明在新生儿中已经出现了触觉和视觉之间的信息整合与跨通道加工。

第二节　视听言语知觉的发展

语言加工是个体成长中非常重要的部分，不仅关系到认知的发展，还会影响个体的社会关系形成。尤其在发展早期，能否用语言清晰地表达自己的需要和想法对儿童建构亲密关系、提高自己的生活质量具有重要影响。早期对语言信号的加工，尤其是从语言信号中提取出相应的意义，对习得语言功能具有重要作用。比如妈妈说话的声音（听觉）和妈妈说话时的口型（视觉），这种多通道的信号影响着儿童习得言语，获得人际交流的能力。那么，从出生开始，个体是如何对这些多通道的言语信息进行加工的？

一　婴儿的视听言语知觉能力

成人后不论是对复杂环境中简单信号的觉察、识别和整合能力，还是对社会环境中人际交往信号（如他人的表情、语音语调等）的识别、理解能力，均需要个体在生命早期就拥有整合不同感觉通道信息的技能。比如，在婴儿时期，除感受周围他人的语音语调，还能从这些简单音节中抽取出其中的语义甚至情感信号，都对这个婴儿在成年后的社会交往技能产生重要影响。我们感受到的儿童早期言语表达的流畅性，从更加微观的角度来看，实际上，来自面部（视觉）和发音系统（听觉）信号的重叠，并且这些信号在时间和空间上产生重叠。

用于解释这些现象的观点有如下几种：

首先是经典的发展整合观（Developmental Integration View），此观点认为在生命早期，婴儿并不能感知跨通道信号之间的一致性和相关性，只是分离的感受单通道信号，由于经验的影响才逐渐获得整合不同单通道信号的能力。[1][2][3]

其次是另一个较为经典的发展分化观（Developmental Differentiation View）[4]，此观点认为，一些基础的多感官知觉能力在出生时就已经存在了。与发展整合观一致的是，发展分化观也认为，通过对周围越来越复杂的环境中的不同信息进行知觉学习，婴儿逐渐认识到所处环境中那些单通道信息的复杂性，以及这些复杂的单通道信息之间的相关。

随着相关研究的不断深入，越来越多的研究发现，上述两种观点并非渐行渐远，而是有大量研究证实，不断发展的整合能力和分化过程能够共同作用于婴儿的整合加工能力的出现。事实上，有研究已经发现，早在婴儿时期就已经出现了某些相对原始的通道间的知觉能力[5]；并且，由于婴儿自身的发展需要更复杂的知觉经验，

---

[1] Birch H. G. & Belmont L., Auditory Visual Integration in Normal and Retarded Readers, *Annals of Dyslexia*, No. 15, 1964, pp. 48 – 96.

[2] Birch H. G. & Lefford A., Visual Differentiation, Intersensory Integration, and Voluntary Motor Control, *Monographs of the Society for Research in Child Development*, No. 32, 1967, pp. 1 – 87.

[3] Piaget J., *The origins of intelligence in children*. New York: International Universities Press, 1952.

[4] Gibson E. J., *Principles of Perceptual Learning and Development*. New York: Appleton, 1969.

[5] Lewkowicz D. J., The Development of Intersensory Temporal Perception: An Epigenetic Systems/limitations View, *Psychological Bulletin*, Vol. 126, No. 2, March 2000, pp. 281 – 308.

他们在生长过程中也逐渐被置于充满各种通道信息的环境中，这就进一步促进了其自身有关多通道信息的整合和加工能力。由此看来，无论是基于"生来就有"的发展整合观，还是基于"经验驱使"的发展分化观，婴儿的多通道知觉能力是遗传与环境的共同产物。

但是，最近有研究发现，婴儿有关通道间信息的加工能力并不总是一直在发展。比如，有研究者利用面孔和声音信息作为实验材料，发现年幼的婴儿能匹配其他物种的面孔及其声音[①②]，或者非原生的视觉和听觉信息[③]。但是，随着年龄逐渐增长，他们却在对后者的匹配中以失败告终。

有关婴儿期视听双通道信息的整合加工能力到底是怎样的过程，其中又存在哪些特点等问题，均是基于早期整合能力与神经系统发育成熟度和复杂的知觉经验之间的不平衡关系所提出的，因此仍然有几个亟待解决的问题。比如，对于整合视听双通道的言语信息的能力是在发展的哪个时间段获得的；当这种能力出现的时候，还有哪些认知过程会促进婴儿对于视听双通道信息的整合加工；这些认知过程是否先于视听整合加工出现等。

二　从儿童到成年期视听言语加工的发展

从上文我们可知，很多研究均揭示了早在婴儿期个体就获得了

---

① Lewkowicz D. J., Leo I. & Simion F., Intersensory Perception at Birth: Newborns Match Nonhuman Primate Faces and Voices, *Infancy*, No. 15, Jannuary 2010, pp. 46–60.
② Lewkowicz D. J. & Ghazanfar A. A., The Decline of Cross-species Intersensory Perception in Human Infants, *Proceedings of the National Academy Sciences USA*, No. 10, 2006, pp. 6771–6774.
③ Pons F., Lewkowicz D. J., Soto-Faraco S. & Sebastián-Gallés N., Narrowing of Intersensory Speech Perception in Infancy, *Proceedings of the National Academy of Sciences USA*, No. 106, 2009, pp. 10598–10602.

视听整合加工的能力[1][2][3][4],同时相关研究也指出,视听整合加工能力的发展,不仅仅依赖于先天因素,后天经验的学习和积累同样重要[5][6][7][8]。基于这些理论可以推测,在儿童期仍然会延续婴儿期视听整合加工能力的发展。

McGurk 效应就是一个很好的例证。McGurk 和 MacDonald 的研究采用了不同年龄阶段的被试,如 3—5 岁的幼儿、7—8 岁的儿童以及 18—40 岁的成年人,结果发现在童年中期和成年期之间有一个明显的中断,表现为幼儿和儿童期的被试比成年被试更不稳定,他们在接下来的一系列实验中均表现出这种趋势[9][10]。有研究者认为,这种发展趋势可以被解释为对于年龄较小的被试,他们的视觉言语经验的接收量要比成年人少很多。Massaro 等人也认为,这些年龄较小的被试之所以呈现这种特点,主要在于他们从周围刺激中

---

[1] Burnham D., Visual Recognition of Mother by Young Infants: Facilitation by Speech, *Perception*, Vol. 22, No. 10, 1993, pp. 1133 – 1153.

[2] Kuhl P. & Meltzoff A., The Bimodal Perception of Speech in Infancy, *Science*, Vol. 218, No. 4577, December 1982, pp. 1138 – 1141.

[3] Kuhl P. K. & Meltzoff A. N., Speech as an Intermodal Object of Perception. In A. Yonas (Ed.), *Perceptual development in infancy. The Minnesota Symposia on Child Psychology*. Hillsdale, NJ: Erlbaum, 1988, pp. 235 – 266.

[4] Lewkowicz D. J. & Turkewitz G., Intersensory Interaction in Newborns: Modification of Visual Preferences Following Exposure to Sound, *Child Development*, No. 52, September 1981, pp. 827 – 832.

[5] MacKain K., Studdert – Kennedy M., Spieker S. & Stern D., Infant Intermodal Speech Perception is a Left-hemisphere Function, *Science*, Vol. 219, No. 4590, March 1983, pp. 1347 – 1349.

[6] Patterson M. L. & Werker J. F., Matching Phonetic Information in Lips and Voice is Robust in 4.5-month-old Infants, *Infant Behavior and Development*, No. 22, December 1999, pp. 237 – 247.

[7] Patterson M. L. & Werker J. F., Two-month-old Infants Match Phonetic Information in Lips and Voice, *Developmental Science*, Vol. 6, No. 2, 2003, pp. 191 – 196.

[8] Sai F. Z., The Role of the Mother's Voice in Developing Mother's Face Preference: Evidence for Intermodal Perception at Birth, *Infant and Child Development*, No. 14, 2005, pp. 29 – 50.

[9] Desjardins R. N., Rogers J. & Werker J. F., An Exploration of Why Preschoolers Perform Differently than Do Adults in Audiovisual Speech Perception Tasks, *Journal of Experimental Child Psychology*, Vol. 66, No. 1, July 1997, pp. 85 – 110.

[10] Sekiyama K. & Burnham D., Impact of Language on Development of Auditory-visual Speech Perception, *Developmental Science*, Vol. 11, No. 2, March 2008, pp. 306 – 320.

抽取的刺激少于成年人，因此，在 McGurk 效应中，和成年人相比，年幼的儿童有更差的读唇技能。

从上述研究中可以看出，年幼的婴儿能在实验中展现出 McGurk 效应，他们能从周围的刺激物中抽取足够的视觉信息来习得、区分语言。这能够说明在视听整合能力的发展中，视觉经验并不是唯一的影响因素，或者说，很少量的视觉经验就足够建立视听整合机制。

在童年晚期的言语知觉中，视觉经验的影响逐渐增加的趋势也受到其他环境因素的调节，比如语言环境，甚至可以推广到不同的文化背景下。这个论断在以不同语言体系的成年人为被试的实验中已经被证实。比如，与西方文化的被试相比，日本被试很少能全面展示 McGurk 效应和视听言语整合。[1][2] 对于这种和语言相关的视听整合加工的差异，不同研究者给出的解释不尽相同。有研究者从个体在交流时对对方面孔的关注程度上进行解释：在日本文化下，交流时直接注视对方的比在西方文化下少得多，这就导致语音的视觉经验较少，也就减少了语音的视觉经验对视听语言整合加工的影响。但是，也不能完全按照这种文化差异来解释所有的具有语言差异的视听语言加工，比如，Aloufy 等人发现，与说英语的被试相比，说希伯来语的被试的视觉影响也减少了。也有研究者从其他角度来解释这种差异，比如日语的音位库没有英语的音位库拥挤，日语使用者在日常口语交流中较少使用视觉线索来辅助交流，从而产

---

[1] Sekiyama K. & Burnham D., Impact of Language on Development of Auditory-visual Speech Perception, *Developmental Science*, Vol. 11, No. 2. March 2008, pp. 306–320.

[2] Sekiyama K. & Tohkura Y., McGurk Effect in Non-English Listeners: Few Visual Effects for Japanese Subjects Hearing Japanese Syllables of High Auditory Intelligibility, *Journal of the Acoustical Society of America*, Vol. 90, No. 4, October 1991, pp. 1797–1805.

生较少依赖语音中的视觉线索的结果。[1][2]

在成年期，影响视听整合加工能力的另一个比较重要的因素可能是感觉敏锐度的变化。有研究者认为，多感觉整合能力在老年期会变得比年轻的时候更加重要，因为在老年期，单个感官通道的处理信息的能力显著下降，这就使得大脑整合不同通道的信息变得更为重要。但也有研究者持相反观点：比如 Ross 等人的研究采用了18—59 岁的被试，发现年龄与视听整合加工能力呈显著负相关，也就是说，随着年龄增长，视听整合加工能力明显下降。[3] 目前，有关年龄和多感觉整合能力（尤其是视听整合加工能力）的关系还在进一步探讨中。

三 视听言语加工能力发展的神经基础

从新生儿到老年期有关视听言语加工能力的发展，不仅依赖于各个单通道能力的发展，其最本质的基础来自神经系统结构和机能的不断变化。因此，想要探明视听言语加工能力的发展趋势，一个重要的知识基础便是与此相关的神经系统结构和机能的发展特点。

由于研究手段和技术的限制，只有很少一部分研究考察了婴儿的视听语音感知的神经基础。比如，一些研究者发现，婴儿在出生

---

[1] Aloufy S., Lapidot M. & Myslobodsky M., Differences in Susceptibility to the "Blending Illusion" among Native Hebrew and English Speakers, *Brain and Language*, Vol. 53, No. 1, April 1996, pp. 51 – 57.

[2] Sekiyama K. & Burnham D., Impact of Language on Development of Auditory-visual Speech Perception, *Developmental Science*, Vol. 11, No. 2, March 2008, pp. 306 – 320.

[3] Ross L. A., Saint – Amour D., Leavitt V. M., Javitt D. C. & Foxe J. J., Do You See What I am Saying? Exploring Visual Enhancement of Speech Comprehension in Noisy Environments, *Cerebral Cortex*, Vol. 17, No. 5, May 2007, pp. 1147 – 1153.

后的几个月中出现了早期视听匹配和整合加工的能力。① 其中最值得一提的一项研究是 MacKain 等人以 5—6 个月大的婴儿为被试所做的研究，实验中向这些婴儿呈现一串双音节假词（如/vava//zu-zu/）以及说话的人脸面孔视频片段。这两个面孔都说出了双音节假词，与声音呈现的音节在时间上是同步的，但只有一个视觉刺激和听觉刺激的内容是一致的。结果发现，这些婴儿喜欢有选择地看在语言与配乐上一致的视频片段，但是这个结果的发生是有限制条件的：只有上述材料出现在婴儿右侧视频时，此结果才会出现。这个结果表明，婴儿期语音视听匹配的相关脑区是左半球。

Kushnerenko 等人采用电生理技术考察了 5 个月婴儿的跨通道言语感知能力。② 在实验中，让这些婴儿被试听和看音节/ba/和/ga/，同时记录他们的脑电活动。视觉和听觉实验材料在内容上组成跨通道匹配或不匹配的两组：在不匹配条件中，听觉/ba/和视觉/ga/同时呈现，此时产生了与预期相一致的感觉整合结果（"da"），在这种情况下，电生理结果与跨通道匹配刺激（/ba/ + [ba] 或/ga/ + [ga]）没有差异。最重要的是，在另一个不匹配的条件下，听觉的/ga/和视觉的 [ba] 同时呈现。在这种条件下，由跨通道不匹配条件刺激引发的电生理结果与由跨通道匹配条件刺激引发的电生理结果产生显著差异。诱发电位差异的时间和头皮分布表明，视听整合加工的效应可以体现在听觉皮层。视听整合在早期感觉阶段的表现与成年人的表现相吻合，因此，Kusherenko 等人的结果表明，类似成年人的视听整合网络的组织在生命早期就开始了。

---

① Baier R., Idsardi W. & Lidz J., Two-month-olds are Sensitive to Lip Rounding in Dynamic and Static Speech Events. Paper Presented in the International Conference on Auditory-Visual Speech Processing（AVSP2007）, Kasteel Groenendaal, Hilvarenbeek, The Netherlands, 31 August-3 September 2007.

② Kushnerenko E., Teinonen T., Volein A. & Csibra G., Electrophysiological Evidence of Illusory Audiovisual Speech Percept in Human Infants, *Proceedings of the National Academy of Sciences U. S. A.*, Vol. 105, No. 32, August 2008, pp. 11442 – 11445.

Bristow 及其同事以 10 周大的婴儿为被试，以视听双通道的信号为刺激，发现婴儿在经过短暂的对相同或不同的元音（如/i/）的习惯期后，对听觉呈现的元音（如/a/）产生了失匹配的脑电波形，无论在习惯期以何种感官方式呈现元音（听觉或视觉），这种波形都非常相似。① 这种结果标明本实验中此年龄段的婴儿有跨通道或单通道的音位表征，这与行为研究的结果相一致，说明仅 10 周大的婴儿便有能力对语音进行感觉通道内的匹配。②③ 有趣的是，头皮分布和失匹配反应的脑电结果显示，和语音匹配有关的左侧皮质网络与对其他类型的跨通道匹配（如脸部—声音—性别）敏感的区域是没有显著相关的。同时值得注意的是，在 10 周大的时候，这个网络已经与通常在成人身上看到的视听整合区域有大量重叠，包括额部（左下额皮质）和颞部（左上和左下颞回）区域。

Dick 等人以年龄更大一些的儿童为被试对视听整合涉及的相关脑区进行考察。④ 结果发现，到 9 岁时，儿童依赖成人用于视听语音处理的相同脑区网络工作。研究者又采用结构方程模型比较了成人和儿童被试电生理的结果，表现为额下回后部/外侧前运动皮层对边缘上回的调节效应在不同年龄组中存在差异，研究者认为，这可能是语言经验调节的成熟过程的结果。

不难发现，上述研究结果证实视听整合的基本脑机制尽管不成熟，但在生命早期就已经出现，这些机制及其相关的神经生理基础

---

① Bristow D., Dehaene-Lambertz G., Mattout J., et al., Hearing Faces: How the Infant Brain Matches the Face It Sees with the Speech it Hears, *Journal of Cognitive Neuroscience*, Vol. 21, No. 5, May 2008, pp. 905–921.

② Kuhl P. & Meltzoff A., The Bimodal Perception of Speech in Infancy, *Science*, Vol. 218, No. 4577, December 1982, pp. 1138–1141.

③ Patterson M. L. & Werker J. F., Matching Phonetic Information in Lips and Voice is Robust in 4.5-month-old Infants, *Infant Behavior and Development*, No. 22, December 1999, pp. 237–247.

④ Dick A. S., Solodkin A. & Small S. L., Neural Development of Networks for Audiovisual Speech Comprehension, *Brain and Language*, Vol. 114, No. 2, August 2010, pp. 101–114.

伴随着视听整合加工过程经历了一个缓慢的发展阶段——从婴儿早期到成年早期。这种观点与之前关于"婴儿和成人的视听整合机制没有显著差异"的说法相吻合。从另一个角度说，正是从婴儿到成人期的漫长岁月，才使得个体在发展过程中习得更多的经验，来作用于与视听整合加工相关的脑结构和机能的发展。

第三章

特殊群体的多感觉整合加工

一直以来，特殊群体的心理与行为的特点和发生、发展机制受到了研究者的广泛关注，但聚焦多感觉整合加工的研究少之又少，例如，发展性阅读障碍最初被定性为"字盲"，研究者很少考虑这种障碍本身是否与知觉加工缺陷有关。像自闭症这样的神经发育障碍群体，研究者对于他们的知觉加工特性关注较少，可能原因在于自闭症群体本身的社会交往能力缺陷，导致他们无法有效配合基础研究开展。但是，无论如何，作为重要的知觉加工过程，多感觉整合加工都不应该被研究者忽略。探讨特殊群体的基础认知加工过程，有利于我们更好地了解这些特殊群体的其他临床表征及其潜在的心理机制。

第一节　听障与视障群体的多感觉整合加工

一　听障群体的多感觉整合加工

有 90%—95% 的聋哑儿童出生在健康的听力环境中。由于他们的父母是正常人群，所以，在这样的环境里，这些聋哑儿童能够随时随地感受与口语有关的视觉因素。[1] 对于聋哑儿童来说，在他们言语感知能力的发展过程中较为重要的因素是视觉方面的刺激，这些视觉刺激是语言理解能力的核心，尤其是涉及唇语阅读方面的经验，决定了这些聋哑儿童是否能达到与人交往的正常水平。因此，对于这些聋哑儿童的健康发展，尤其是对于他们言语能力的发展来说，他们的言语能力是否能在后天训练中得到改善是非常值得我们去思考与探索的。

一些研究对比了聋哑群体和正常人，考察了这两类人群与唇读能力有关的内容。比如，有研究发现，一部分先天性耳聋的人比正常听力的人有更好的唇读能力。[2][3][4] 另有研究考察了读唇术训练的效果，结果发现，至少在短期训练（如5周）的情况下，无论是听力正常群体还是聋人群体的训练效果都没有预期的好，这表明要发展读唇术这项技能可能需要更长期的训练与经验的积累。[5] 还有研究对比了先天性聋人和发育性聋人之间的差异，发现影响有效语音阅读能力发展的一个关键因素是早期对听觉和视觉语音之间的对应

---

[1] Campbell R. & MacSweeney M., Neuroimaging Studies of Crossmodal Plasticity and Language Processing in Deaf People, In *The handbook of multisensory processes* (ed. G. A. Calvert, C. Spence, and B. A. Stein), 2004, pp. 773 – 778. MIT Press, Cambridge, M. A.

[2] Auer E. T. & Jr. Bernstein L. E., Enhanced Visual Speech Perception in Individuals with Early-onset Hearing Impairment, *Journal of Speech, Language and Hearing Research*, Vol. 50, No. 5, October 2007, pp. 1157 – 1165.

[3] Bernstein L. E., Demorest M. E. & Tucker P. E., Speech Perception without Hearing, *Perception and Psychophysics*, Vol. 62, No. 2, 2000, pp. 233 – 252.

[4] Mohammed T., Campbell R., MacSweeney M., Milne E., Hansen P. & Coleman M., Speechreading Skill and Visual Movement Sensitivity are Related in Deaf Speechreaders, *Perception*, Vol. 34, No. 2, 2005, pp. 205 – 216.

[5] Bernstein L. E., Auer E. T. & Tucker P. E., Enhanced Speechreading in Deaf Adults: Can Shortterm training/practice Close the Gap for Hearing Adults, *Journal of Speech, Language and Hearing Research*, Vol. 44, No. 1, February 2001, pp. 5 – 18.

关系的体验。[1]

在聋哑人群中考察其视听整合能力的困难比较大，因此，需要依赖外界工具来帮助这些聋哑群体获得听觉体验。人工耳蜗是一种基于电刺激听觉神经的技术，被广泛应用于聋哑群体中。人工耳蜗的使用使听障人群有机会获得正常或接近正常的声音输入，这也使相关研究人员有机会进一步探讨这部分人群的视听整合加工能力。研究发现，如果在婴儿期就植入人工耳蜗，多年后，聋人在视听语言感知中仍会保持明显的视觉优势。[2] 比如，Rouger 等人发现对于 McGurk 效应来说，正常听力被试的典型整合反应是"da"，而对于晚期植入人工耳蜗的被试来说，其整合反应是当"ga"在视觉上呈现而"ba"在听觉上呈现时报告"ga"，也就是说，他们显示出更高的视觉主导反应；而对于那些人工耳蜗在 30 个月前被植入的被试来说，他们会表现出与正常人群相同的 McGurk 效应。[3][4]

因此，上述有关人工耳蜗的使用与视听整合加工关系的研究表明，聋人的大脑早期倾向于从视觉上解码语音，而当他们的听觉有明显改善时（植入人工耳蜗 6 个月后），他们对视觉语音信息的强烈偏向不受影响。然而，在发展的早期阶段，足够的经验会导致正常语音（没有视觉偏见的）的视听整合。此外，接受人工耳蜗的人

---

[1] Auer E. T. & Jr. Bernstein L. E., Enhanced Visual Speech Perception in Individuals with Early‐onset Hearing Impairment, *Journal of Speech, Language and Hearing Research*, Vol. 50, No. 5, October 2007, pp. 1157–1165.

[2] Rouger J., Fraysse B., Deguine O. & Barone P., McGurk Effects in Cochlear‐implanted Deaf Subjects, *Brain Research*, No. 1188, January 2008, pp. 87–99.

[3] Barker B. A. & Tomblin J. B., Bimodal Speech Perception in Infant Hearing Aid and Cochlear Implant Users, *Archives of Otolaryngology-Head and Neck Surgery*, Vol. 130, No. 5, May 2004, pp. 582–586.

[4] Schorr E. A., Fox N. A., van Wassenhove V. & Knudsen E. I., Auditory-Visual Fusion in Speech Perception in Children with Cochlear Implants, *Proceedings of the National Academy of Sciences USA*, Vol. 102, No. 51, December 2005, pp. 18748–18750.

似乎在将唇读的视觉信息与新的声学输入整合的能力方面（比健康对照组）表现得更强。①

在神经水平上，聋人的初级听觉皮层经历了与正常听力群体相似的结构发展（例如在大小方面），因此，表明该区域可以在没有任何听觉输入的情况下被其他通道所使用。②③ 事实上，现有的证据表明在感知视觉语言和非语言刺激时，聋人的听觉联想和多感觉区（如颞上回和沟）的参与程度比正常听力的人要高。④⑤ 这种功能重组似乎是在耳聋发生后迅速产生的。比如，有研究者认为，重组功能的产生可能是由于先前存在的多感官神经回路中相对快速的适应过程的结果⑥；有研究者采用 fMRI 技术发现先天性聋人在进行视觉语音感知时，外侧上颞的活动没有增多，这就表明一些预先就存在的并且专门用于整合视听语音信息的工作回路，需要在视觉上

---

① Rouger J., Lagleyre S., Fraysse B., Deneve S., Deguine O. & Barone P., Evidence That Cochlearim Planted Deaf Patients are Better Multisensory Integrators, *Proceedings of the National Academy of Sciences USA*, Vol. 104, No. 17, April 2007, pp. 7295 – 7300.

② Emmorey K., Allen J. S., Bruss J., Schenker N. & Damasio H., A Morphometric Analysis of Auditory Brain Regions in Congenitally Deaf Adults, *Proceedings of the National Academy of Sciences USA*, Vol. 100. No. 17, August 2003, pp. 10049 – 10054.

③ Penhune V. B., Cismaru R., Dorsaint – Pierre R., Petitto L. A. & Zatorre R. J., The Morphometry of Auditory Cortex in the Congenitally Deaf Measured Using MRI, *Neuroimage*, Vol. 20. No. 2, October 2003, pp. 1215 – 1225.

④ Lee H. J., Tru E., Mamou G., Sappey-Marinier D. & Giraud A. L., Visual Speech Circuits in Profound Acquired Deafness: A Possible Role for Latent Multimodal Connectivity, *Brain*, Vol. 130, No. 11, November 2007, pp. 2929 – 2941.

⑤ Finney E. M., Clementz B. A., Hickok G. & Dobkins K. R., Visual Stimuli Activate Auditory Cortex in Deaf Subjects: Evidence from MEG, *Neuroreport*, Vol. 14, No. 11, August 2003, pp. 1425 – 1427.

⑥ Lee H. J., Tru E., Mamou G., Sappey – Marinier D. & Giraud A. L., Visual Speech Circuits in Profound Acquired Deafness: A Possible Role for Latent Multimodal Connectivity, *Brain*, Vol. 130, No. 11, November 2007, pp. 2929 – 2941.

利用更多的视听多感官区域[1][2]。

二 视障群体的多感觉整合加工

一般认为,那些从未经历过语言视觉相关因素的先天性盲人似乎完全能够使用(包括理解和产生)口语,这一事实证明了视听结合在语言感知发展中具有重要作用。有研究者发现,盲人和视力正常的人在涉及视觉上独特的发音,比如在"p"的发音上有轻微的差异,但是,这些差异非常小,并未达到显著性水平。[3] 针对盲人的言语感知能力的相关研究非常少,仅有的几项研究发现:由于补偿机制,盲人的声学感知(以及因此而产生的听觉言语感知)要优于视力正常的人。与这一观点相一致的是,Lucas 的研究表明,盲童在发现口头故事中的错误拼写方面有更高的能力[4];Muchnik 等人的研究表明,盲人比视力正常的人更少受到语音中噪声的影响[5]。那么是否可以说明盲人在语音感知方面的优势,可能预示着视觉语音在语言获得过程中的作用并不是必需的?但是,目前为止,关于盲人的言语感知是否存在优越性,我们还没得到充分的证据,这也有待于未来研究给出答案。

---

[1] Campbell R. & MacSweeney M., Neuroimaging Studies of Crossmodal Plasticity and Language Processing in Deaf People, In *The handbook of multisensory processes* (ed. G. A. Calvert, C. Spence, and B. A. Stein), 2004, pp. 773 – 778. MIT Press, Cambridge, M. A.

[2] MacSweeney M., Calvert G. A., Campbell R., et al., Speechreading Circuits in People Born Deaf, *Neuropsychologia*, Vol. 40, No. 7, 2002, pp. 801 – 807.

[3] Ménard L., Dupont S., Baum S. R. & Aubin J., Production and Perception of French Vowels by Congenitally Blind Adults and Sighted Adults, *Journal of the Acoustical Society of America*, Vol. 126, No. 3, September 2009, pp. 1406 – 1414.

[4] Lucas S. A., Auditory Discrimination and Speech Production in the Blind Child, *International Journal of Rehabilitation Research*, No. 7, 1984, pp. 74 – 76.

[5] Muchnik C., Efrati M., Nemeth E., Malin M. & Hildesheimer M., Central Auditory Skills in Blind and Sighted Subjects, *Scandinavian Journal of Audiology*, Vol. 20, No. 1, 1991, pp. 19 – 23.

第二节 自闭症群体的多感觉整合

自闭症谱系障碍（Autism Spectrum Disorders，ASD）是一种发育障碍，其特征是社会互动和交流受损，以及行为、兴趣和活动的限制性、重复性和刻板性模式。根据第五版《精神疾病诊断与统计手册》（DSM-V）对自闭症谱系障碍的统一诊断标准，目前对这种神经发育障碍的"谱系"特点有了更加清晰的认识。[1] 尤其是针对自闭特质，研究者一致认为，这种第六大人格特质在 ASD 和正常人群中广泛存在，只不过与 ASD 相关的症状在严重性上具有量化的差异。

除此之外，在 ASD 中开展的研究包括在认知、情感和行为领域，均发现了 ASD 和正常人群的显著差异。在多通道加工能力方面，也有不少研究者利用不同的研究方法和技术展开探索。一些研究者认为，多感官整合的障碍可能是 ASD 的核心缺陷。[2][3][4][5] 比如，Foxe 和 Molholm 发现，在整合或结合不同的感觉刺激（例如将弹跳

---

[1] American Psychiatric Association. Diagnostic and Statistical Manual of Mental Disorders (DSM-5). 2013; American Psychiatric Association, Washington, D. C.

[2] Bahrick L. E., Intermodal Perception and Selective Attention to Intersensory Redundancy: Implications for Typical Social Developmental and Autism, In *The Wiley – Blackwell Handbook of Infant Development*, 2nd edn. (eds. J. G. Bremner, and T. D. Wachs), 2010, pp. 120 – 166. Wiley – Blackwell, Oxford, UK.

[3] Bahrick L. E. & Todd J. T., Multisensory Processing in Autism Spectrum Disorders: Intersensory Processing Disturbance as a Basis for Atypical Development, In *The new handbook of multisensory processes* (ed. B. E. Stein), 2012, MIT Press, Cambridge, M. A.

[4] Foxe J. J. & Molholm S., Ten Years at the Multisensory Forum: Musings on the Evolution of a Field, *Brain Topography*, Vol. 21. No. 3, May 2009, pp. 149 – 154.

[5] Oberman L. S. & Ramachandran V. S., Preliminary Evidence for Deficits in Multisensory Integration in Autism Spectrum Disorders: The Mirror Neuron Hypothesis, *Social Neuroscience*, Vol. 3, No. 3, 2008, pp. 348 – 355.

球的运动与球落地的声音联系起来）时，ASD 存在明显缺陷。①Foxe 和 Molholm 认为，正是这种缺陷可能导致 ASD 患者的混乱，从而进一步引发 ASD 的核心缺陷症状，如社会退缩。Bahrick 及其同事对 ASD 的多感觉整合加工的起源问题进行了考察，认为婴儿早期对感官内冗余的参与和脱离注意力不足，可能导致对社会刺激的定向出现特殊问题，从而解释了后来 ASD 儿童在社会交往中的困难。②③

其他研究者针对 ASD 的多感觉整合能力缺陷提出了不同的解释。比如，Oberman 和 Ramachandran 认为，"镜像神经元系统"的异常是导致 ASD 的核心因素。④⑤ 镜像神经元系统是能将有关他人行动的感觉刺激转换为观察者的类似（镜像）感觉运动表征的大脑网络。⑥ 一些研究者还认为，这些系统可以抑制其他人对思想、情感和行为的理解，对个体发展过程中的模仿、心理理论、语言、共情能力和识别能力都具有重要影响。然而，值得注意的是，尽管 Oberman 和 Ramachandran 一致认为，镜像神经元的缺陷可能与多感

---

① Foxe J. J. & Molholm S., Ten Years at the Multisensory Forum: Musings on the Evolution of a Field, *Brain Topography*, Vol. 21. No. 3, May 2009, pp. 149 – 154.

② Bahrick L. E., Intermodal Perception and Selective Attention to Intersensory Redundancy: Implications for Typical Social Developmental and Autism, In *The Wiley – Blackwell handbook of infant development*, 2nd edn. (eds. J. G. Bremner, and T. D. Wachs), 2010, pp. 120 – 166. Wiley – Blackwell, Oxford, UK.

③ Bahrick L. E. & Todd J. T., Multisensory Processing in Autism Spectrum Disorders: Intersensory Processing Disturbance as a Basis for Atypical Development, In *The new handbook of multisensory processes* (ed. B. E. Stein), 2012, MIT Press, Cambridge, M. A.

④ Oberman L. M. & Ramachandran V. S., The Simulating Social Mind: The Role of the Mirror Neuron System and Simulation in the Social and Communicative Deficits of Autism Spectrum Disorders, *Psychological Bulletin*, Vol. 133, No. 2, March 2007, pp. 310 – 327.

⑤ Oberman L. S. & Ramachandran V. S., Preliminary Evidence for Deficits in Multisensory Integration in Autism Spectrum Disorders: The Mirror Neuron Hypothesis, *Social Neuroscience*, Vol. 3, No. 3, 2008, pp. 348 – 355.

⑥ Rizzolatti G. & Craighero L., The Mirror Neuron System, *Annual Review of Neuroscience*, No. 27, 2004, pp. 169 – 192.

觉整合的缺陷有关，但这个观点并没有得到验证，主要原因在于，在这个观点中到底是镜像神经元影响多感觉整合，还是多感觉整合影响镜像神经元病并没有解释清楚。目前在这方面仍存在争议，比如一些研究者发现 ASD 患者存在镜像神经元系统的异常，但也有研究发现 ASD 个体的模仿能力与正常个体无异。

Gergely 的观点与上述观点基本相似，他特别关注视觉本体感觉偶然性，认为婴儿期对这种偶然性注意的典型发育变化过程不会发生在 ASD 中。[1] 正在发育的婴儿通常会经历注意的变化，他们从喜欢完美的视觉本体感觉偶然性（当他们看到自己的身体产生移动时会有这种感受），过渡到喜欢不完美的偶然性（当他们看到另一个人响应自己的动作而移动时就会有这种感受）。研究发现，这种"偶然性的变化"发生在 3 个月左右的正常儿童中，是潜藏在社会导向行为背后的重要过程。Gergely 认为，这种转变不会发生在患有 ASD 的个体中，因而提出了 ASD 群体不会出现典型的社会性导向行为。[2]

尽管研究者对 ASD 多感觉加工的起源问题存在争论，但到目前为止，相关的经验数据相对较少，也很少有证据能证明这些争论到底谁是谁非。最近的一些研究发现，多感觉整合加工障碍可能是 ASD 相关研究领域的重要突破。一些直接采用 ASD 个体作为被试的研究发现，这些患者对一种感觉信息的注意会损坏对另一种感觉的感知和注意。

一些研究者采用较小的被试（6—12 个月的婴儿）进行考察，

---

[1] Gergely G., The Object of Desire: "Nearly, but Clearly Not, Like Me": Contingency Preference in Normal Children Versus Children with Autism, *Bulletin of the Menninger Clinic*, Vol. 65, No. 3, 2001, pp. 411–426.

[2] Gergely G., The Object of Desire: "Nearly, but Clearly Not, Like Me": Contingency Preference in Normal Children Versus Children with Autism, *Bulletin of the Menninger Clinic*, Vol. 65, No. 3, 2001, pp. 411–426.

发现了他们单通道感知的异常反应,表现为对单个感觉通道的敏感性差异[1][2],因此,研究者认为,这是 ASD 最早的疾病指标之一[3]。这些异常反应不仅出现在婴儿期,在随后的发展阶段中,如在年龄较大的儿童[4][5]、青少年[6]和成人[7]中都发现了这种异常反应。

除感知觉领域外,研究者也开始探索 ASD 的语言加工领域潜在的多感觉整合缺陷。一般认为,语言加工是由多个感官参与的过程,尤其是在语音感知中同时涉及听觉和视觉信息;在阅读过程中,也涉及视听输入和语音发音之间的关系问题。一些研究考察了这些方面,得到了不尽相同的结果。比如,Smith 和 Bennetto 考察了 ASD 和正常青少年的视听加工与唇读之间的关系,结果发现,ASD 青少年在唇读方面明显差于同龄的正常群体,同时在视听言语感知任务中,ASD 青少年从视觉信息中的获益要明显少于正常青少

---

[1] Baranek G. T., Autism during Infancy: A Retrospective Video Analysis of Sensory – motor and Social Behaviors at 9 – 12 Months of Age, *Journal of Autism and Developmental Disorders*, Vol. 29, No. 3, June 1999, pp. 213 – 224.

[2] Dawson G., Osterling J., Meltzoff A. N. & Kuhl P., Case Study of the Development of an Infant with Autism from Birth to 2 Years of Age, *Journal of Applied Developmental Psychology*, Vol. 21, No. 3, May 2000, pp. 299 – 313.

[3] O'Neill M. & Jones R. S. P., Sensory-perceptual Abnormalities in Autism: A Case for More Research, *Journal of Autism and Developmental Disorders*, Vol. 27, No. 3, June 1997, pp. 283 – 293.

[4] Kientz M. A. & Dunn W., A Comparison of the Performance of Children with and without Autism on the Sensory Profile, *American Journal of Occupational Therapy*, Vol. 51, No. 7, August 1997, pp. 530 – 537.

[5] Leekam S. R., Nieto C., Libby S. J., Wing L. & Gould J., Describing the Sensory Abnormalities of Children and Adults with Autism, *Journal of Autism and Developmental Disorders*, Vol. 37, No. 5, May 2007, pp. 894 – 910.

[6] Jones C., Happé F., Baird G., et al., Auditory Discrimination and Auditory Sensory Behaviours in Autism Spectrum Disorders, *Neuropsychologia*, Vol. 47, No. 13, November 2009, pp. 2850 – 2858.

[7] Baron – Cohen S., Ashwin E., Ashwin C., Tavassoli T. & Chakrabati B., Talent in Autism: Hypersystemizing, Hyper-attention to Detail and Sensory Hypersensitivity, *Philosophical Transactions of the Royal Society B: Biological Sciences*, Vol. 364, No. 1522, May 2009, pp. 1377 – 1383.

年。① 因此，Smith 和 Bennetto 认为，这些结果可能反映了 ASD 在视听整合加工中的缺陷。

Oberman 和 Ramachandran 认为，ASD 症状的核心生理机制是镜像神经元系统的受损，基于这个假设，他们考察了"bouble-kiki 效应"②。实验要求被试将无意义的单词与形状配对。正常成人和儿童被试均能正确匹配，表明正常人群能在视觉和听觉刺激之间产生联觉对应，但是，ASD 儿童在这项任务中并不能表现出这种效应。因此，Oberman 和 Ramachandran 认为，这是由于 ASD 不能产生正常整合导致的③。

但也有研究者提出了不同的结果，比如 Williams 等人以 ASD 和正常儿童为被试考察了他们在单通道（视觉、听觉）和双通道条件（需要多感觉整合）下对言语刺激的加工，结果仅在单通道条件下发现了被试间的差异，这就表明 ASD 儿童也能出现正常的多感觉整合。④

综上所述，有关 ASD 是否能产生多感觉整合，以及这种整合能力是否会随着 ASD 个体病情的发展逐渐减退，目前仍是悬而未决的问题，这也有待于未来研究从眼动、脑电等多个技术角度逐一探索。

---

① Smith E. G. & Bennetto L., Audiovisual Speech Integration and Lip-reading in Autism, *Journal of Child Psychology and Psychiatry*, Vol. 48, No. 8, August 2007, pp. 813–821.

② Köhler W., *Gestalt psychology*. Liveright, New York, 1929.

③ Oberman L. S. & Ramachandran V. S., Preliminary Evidence for Deficits in Multisensory Integration in Autism Spectrum Disorders: The Mirror Neuron Hypothesis, *Social Neuroscience*, Vol. 3, No. 3, 2008, pp. 348–355.

④ Williams J. H., Massaro D. W., Peel N. J., Bossele A. & Suddendorf T., Visual-auditory Integration dring Speech Imitation in Autism, *Research in Developmental Disabilities*, Vol. 25, No. 6, December 2004, pp. 559–575.

第三节 发展性阅读障碍群体的多感觉整合

发展性阅读障碍（Developmental Dyslexia，DD）个体在阅读能力和智力能力之间表现出非常显著的差异，这种差异是教学无法弥补的。被诊断有 DD 的个体可能无法学习字母表，无法区分发音相似的单词，存在书写错误（如字母颠倒），并且拼写能力极差。同时，DD 还与口语和书面语言习得、数学、视觉空间能力、运动协调和注意力缺陷有关。

阅读是我们日常生活、学习、工作的重要技能，它要求我们在书面语言（视觉）和语音（听觉）之间进行快速的加工。因此，阅读是涉及视觉和听觉通道快速整合的重要过程。由于这种视听整合特性，相关研究人员开始探索 DD 个体是否由于视听整合缺陷导致的阅读和听写障碍。早在 20 世纪 60 年代就有研究发现，DD 儿童在识别听觉呈现的敲击音和视觉呈现的线条之间是否存在一致性中存在困难，因此得出结论，视觉和听觉的平衡存在缺陷因此导致阅读障碍。[1][2]

Snowling 考察了 DD 儿童的视听对应能力。在实验中，儿童被试进行伪词的识别记忆任务，要求被试进行字素—音素的匹配。结果发现，与阅读能力匹配的对照组相比，患有 DD 的儿童在识别跨通道刺激时存在缺陷，而在识别通道内刺激时与正常儿童并没有显著差异。[3] 在最近的一项研究中，Hairston 和他的同事发现，在处理

---

[1] Birch H. G. & Belmont L., Auditory Visual Integration in Normal and Retarded Readers, *Annals of Dyslexia*, No. 15, 1964, pp. 48-96.

[2] Critchley M., *The dyslexic child*. Heinemann, London, 1970.

[3] Snowling M. J., The Development of Grapheme-phoneme Correspondence in Normal and Dyslexic Readers, *Journal of Experimental Child Psychology*, Vol. 29, No. 2, April 1980, pp. 294-305.

时间信息方面，患有 DD 的成年人和对照组之间的多感觉交互作用存在差异。Hairston 等人使用视觉"时序判断"（TOJ）任务，实验中向被试呈现两个视觉刺激，让被试判断在固定十字架上方或下方的两个刺激哪一个先出现在屏幕上。结果发现，患有 DD 的被试在分辨刺激的时间顺序方面的阈值高得多。也就是说，他们需要在刺激之间有更长的时间间隔才能对其时间顺序做出适当的反应。在其他条件下，听觉刺激对 DD 组的促进作用要大于对照组，而且 DD 组发生这种促进作用的时间窗口更大。Hairston 等人认为，患有 DD 的成年人对听觉和视觉信息的多感官整合的时间窗口扩大，这种扩大的处理多感官信息的时间窗口可能导致多感官整合错误的数量增加。[1] 也就是说，将视觉和听觉信息联系在一起所需时间的增加，从而可能导致更多的阅读错误，进而导致阅读能力的普遍减慢。

　　因此，一些研究表明，DD 患者存在多感觉整合加工的缺陷。然而，多感觉整合是阅读障碍的重要致病原因之一的观点缺乏大量研究支持，有关 DD 个体的多感觉整合加工的研究结果也缺乏一致性。

---

[1] Hairston W. D., Burdette J. H., Flowers D. L., Wood F. B. & Wallace M. T., Altered Temporal Profile of Visual–auditory Multisensory Interactions in Dyslexia, *Experimental Brain Research*, Vol. 166, No. 3, October 2005, pp. 474–480.

第 四 章

注意与多感觉整合加工的关系

随着相关研究的不断深入,研究者们开始关注多感觉整合与注意的关系。结合先进技术手段的发展,这些研究可以为我们探索不同皮层间相互作用的模式与时间进程提供更好的视角。众多研究热点中比较受到当前研究者关注的一个重要问题是多感觉整合的产生是否依赖于注意。一些研究者提出了不同的观点。比如,有研究者对腹语术效应与注意的关系进行了考察,发现作为多感觉整合现象中最为典型的例子,腹语术效应发生在注意之前,即不受注意影响。同时有研究发现,腹语术效应不依赖于有意和无意的空间注意转移,因此得出结论,多感觉整合不需要注意的参与。[1][2] 另有研究者认为,多感觉整合必须发生在当双通道目标被注意时,在不注意条件下不会产生整合效应。[3] 由此可见,有关多感觉整合与注意关系的研究结果较为复杂,目前仍没有定论。

---

[1] Vroomen J., Bertelson P. & de Gelder B., Directing Spatial Attention towards the Illusory Location of a Ventriloquized Sound, *ActaPsychologica*, Vol. 108, No. 1, June 2001, pp. 21 – 33.

[2] Vroomen J., Bertelson P. & de Gelder B., The Ventriloquist Effect Does Not Depend on the Direction of Automatic Visual Attention, *Perception & Psychophysics*, Vol. 63, No. 4, May 2001, pp. 651 – 659.

[3] Talsma D. & Woldorff M. G., Selective Attention and Multisensory Integration: Multiple Phases of Effects on the Evoked Brain Activity, *Journal of Cognitive Neuroscience*, Vol. 17, No. 7, July 2005, pp. 1098 – 1114.

第一节　早期整合模型：多感觉整合不依赖于注意

早期整合模型认为，多感觉整合发生在较早的感觉阶段，其在较晚的阶段才会捕获注意。这个模型表明，多感觉整合的产生不需要注意参与。一些行为研究结果与此观点一致。比如，除上文提到的腹语术效应之外，Van der Burg、Olivers、Bronkhorst 和 Theeuwes 发现多感觉整合的另一个典型例子——凸显效应（the pip and pop effect）——也发生在注意之前[1]。在实验中，他们向被试呈现不同方向的线段（干扰刺激）。被试的任务是在这些线段中快速地搜索水平或垂直的线段（目标刺激）。干扰刺激和目标刺激的颜色在红色和绿色之间随机改变。实验分为有声音条件和无声音条件：在有声音条件中，目标刺激颜色的改变总是伴随着一个短音，这个短音不提供关于目标刺激的任何信息，比如颜色，位置等，只是与目标刺激颜色的改变同时呈现；在无声音条件中，不呈现短音。两种条件下被试的任务完全相同。结果发现，在有声音条件下，被试对同步呈现的目标物体的搜索时间明显减少。Van der Burg 等人认为，这种听觉刺激导致视觉刺激的凸显现象可能是由于两种通道（视觉和听觉）的刺激整合所带来的行为上的收益，也可能是由于听觉刺激的警报作用所导致的。为验证这两种可能性，Van der Burg 等人在第二个实验中加入视觉警报信号，以考察视觉警报信号对视觉刺激的指导作用。第二个实验与第一个实验设置完全相同，唯一不同的是将第一个实验中的短音替换为视觉信号（闪光或注视点的消

---

[1] Van der Burg E., Olivers C. N., Bronkhorst A. W. & Theeuwes J., Audiovisual Events Capture Attention: Evidence from Temporal Order Judgments, *Journal of vision*, Vol. 8, No. 5, May 2008, pp. 1–10.

失)。他们假设：如果视觉信号能指导注意以增强警报作用，并使目标的改变更为明显，那么在呈现这些视觉信号的条件下会有行为表现的增强，即对目标刺激搜索时间的缩短；如果没有发现行为表现的增强，则表明凸显效应是由于两种通道的刺激产生整合而造成的。结果发现，不论用闪光还是注视点的消失作为视觉信号，均没有发现任何搜索时间的改变。在后续实验中，Van der Burg 等人采用另一种新的搜索任务，在呈现两种（视觉和听觉）信号的条件下比较被试的行为表现。结果发现，听觉信号比视觉信号能更为有效地指导被试的行为，表现为对目标刺激搜索时间的减少。Van der Burg 等人认为，凸显效应的发生并不是归因于听觉信号（短音）的警报作用，而是由于听觉信号的时间信息与视觉信号在知觉水平上整合，形成一个相对凸显的特征，并在较晚的阶段吸引注意。

他们在后续研究中考察了视觉与触觉的相互作用与注意的关系。[①] 实验中，同样要求被试在不断改变颜色的干扰刺激中搜索水平或垂直的线段。当目标刺激的颜色改变同时伴随触觉信号时，被试的搜索次数显著减少。此研究结果与上述凸显效应的结果一致表明，多感觉整合发生在前注意阶段，因此符合多感觉整合的早期模型。

最近有研究者认为，早潜伏期的多通道交互作用（early-latency Multisen Sory Interactions，eMSI）可以直接影响行为。[②] 这种观点的出现使多通道加工直接影响知觉和行为看起来更加具有可能性。一些跨物种的研究为这种自下而上的多通道交互作用提供了证据。比

[①] Van der Burg E., Olivers C. N., Bronkhorst A. W. & Theeuwes J., Poke and Pop: Tactile-Visual Synchrony Increases Visual Saliency, *Neuroscience letters*, Vol. 450, No. 1, January 2009, pp. 60–64.

[②] De Meo R., Murray M. M., Clarke S. & Matusz P. J., Top–down Control and Early Multisensory Processes: Chicken Vs. Egg, *Frontiers in integrative neuroscience*, Vol. 9, No. 17, March 2015.

如，有研究者在采用被麻醉的动物作为被试时发现了 eMSI。①② 被麻醉的动物无法进行自上而下的调节，因此表明 eMSI 不受自上而下控制的影响。此外，在考察人类被试的光幻视知觉（phosphene perception）时，有研究者采用经颅磁刺激技术（Transcranial Magnetic Stimulation，TMS）发现，声音能影响低水平视觉皮层的兴奋性。值得注意的是，个体的注意偏好只能影响视觉皮层兴奋性改变的晚期阶段，而非早期阶段。③ 这都为 eMSI 的自下而上的本质提供了证据。④⑤⑥⑦

第二节　晚期整合模型：多感觉整合的产生依赖于注意

支持晚期整合模型的研究者认为，注意会影响个体的感觉输入，个体在较晚的阶段将它们整合成一个单独的知觉。因此，在更

---

① Sarko D. K., Nidiffer A. R., Powers I. I. I. A. R., Ghose D. & Wallace M. T., "Spatial and Temporal Features of Multisensory Processes," in *The Neural Basis of Multisensory Processes*, eds M. M. Murray and M. T. Wallace (Boca Raton, FL: CRC Press), 2012, pp. 191 – 215.

② Rowland B. A. & Stein B. E., A Model of the Temporal Dynamics of Multisensory Enhancement, *Neuroscience & Biobehavioral Reviews*, No. 41, April 2014, pp. 78 – 84.

③ Spierer L., Manuel A. L., Bueti D. & Murray M. M., Contributions of Pitch and Bandwidth to Sound-induced Enhancement of Visual Cortex Excitability in Humans, *Cortex*, Vol. 49, No. 10, January 2013, pp. 2728 – 2734.

④ Romei V., Murray M. M., Merabet L. B. & Thut G., Occipital Transcranial Magnetic Stimulation Has Opposing Effects on Visual and Auditory Stimulus Detection: Implications for Multisensory Interactions, *The Journal of neuroscience*, Vol. 27, No. 43, November 2007, pp. 11465 – 11472.

⑤ Romei V., Murray M. M., Cappe C. & Thut G., Preperceptual and Stimulus-selective Enhancement of Low-level Human Visual Cortex Excitability by Sounds, *Current Biology*, Vol. 19, No. 21, November 2009, pp. 1799 – 1805.

⑥ Romei V., Murray M. M., Cappe C. & Thut G., The Contributions of Sensory Dominance and Attentional Bias to Cross-modal Enhancement of Visual Cortex Excitability, *Journal of Cognitive Neuroscience*, Vol. 25. No. 7, July 2013, pp. 1122 – 1135.

⑦ Spierer L., Manuel A. L., Bueti D. & Murray M. M., Contributions of Pitch and Bandwidth to Sound-induced Enhancement of Visual Cortex Excitability in Humans, *Cortex*, Vol. 49, No. 10, January 2013, pp. 2728 – 2734.

高的多模态脑区（hetero-modal）水平上产生整合之前，多通道刺激首先通过注意被增强，这就导致多感觉整合的发生需要注意参与。一些研究支持这个观点。比如，Talsma、Doty 和 Woldorff 采用快速系列视觉呈现（Rapid Serial Visual Presentation，RSVP）范式在注视点上方呈现一系列字母，每个字母呈现 150ms，每过 1—10s 不等，就会在字母的位置出现一个数字作为目标刺激。[①] 同时，在注视点下方会出现一个干扰刺激，其大小与字母和数字相同。单通道视觉干扰刺激为四条短横线，单通道听觉干扰刺激为短音，多通道干扰刺激为四条短横线和短音同时呈现。每种干扰刺激均呈现 105ms。实验中要求被试注意双通道刺激（注意条件）或不注意双通道刺激（不注意条件）。被试的任务是通过按键来探测目标刺激，同时记录脑电信号。结果表明，在 P50 成分上观察到一个超加性的视听整合成分，即对视听刺激反应的 P50 波幅大于对单通道听觉刺激和对单通道视觉刺激反应的 P50 波幅之和。当多通道刺激不被注意时，超加性效应被反转，即多通道刺激脑电数据中的 P50 波幅小于单通道刺激之和。

在另一项 ERP 研究中，Talsma 和 Woldorff[②] 针对已有研究可能将关联性负变（Contingent Negative Variation，CNV）当作早期整合效应 ERP 成分的潜在问题，对传统实验范式做出调整。为减少预期 ERP 的形成，他们采用随机变化的 SOA（350—650ms）呈现所有刺激，这些刺激以相等的概率呈现在左侧或右侧视野，要求被试注意指定一侧的所有刺激，并对目标刺激进行按键反应，同时记录

---

① Talsma D., Doty T. J. & Woldorff M. G., Selective Attention and Audiovisual Integration: Is Attending to Both Modalities a Prerequisite for Early Integration, *Cerebral Cortex*, Vol. 17, No. 3, March 2007, pp. 679–690.

② Talsma D. & Woldorff M. G., Selective Attention and Multisensory Integration: Multiple Phases of Effects on the Evoked Brain Activity, *Journal of Cognitive Neuroscience*, Vol. 17, No. 7, July 2005, pp. 1098–1114.

被试的脑电成分。数据分析主要关注对非目标刺激的反应。他们认为，虽然这种呈现刺激的方式能有效减少预期 ERP 的形成，但也可能会产生相邻刺激反应的 ERP 重叠的问题。因此，他们在实验中增加了无刺激的试次，即试次中没有任何刺激，这样就有效减少了相邻刺激反应的 ERP 重叠问题。他们的研究发现，与非注意条件相比，注意条件下与多感觉整合效应有关的 ERP 波幅更大，这说明注意能够调节多感觉整合。他们的研究验证了多感觉整合的晚期整合模型，即多感觉整合受注意的影响，表现为多感觉整合效应只有在被注意的条件下才会产生。

第三节　注意影响多感觉整合加工的机制

近几年，不少研究者采用不同的技术手段对多感觉整合的加工特性及其工作方式进行探索。作为信息加工的最主要方面，视听整合加工成为多感觉整合研究领域的重要部分。随着相关研究的不断深入，越来越多的研究者开始关注注意在视听整合中起的作用。有研究者认为，视听整合是自动化过程，不受自上而下控制（如注意）的影响[1]；另有研究者认为，与不被注意的条件相比，只有当双通道刺激被注意时才会产生视听整合[2]，因此认为，注意在视听整合中起重要作用。需要指出的是，认为视听整合不受自上而下控

---

[1] Vroomen J., Bertelson P. & de Gelder B., Directing Spatial Attention towards the Illusory Location of a Ventriloquized Sound, *ActaPsychologica*, Vol. 108, No. 1, June 2001, pp. 21–33.

[2] Talsma D. & Woldorff M. G., Selective Attention and Multisensory Integration: Multiple Phases of Effects on the Evoked Brain Activity, *Journal of Cognitive Neuroscience*, Vol. 17, No. 7, July 2005, pp. 1098–1114.

制影响的早期研究①多关注的是空间注意；而认为注意能够影响视听整合的研究仅关注注意与非注意条件影响视听整合的差异，而忽略了对注意条件的区分。众所周知，注意除能指向空间位置外，还能指向某个感觉通道。②

Wilschut、Theeuwes 和 Olivers 认为，在认知加工方面，注意系统包括定向（空间转移）和选择性（通道选择）等成分。③ 同时，在行为表现上，对空间位置的注意可以增强个体对此位置上信息的知觉，不论刺激来自哪个通道；而对于通道的注意则会减弱个体对不被注意的通道内的信息加工，在被注意的通道内的信息加工则得到增强。④ 也就是说，空间注意不同于指向通道的注意。因此，视听整合加工不受空间注意影响的结论可能并不适用于指向通道的注意。

同时，偏向竞争模型认为，选择性注意能增强对所选择信息的感觉神经反应，并抑制无关反应。⑤⑥ 根据此模型，当注意集中于一个感觉通道（选择性注意）时，对此通道内信息的神经反应被增强，而被忽视通道内信息的神经反应则被抑制，因此，可能在选择性注意条件下，并不会有视听刺激的整合加工。为检验此假设，本

---

① Vroomen J., Bertelson P. & de Gelder B., The Ventriloquist Effect Does Not Depend on the Direction of Automatic Visual Attention, *Perception & Psychophysics*, Vol. 63, No. 4, May 2001, pp. 651 – 659.

② Talsma D., Predictive Coding and Multisensory Integration: An Attentional Account of the Multisensory Mind, *Frontiers in Integrative Neuroscience*, Vol. 26, No. 6, March 2015.

③ Wilschut A., Theeuwes J. & Olivers C. N., The Time Course of Attention: Selection is Transient, *PLoS One*, Vol. 6, No. 11, 2011, p. e27661.

④ Spence C., Audiovisual Multisensory Integration, *Acoustical Science and Technology*, Vol. 28, No. 2, March 2007, pp. 61 – 70.

⑤ Beck D. M. & Kastner S., Top-down and Bottom – up Mechanisms in Biasing Competition in the Human Brain, *Vision research*, Vol. 49, No. 10, June 2009, pp. 1154 – 1165.

⑥ Mishra J. & Gazzaley A., Attention Distributed across Sensory Modalities Enhances Perception Performance, *The journal of neuroscience*, Vol. 32, No. 35, August 2012, pp. 12294 – 12302.

研究的实验 1 通过线索刺激将注意指向不同感觉通道以形成选择性注意（只注意视觉或只注意听觉通道）与分配性注意（同时注意视觉和听觉通道）两种状态，考察这两种注意条件在影响视听整合加工时的差异。

另一方面，我们生活环境中的刺激除共享时间和空间特征外，还共享语义特征，这就构成了刺激之间的语义联结。有研究者认为，大脑在处理信息时，倾向于将内容上匹配的刺激当作源自相同资源处理，或者说，当两种刺激在内容上相一致（如语义一致）时，大脑更倾向于认为它们来源于同一资源，这样更有益于我们的知觉系统将其整合成统一的知觉。[1] 一些以视听言语知觉为考察对象的研究结果与这种视听语义一致信息的加工优势基本一致。比如，有研究发现，与视听不匹配的刺激对相比，当被试听到的声音与看到的面孔在性别上相匹配[2]，或者当被试听到的词语与看到的嘴唇动作相匹配时，双通道刺激均被优先整合。[3] 由此可见，语义一致的视听刺激对更易产生整合加工。那么，在不同的注意条件下，这种语义一致的视听刺激是否仍然具有加工优势？鉴于此，本研究的实验 2 对实验 1 的听觉刺激进行调整，采用人声读出的单字词（"圆""方"）作为与视觉目标刺激语义一致的听觉刺激，这样二者之间就产生语义联结，同时利用短音与视觉目标配对呈现，使二者之间产生不一致的语义联结，分别在选择性注意和分配性注意

---

[1] Su Y. H., Content Congruency and Its Interplay with Temporal Synchrony Modulate Integration between Rhythmic Audiovisual Streams, *Frontiers in Integrative Neuroscience*, No. 8, February 2014, p. 92.

[2] Vatakis A. & Spence C., Crossmodal Binding: Evaluating the "Unity Assumption" Using Audiovisual Speech Stimuli, *Percept. Psychophys*, Vol. 69, No. 5, July 2007, pp. 744–756.

[3] Ten Oever S., Sack A. T., Wheat K. L., Bien N. & Van Atteveldt N., Audio-visual Onset Differences are Used to Determine Syllable Identity for Ambiguous Audio-visual Stimulus Pairs, *Frontiers in Psychology*, No. 4, June 2013, p. 331.

条件下考察不同语义联结程度的视听刺激的整合加工。

尽管一些研究得出了只有在注意条件下才会进行视听整合加工的结论，但这些研究仍忽视了一个重要问题：可用的注意资源量。有研究者对可用的注意资源量影响多感觉整合的问题进行了考察。比如，Alsius、Navarra 和 Campbell 在双任务范式中考察了被试对 McGurk 效应的反应敏感性。[1] 在 Alsius 等人的实验中，视觉刺激是一个女性读单词的视频片段，被试只可以看到这个女性的面部动作；听觉刺激是单词的发音；视听刺激是将视觉和听觉刺激同时呈现。被试的主要任务是回忆刚才看到和听到的单词。负荷刺激分别通过视觉和听觉呈现。在呈现视觉负荷刺激的条件下，在视频中女性的面部添加一个与所读单词无关的图形（如钟表、橱柜）。被试在完成主要任务的同时还需探测重复呈现的图形。在呈现听觉负荷刺激的条件下，呈现听觉刺激的同时向被试播放一个物品的声音（如狗叫、哨子声）。被试对负荷刺激的任务是探测重复呈现的声音。实验结果发现，在双任务条件下，McGurk 效应的百分比减少。因此，Alsius 等人得出结论，在可用的注意资源减少的情况下，视听言语整合减弱。

但是，Alsius 等人的实验存在以下几点不足：首先，在 Alsius 等人的实验中，负荷任务是要求被试探测重复呈现的刺激。由于被试需要先记住上一次刺激的内容，才能对当前刺激进行判断，在对负荷刺激进行反应时，可能不仅消耗了被试的注意资源，还消耗了一定的记忆资源，因此，其结论并不能单纯认为是注意资源的减少而影响了整合加工。其次，Alsius 等人采用的量化多感觉整合的指标是 McGurk 效应的百分比。与行为研究中常用的竞争模型分析相

---

[1] Alsius A., Navarra J., Campbell R. & Soto-Faraco S., Audiovisual Integration of Speech Falters under High Attention Demands, *Current Biology*, Vol. 15, No. 9, May 2005, pp. 839–843.

比，这种量化方法可能存在一定的主观性，无法客观地反映多感觉整合在有无负荷条件下的差异。因此，研究二将采用已有研究中的双任务范式，在实验2的基础上，在分配性注意条件下分别考察视觉注意负荷和听觉注意负荷对视听言语整合加工的影响。

人的感受性不能长久地保持在稳定状态，而是有规律地增强和减弱，这种现象叫作注意的起伏（fluctuation of attention）。注意起伏除与内部的感觉器官适应性有关之外，还受到外部时间规律的调制。[1][2] 有研究者[3][4]利用动态注意理论（Dynamic Attending Theory, DAT）[5][6][7] 来解释此现象。这个理论认为，注意并不是平均分布在各个时间段内的，而是依赖于内部的"动态震荡器"（dynamic oscillator）进行周期性变化。这些震荡器决定个体注意的节奏，并决定个体对外部事件的期待或者加工的速度是否处于注意节奏的峰值。更为重要的是，外部事件的节奏化与时间进程可能会使内部震荡器与外部事件同步而自动地吸引个体的注意。

Escoffier、Sheng 和 Schirmer 考察了不被注意的音乐节奏对视觉

---

[1] Grahn J. A. & Rowe J. B., Finding and Feeling the Musical Beat: Striatal Dissociations between Detection and Prediction of Regularity, *Cerebral Cortex*, Vol. 23, No. 4, April 2012, pp. 913 – 921.

[2] Nozaradan S., Peretz I., Missal M. & Mouraux A., Tagging Theneuronal Entrainment to Beat and Meter, *Journal of Neuroscience*, Vol. 31, No. 28, July 2011, pp. 10234 – 10240.

[3] Escoffier N., Sheng D. Y. J. & Schirmer A., Unattended Musical Beats Enhance Visual Processing, *Acta Psychologica*, Vol. 135, No. 1, September 2010, pp. 12 – 16.

[4] Brochard R., Tassin M. & Zagar D., Got Rhythm…for Better and for Worse, Cross-modal effects of auditory rhythm on visual word recognition. *Cognition*, Vol. 127, No. 2, May 2013, pp. 214 – 219.

[5] Jones M. R., Time, Our Lost Dimension: Toward a New Theory of Perception, Attention, and Memory, *Psychological Review*, Vol. 83, No. 5, September 1976, pp. 323 – 355.

[6] Jones M. R. & Boltz M., Dynamic Attending and Responses to Time, *Psychological Review*, Vol. 96, No. 3, July 1989, pp. 459 – 491.

[7] Large E. W. & Jones M. R., The Dynamics of Attending: How People Track Time Varying Events, *Psychological Review*, Vol. 106, No. 1, January 1999, pp. 119 – 159.

加工的影响。① 在他们的实验中，节奏化条件是在一小段音乐节奏的最后一拍中呈现一张图片，非节奏化条件是呈现的图片在最后一拍之前 250ms。被试的任务是忽视音乐节奏，同时判断这张图片是正立还是倒立的。结果发现，与非节奏化条件相比，当图片与音乐节奏合拍，即图片恰好与音乐节奏的最后一拍同时呈现时，被试对图片的判断速度最快。也就是说，不被注意的音乐节奏促进的视觉加工是跨通道的。根据 DAT 理论，这可能是由于图片所处的位置恰好位于动态注意的峰值。个体对任何与注意峰值同相位的知觉事件更为期待，因此分配给这些事件更多资源，这些事件也就被更好地加工。② 那么，当双通道刺激恰好处于动态注意的峰值时，是否能促进双通道刺激中的视觉和听觉成分的整合？研究三的实验 6 将采用节奏化的视听线索，在实验 2 的基础上，进一步考察分配性注意条件下的注意起伏对视听言语整合加工的影响。

从已有研究中可以推测，与节奏化线索合拍的目标刺激可能会产生视听整合。但是，这种整合在何时产生仍是悬而未决的问题。其主要原因在于已有的行为研究所依托的反应时等指标只能反映心理加工的综合结果，对于发生在加工早期的感觉整合过程很难进行有效的观察与测量，因而无法揭示感觉整合在何时产生这一动态的过程及其机制。由于事件相关电位具有很高的时间分辨率能够对认知神经活动特征提供即时的评价，从加工的初始就可以对单个的认

---

① Escoffier N., Sheng D. Y. J. & Schirmer A., Unattended Musical Beats Enhance Visual Processing, *Acta Psychologica*, Vol. 135, No. 1, September 2010, pp. 12 – 16.

② Brochard R., Tassin M. & Zagar D., Got Rhythm…for Better and for Worse, Cross – modal effects of auditory rhythm on visual word recognition. *Cognition*, Vol. 127, No. 2, May 2013, pp. 214 – 219.

知过程进行识别和分离①,因此,研究三的实验 5 将采用事件相关电位技术考察注意的起伏影响视听整合的时间进程及其机制。

综上所述,注意对视听整合加工的影响仍有以下几方面需要进一步探讨的问题:

第一,指向不同感觉通道的注意在影响视听整合加工时是否存在差异?如果存在差异的话,这种差异是如何体现的?

第二,一些研究发现,视听语义一致能够促进视听整合,那么,此结论在不同注意条件下是否仍然成立?或者说,不同注意条件下的视听言语整合是否存在差异?

第三,注意资源量(注意负荷)的多少是否能够影响视听言语整合加工?

第四,注意的起伏在视听言语整合加工中是否存在调制作用?这种效应的时间进程是怎样体现的?

---

① Rhodes S. M. & Donaldson D. I., Association and Not Semantic Relationships Elicit the N400 Effect: Electrophysiological Evidence from an Explicit Language Comprehension Task, *Psychophysiology*, Vol. 45, No. 1, January 2008, pp. 50–59.

第 五 章

注意影响视听整合加工的实验研究

注意与多感觉整合加工的关系一直受到研究者关注,尤其是注意对多感觉整合的影响及其心理和神经机制并未被厘清。本章通过行为和脑电实验的方式简要介绍了注意对视听整合加工的作用及其机制。

第一节 选择性注意和分配性注意对视听整合加工的影响

目前,关于注意在多感觉整合中所起的作用仍存在争议。其争议的焦点在于,注意能否影响多感觉整合。比如,有研究者认为多感觉整合是自动化过程,不受自上而下控制的影响。[1][2] 也就是说,这些研究者认为,注意并不能影响多感觉整合。另有研究者认为,

---

[1] Bertelson P., Vroomen J., De Gelder B. & Driver J., The Ventriloquist Effect Does Not Depend on the Direction of Deliberate Visual Attention, *Perception and Psychophysics*, Vol. 62, No. 2, February 2000, pp. 321–332.

[2] Vroomen J., Bertelson P. & De Gelder B., Directing Spatial Attention towards the Illusory Location of a Ventriloquized Sound, *ActaPsychologica*, Vol. 108, No. 1, June 2001, pp. 21–33.

与不被注意的条件相比,只有当双通道刺激被注意时才会产生多感觉整合[1],因此认为,注意在多感觉整合中起重要作用。

需要指出的是,认为多感觉整合不受自上而下控制影响的早期研究多关注的是空间注意[2],即:他们的观点代表的是空间注意不会影响多感觉整合;而认为注意能够影响多感觉整合的研究仅关注注意与非注意条件影响多感觉整合的差异,而忽略了对注意条件的区分。众所周知,注意除能指向空间位置外,还能指向某个感觉通道。[3] 那么,多感觉整合不受空间注意影响的结论是否适用于指向感觉通道的注意?

偏向竞争模型认为,选择性注意能增强对所选择信息的感觉神经反应,并抑制无关反应。[4][5] 根据此模型,当注意集中于一个感觉通道时,对此通道内信息的神经反应被增强,而被忽视通道内信息的神经反应则被抑制,因此可能不会产生双通道刺激的整合加工。鉴于此,本研究的实验1通过线索刺激将注意指向不同通道以形成选择性注意(只注意视觉、只注意听觉)与分配性注意(同时注意视觉和听觉)两种条件,考察在这两种条件下视听整合加工是否存在差异。此外,有研究发现,视听刺激之间的语义联结可能

---

[1] Talsma D. & Woldorff M. G., Selective Attention and Multisensory Integration: Multiple Phases of Effects on the Evoked Brain Activity, *Journal of Cognitive Neuroscience*, Vol. 17, No. 7, July 2005, pp. 1098–1114.

[2] Vroomen J., Bertelson P. & De Gelder B., The Ventriloquist Effect Does Not Depend on the Direction of Automatic Visual Attention, *Perception & Psychophysics*, Vol. 63, No. 4, May 2001, pp. 651–659.

[3] Talsma D., Predictive Coding and Multisensory Integration: An Attentional Account of the Multisensory Mind, *Frontiers in Integrative Neuroscience*, Vol. 26, No. 6, March 2015.

[4] Beck D. M. & Kastner S., Top-down and Bottom-up Mechanisms in Biasing Competition in the Human Brain, *Vision research*, Vol. 49, No. 10, June 2009, pp. 1154–1165.

[5] Mishra J. & Gazzaley A., Attention Distributed across Sensory Modalities Enhances Perception Performance. *The Journal of Neuroscience*, Vol. 32, No. 35, August 2012, pp. 12294–12302.

会对视听整合加工有一定的影响①，表现为视听一致的刺激更易产生整合加工。那么，在不同注意条件下，这种视听一致刺激的加工优势是否仍然存在？鉴于此，本研究的实验2在实验1的基础上进行调整，以人声读出的单字词作为听觉刺激，与视觉刺激（简单图形）进行匹配，形成语义一致和语义两种刺激对，分别在选择性注意和分配性注意条件下考察视听言语整合加工的差异。

一 实验1：选择性注意和分配性注意对简单视听刺激整合加工的影响

（一）目的

考察指向不同感觉通道的注意对视听整合加工的影响是否存在不同。

（二）假设

指向不同感觉通道的注意对视听整合加工的影响存在不同：在指向某个具体通道的注意（选择性注意）条件下不会产生视听整合加工，在同时注意视觉和听觉两个通道（分配性注意）条件下会产生视听整合加工，表现为被试对双通道目标的反应最快。

（三）方法

1. 被试

从天津市某高校随机选取25名在校大学生（男生14人，女生11人）作为被试，平均年龄为19岁。所有被试的视力或矫正视力正常，听力正常，均为右利手，身体健康，无精神系统疾病，没有脑部损伤史。每位被试在完成实验后会得到一个小礼物作为报酬。

2. 实验仪器和材料

实验刺激采用E-prime 1.1软件编制实验程序。视觉刺激通过

---

① Laurienti P. J., Kraft R. A., Maldjian J. A., Burdette J. H. & Wallace M. T., Semantic Congruence is a Critical Factor in Multisensory Behavioral Performance, *Experimental Brain Research*, Vol. 158, No. 4, October 2004, pp. 405 – 414.

17英寸液晶显示器呈现，听觉刺激通过入耳式耳机呈现，响度调整至被试感觉舒服为宜。被试眼睛正对电脑显示器中央位置，距离约50cm。实验中的线索包括三种："请注意看""请注意听""请注意看和听"，这三种线索均用30号白色宋体字呈现于黑色背景中央。单通道视觉目标刺激为白色圆形和白色正方形，视角为3.4°。单通道听觉目标刺激为双耳呈现的高音（1200Hz）和低音（400Hz）。双通道目标刺激为视觉刺激和听觉刺激同时呈现。

3. 实验程序与实验设计

在每个试次中，首先在黑色屏幕上呈现白色十字注视点，呈现时间为1000—1200ms之间的随机时间。随后注视点消失，在屏幕中央呈现线索。线索呈现1s，之后白色十字注视点出现在屏幕中央，呈现时间为1000—1200ms之间的随机时间。注视点消失后，呈现目标刺激。视觉刺激、听觉刺激和视听双通道刺激均呈现200ms，被试进行按键反应。如果超过3000ms不做反应，该试次记为错误，自动进入下一试次。随后呈现1000ms的空屏作为试次间隔。被试的任务是根据线索的要求进行按键反应：当线索为"请注意看"时，被试需要忽略听到的内容，只对看到的内容进行按键反应；当线索为"请注意听"时，被试需要忽略看到的内容，只对听到的内容进行按键反应；当线索为"请注意看和听"时，被试需要同时关注看到的和听到的内容进行按键反应。

当出现圆形、高音或圆形和高音同时呈现时按F键；当出现正方形、低音或正方形和低音同时呈现时按J键。为防止被试产生按键策略，将圆形和低音同时呈现、正方形和高音同时呈现作为填充刺激，不需要被试反应。按键顺序在被试间进行平衡。在整个实验过程中，要求被试双眼注视屏幕正中央，既快又准确地做出反应。实验流程如图5-1所示。

根据线索的要求，实验设置不同的试次类型。当线索为"请注

注视点（1000—1200ms）

线索刺激（1000ms）

注视点（1000—1200ms）

目标刺激（200ms）

反应窗口

试次间隔（1000ms）

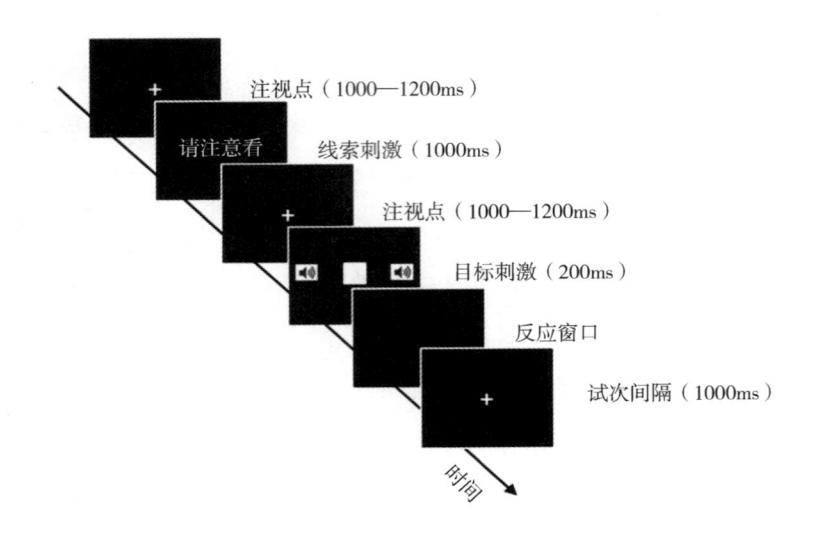

时间

图 5-1　实验 1：注意视觉时呈现双通道目标的试次流程

意看"（注意视觉）时，目标刺激为单通道视觉刺激或者多通道刺激中的视觉成分；当线索为"请注意听"（注意听觉）时，目标刺激为单通道听觉刺激或者多通道刺激中的听觉成分；当线索为"请注意看和听"（同时注意视觉和听觉）时，目标刺激为单通道视觉刺激、单通道听觉刺激或者同时呈现的多通道刺激。具体来说，试次类型包括 8 种：注意视觉—单通道视觉目标；注意视觉—双通道目标中的视觉成分；注意听觉—单通道听觉目标；注意听觉—双通道目标中的听觉成分；注意视听—单通道视觉目标；注意视听—单通道听觉目标；注意视听—双通道目标；注意视听—填充刺激。其中，当线索为"请注意看"和"请注意听"时，该试次属于选择性注意条件；当线索为"请注意看和听"时，该试次为分配性注意条件。

实验采用 2（注意条件：分配性注意、选择性注意）×3（目标刺激类型：单通道视觉、单通道听觉、多通道）的被试内设计。

实验中，每个试次持续约5s。实验共有240个试次，整个实验约持续20分钟。在正式实验之前有32个试次作为练习，正式实验中每80个试次结束安排短暂休息，被试按空格键可以继续进行实验。

（四）结果

对被试的反应时和正确率进行初步统计分析。删除反应错误的、反应时小于200ms和大于1000ms的以及反应时超出平均反应时3个标准差的数据。删除数据约占总数据的4.48%。3名男性被试因错误率较高（大于30%）而被剔除，剩余有效被试为22人（男女各半）。结果见表5-1。

表5-1　　实验1：不同注意条件下对三种目标的正确率和反应时（N=22）

目标刺激类型	正确率（%）		反应时（ms）	
	选择性注意	分配性注意	选择性注意	分配性注意
单通道听觉目标	96.00（0.92）	88.02（2.25）	553.18（100.69）	636.64（101.07）
单通道视觉目标	96.35（0.93）	93.33（2.12）	547.99（84.24）	668.26（101.50）
视听双通道目标	97.46（0.54）	99.67（0.21）	562.58（97.56）	611.05（117.73）

注：括号中为标准差。

对于正确率数据，重复测量方差分析结果表明，注意条件主效应显著，$F(1, 21) = 5.46$，$p < 0.05$，$\eta^2 = 0.21$。目标刺激类型主效应显著，$F(2, 42) = 18.43$，$p < 0.001$，$\eta^2 = 0.47$。注意条件和目标刺激类型的交互作用显著，$F(2, 42) = 10.93$，$p < 0.001$，$\eta^2 = 0.34$。进一步分析表明，在分配性注意条件下，被试对单通道听觉目标的反应正确率显著低于对单通道视觉目标，$p < 0.05$；低于双通道目标的反应正确率，$p < 0.001$；对单通道视觉目标的反应正确率显著低于对双通道目标的反应正确率，$p < 0.05$。

而在选择性注意条件下，三种类型的目标正确率之间均无显著差异，$ps > 0.05$。

对于反应时数据，重复测量方差分析表明，注意条件主效应显著，$F(1, 21) = 23.49$，$p < 0.001$，$\eta^2 = 0.53$。目标刺激类型主效应显著，$F(2, 42) = 3.31$，$p < 0.05$，$\eta^2 = 0.14$。注意条件与目标刺激类型的交互作用（见图 5-2）显著，$F(2, 42) = 11.42$，$p < 0.001$，$\eta^2 = 0.35$。进一步分析表明，在分配性注意条件下，被试对双通道目标的反应时显著短于对单通道听觉目标，$p < 0.05$；短于单通道视觉目标的反应时，$p < 0.001$；对单通道听觉目标的反应时显著短于对单通道视觉目标的反应时，$p < 0.01$。而在选择性注意条件下，被试对三种目标刺激的反应时之间无显著差异，$ps > 0.1$。也就是说，只有在分配性注意条件下才表现出冗余信号效应，而在选择性注意条件下并没有表现出冗余信号效应。

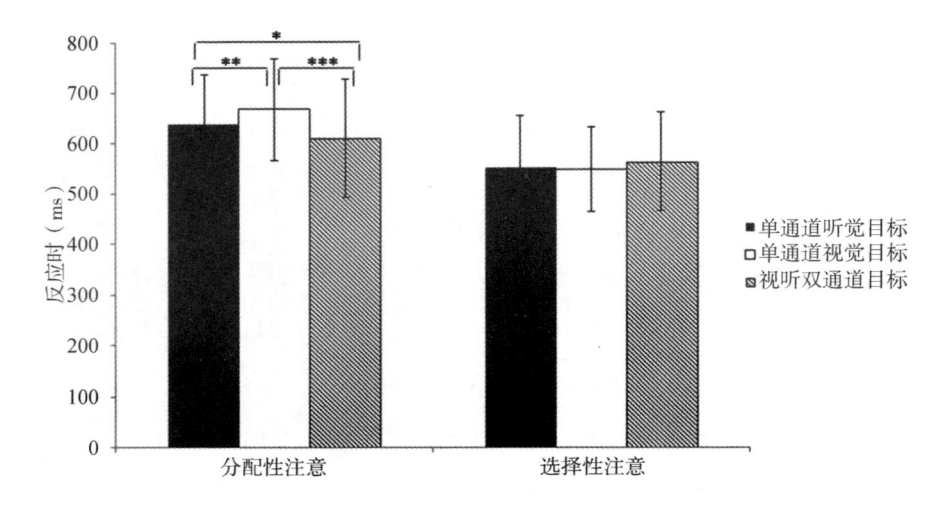

图 5-2 实验 1：不同注意条件下被试对三种目标的反应时

有研究者针对冗余信号效应做出了解释。Raab 提出的竞争模型[1]认为，在个体加工多通道刺激时，多通道刺激的每个单通道成分在不同的感觉通道中分别被加工，在行为结果中出现对多通道刺激加工优势（冗余信号效应）的原因是：来自不同感觉通道的刺激之间相互竞争，被试最终的反应由最先完成加工的那个感觉通道所触发。以掷骰子为例，当我们想得到一个 6 点时，掷两个骰子得到一个 6 点的概率要大于掷一个骰子得到一个 6 点的概率。[2] 另一个模型与竞争模型相反。共激活模型认为，来自不同感觉通道的信息均被激活，这些信息在特定的时间点上被整合为统一的直觉信息，共同作用于随后的额加工，因此产生了冗余信号效应。[3][4] 针对这两种模型，Miller 提出了竞争模型不等式。

$$P(RT_{av}<t) \leqslant [P(RT_v<t) + P(RT_a<t)] - [P(RT_v<t) \times P(RT_a<t)]$$ [5]

上述不等式中的 P 代表的是反应时概率的累积量分布函数（Cumulative Distribution Function，CDF），表示在任意给定时间 t 内做出某个反应的概率。不等式的左边代表在任意给定时间 t 内个体对同时呈现的双通道刺激的反应时的累积概率值，右边代表竞争模型预测值。这一不等式的含义是：在任意给定时间点上，如果个体

---

[1] Raab D. H., Statistical Facilitation of Simple Reaction Times, *Transactions of the New York Academy of Sciences*, Vol. 24, March 1962, pp. 574–590.

[2] 刘强：《多感觉整合的脑机制研究》，博士学位论文，西南大学，2010 年。

[3] Miller J., Divided Attention: Evidence for Coactivation with Redundant Signals, *Cognitive psychology*, Vol. 14, No. 2, April 1982, pp. 247–279.

[4] Miller J., Timecourse of Coactivation in Bimodal Divided Attention, *Perception & Psychophysics*, Vol. 40, No. 5, November 1986, pp. 331–343.

[5] Miller J., Divided Attention: Evidence for Coactivation with Redundant Signals, *Cognitive psychology*, Vol. 14, No. 2, April 1982, pp. 247–279.

对多通道刺激的反应概率显著大于竞争模型预测值，那么对多通道刺激的反应偏离竞争模型，这就表明组成多通道刺激的两个单通道刺激产生了神经上的整合，因此，导致了冗余信号效应。

为考察在本研究的反应时结果中所发现的冗余信号效应是否来源于视听刺激的整合，对被试的反应概率进行竞争模型分析。由于只在分配性注意条件下表现出冗余信号效应，因此只对分配性注意条件下的数据进行竞争模型分析（见图5-3）。

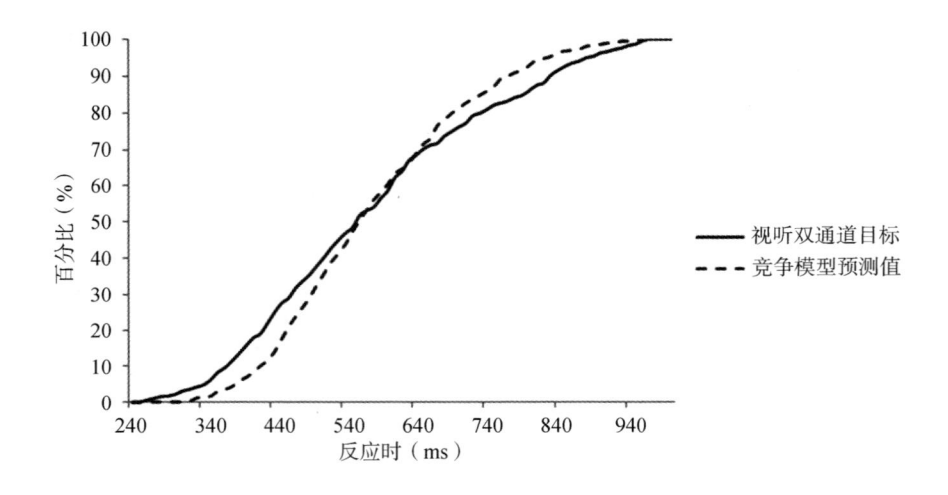

图5-3 实验1：分配性注意条件下的竞争模型分析

首先，计算反应时的累积量分布函数单通道视觉 $P(RTv<t)$、单通道听觉 $P(RTa<t)$ 和多通道 $P(RTav<t)$。其次，根据已有研究计算出竞争模型预测值 $[P(RTv<t)+P(RTa<t)] - [P(RTv<t) \times P(RTa<t)]$。最后，为考察实验值与竞争模型预测值之间是否存在显著差异，在每10%的时间点上将多通道 $P(RTav<t)$ 与竞争模型预测值进行配对 t 检验。结果发现，在310—490ms 上多通道 $P(RTav<t)$ 显著大于竞争模型预测值（310ms，$t=2.26$，$p<0.05$；320ms，$t=2.37$，$p<0.05$；330ms，$t=2.46$，$p<0.05$；

340ms，$t=2.40$，$p<0.05$；350ms，$t=2.86$，$p=0.01$；360ms，$t=2.92$，$p=0.01$；370ms，$t=3.01$，$p=0.01$；380ms，$t=3.15$，$p=0.01$；390ms，$t=3.01$，$p=0.01$；400ms，$t=3.61$，$p<0.01$；410ms，$t=3.58$，$p<0.01$；420ms，$t=3.61$，$p<0.01$；430ms，$t=3.93$，$p=0.001$；440ms，$t=4.12$，$p=0.001$；450ms，$t=4.31$，$p=0.001$；460ms，$t=2.67$，$p=0.01$；470ms，$t=2.73$，$p=0.01$；480ms，$t=2.79$，$p=0.01$；490ms，$t=2.54$，$p<0.05$），即此结果违背竞争模型。这表明在反应时数据中出现的冗余信号效应源自双通道刺激中视觉刺激和听觉刺激产生的多感觉整合。

（五）讨论

本研究的实验1采用简单图形和短音作为实验材料，通过线索刺激指导被试注意不同的感觉通道，形成选择性注意（只注意视觉、只注意听觉）和分配性注意（同时注意视觉和听觉）两种条件，考察了在这两种条件下视听整合加工的差异。实验1的结果发现，在被试只注意一个通道时，无论在正确率还是在反应时上均没有表现出对双通道目标的加工优势。这可能是由于，在选择性注意状态下，被试尝试过滤掉不相关感觉通道的信息[①]。具体而言，当注意指向视觉时，听觉信息被忽略，被试尝试过滤掉不相关的听觉信息；而当注意指向听觉时，视觉信息被忽略，被试尝试过滤掉不相关的视觉信息。结果不论在注意视觉还是在注意听觉时，另一个不相关通道的信息均被忽略。由于被试对忽略通道内信息的加工效能降低，因此不被注意的通道内的信息不能被有效加工。这样，在只注意一个感觉通道时，被试对双通道信息的加工并不完全，因此

---

① Talsma D. & Woldorff M. G., Selective Attention and Multisensory Integration: Multiple Phases of Effects on the Evoked Brain Activity, *Journal of Cognitive Neuroscience*, Vol. 17, No. 7, July 2005, pp. 1098-1114.

无法体现出对双通道信息的加工优势,因而没有产生冗余信号效应,表现为被试对三种类型的目标反应时无显著差异。

更为重要的是,本研究的实验 1 发现,当被试同时注意两个通道(分配性注意)时,与单通道目标相比,被试对双通道目标的加工既快又准确,即产生冗余信号效应。为检验这种效应是否来源于双通道信息的整合加工,实验 1 采用行为研究中较为常见的竞争模型分析法对分配性注意条件下的反应时进行竞争模型分析。结果发现,这种冗余信号效应的确源自视听双通道刺激的视觉成分和听觉成分的整合加工。简言之,实验 1 结果表明,与选择性注意于一个通道(选择性注意)相比,只有在同时注意两个通道(分配性注意)的条件下才会产生多感觉整合。这个结果可能与信息加工时的皮层活性有关。有研究发现,当个体只注意一个感觉通道时,被忽略通道所在皮层的活性会被抑制[1][2],从而导致在被忽视的皮层中,用于产生多感觉整合的信息减少,因此与分配性注意相比,选择性注意于一个通道难以产生多感觉整合。而在分配性注意时,两个被注意的通道皮层均被激活,这样就保证了多感觉整合所需的资源量,因此能够产生整合。

最近有研究与实验 1 的结果基本一致。Mittag、Alho、Takegata、Makkonen 和 Kujala 采用视听 oddball 范式,以音节作为刺激材料,在音节的不同视觉形式下考察了注意在字母—语音整合加工中的作用。[3] 他们的研究发现,当注意被指向视听双通道和视觉通道

---

[1] Farb N. A., Segal Z. V. & Anderson A. K., Attentional Modulation of Primary Interoceptive and Exteroceptive Cortices, *Cerebral Cortex*, Vol. 23, No. 1, January 2013, pp. 114 – 126.

[2] Alho K., Rinne T., Herron T. J. & Woods D. L., Stimulus-dependent Activations and Attention-related Modulations in the Auditory Cortex: A Meta-analysis of FMRI Studies, *Hearing Research*, Vol. 307, January 2014, pp. 29 – 41.

[3] Mittag M., Alho K., Takegata R., Makkonen T. & Kujala T., Audiovisual Attention Boosts Letter-speech Sound Integration, *Psychophysiology*, Vol. 50, No. 10, October 2013, pp. 1034 – 1044.

时，字母和语音之间会产生整合加工，即对视听双通道目标具有加工优势，而在注意单通道听觉和不注意刺激的条件下不会产生视听刺激的整合加工。本研究的实验 1 与 Mittag 等人的研究均发现，在注意的同时呈现视听刺激会产生多感觉整合。但是 Mittag 等人的实验还发现，只注意一个通道（视觉通道）也会产生多感觉整合。这与实验 1 的结果不一致。产生这种差异的原因可能是，在 Mittag 等人的实验中采用 oddball 范式，被试的任务是当目标刺激出现时只需按一个键对其进行探测反应。而在本实验中，要求被试对呈现的圆形和方形或者高低音分别按键，即本实验采用的是辨别反应。在被试探测到目标刺激之后，还要进行对目标的分类。因此与探测反应相比，在本实验的选择性注意状态下，被试对双通道刺激的分类反应更难一些，不容易产生多感觉整合。

尽管本研究的实验 1 发现，只有在分配性注意条件下才会产生视听刺激的整合加工，但是，日常生活中的信息并不仅仅是简单刺激，更多的信息以语义的形式被我们的脑整理、分析并加工。同时，有研究者认为，当刺激在内容上匹配时，被试更倾向于认为其来源于同一资源，可能与在内容上不匹配的刺激相比更容易被知觉系统整合。[1] 从这个角度出发，我们可以推测，视听刺激的视觉和听觉成分如果存在内容上的匹配，或者语义上的一致性，与视听内容不匹配或语义不一致的刺激信息相比，更易被我们的脑整合。那么，在不同注意条件（选择性注意和分配性注意）下，被试对语义一致视听刺激的加工优势是否继续存在？因此，实验 2 将调整实验 1 中的听觉刺激，采用人声读出的单字词与视觉简单图形相匹配，

---

[1] Su Y. H., Content Congruency and Its Interplay with Temporal Synchrony Modulate Integration between Rhythmic Audiovisual Streams, *Frontiers in Integrative Neuroscience*, No. 8, February 2014, p. 92.

以形成视听语义一致和视听语义不一致两种类型的视听刺激，考察在不同注意条件下，被试在视听言语整合加工上的差异。

（六）小结

上述实验的结果发现，在选择性注意条件下，视听双通道目标不具有加工优势。而在分配性注意条件下，被试对视听双通道目标的反应最快，即产生冗余信号效应。竞争模型分析发现，这种分配性注意条件下视听双通道目标的加工优势源自视听双通道目标的视觉和听觉成分的整合。也就是说，上述实验发现，只有在分配性注意条件下才会产生视听整合加工，在选择性注意条件下并没有产生视听整合加工。

二 实验2：选择性注意和分配性注意对视听言语整合加工的影响

（一）目的

以具有一定语义联结的视听刺激为材料，考察选择性注意和分配性注意下视听言语整合加工是否存在差异。

（二）假设

（1）视听语义一致的双通道目标刺激在分配性注意条件下才会产生视听整合，而在选择性注意条件下，即使视听刺激语义一致，仍无法产生整合加工；

（2）语义不一致的视听刺激在分配性注意和选择性注意条件下均无法产生整合加工。

（三）方法

1. 被试

从天津市某高校随机选取26名在校大学生（男生16人，女生10人）作为被试，这些被试并没有参与过实验1，其平均年龄为20岁。所有被试的视力或矫正视力正常，听力正常，均为右利手，身体健康，无精神系统疾病，没有脑部损伤史。每位被试在完成实验后会得到一个小礼物作为报酬。

2. 实验仪器和材料

实验刺激采用 E-prime 1.1 软件编制实验程序。视觉刺激通过 17 英寸液晶显示器呈现，听觉刺激通过入耳式耳机呈现，响度调整至被试感觉舒服为宜。被试眼睛正对电脑显示器中央位置，距离约 50cm。实验中的线索包括三种："请注意看""请注意听""请注意看和听"，这三种线索均用 30 号白色宋体字呈现于屏幕中央（黑色背景）。单通道视觉目标刺激为白色圆形、白色正方形和白色三角形，视角为 3.4°。单通道听觉目标刺激采用 Sound Forge 9.0 软件制作和处理，为同一女声读出的"圆""方"和 400Hz 的短音。双通道目标刺激为视觉和听觉刺激同时呈现。

3. 实验程序与实验设计

在每个试次中，首先在黑色屏幕上呈现白色十字注视点，呈现时间为 1000—1200ms 之间的随机时间。注视点消失后在屏幕中央呈现线索。线索呈现 1s，随后白色十字注视点出现在屏幕中央，呈现时间同样为 1000—1200ms 之间的随机时间。注视点消失后呈现目标刺激。视觉刺激、听觉刺激和视听双通道刺激均呈现 200ms，随后被试进行按键反应，按键后自动进入下一个试次。如果超过 3000ms 不做反应，该试次记为错误，也自动进入下一试次。随后呈现 1000ms 的空屏作为试次间隔。实验中人声读出的"圆""方"分别与圆形和正方形形成具有语义联结的刺激对，同时，分别将白色三角形与"圆""方"匹配，将短音与圆形和正方形匹配，以形成语义不一致的刺激对。被试的任务是根据线索的要求进行按键反应：当线索为"请注意看"时，被试需要忽略听到的内容，只对看到的内容进行按键反应；当线索为"请注意听"时，被试需要忽略看到的内容，只对听到的内容进行按键反应；当线索为"请注意看和听"时，被试需要同时关注看到的和听到的内容并进行按键反应。当看到圆形、听到"圆"或看到的圆形和听到的"圆"同时呈现时，按 F 键；当看到正方形、听到"方"或者看到正方形和听到"方"同时呈现时，按 J 键。在整个实验过程中，要求被试双眼注视屏幕正中央，既快又准确地做出反应。实验流程见图 5-4。

注视点（1000—1200ms）
线索刺激（1000ms）
注视点（1000—1200ms）
目标刺激（200ms）
反应窗口
试次间隔（1000ms）
时间

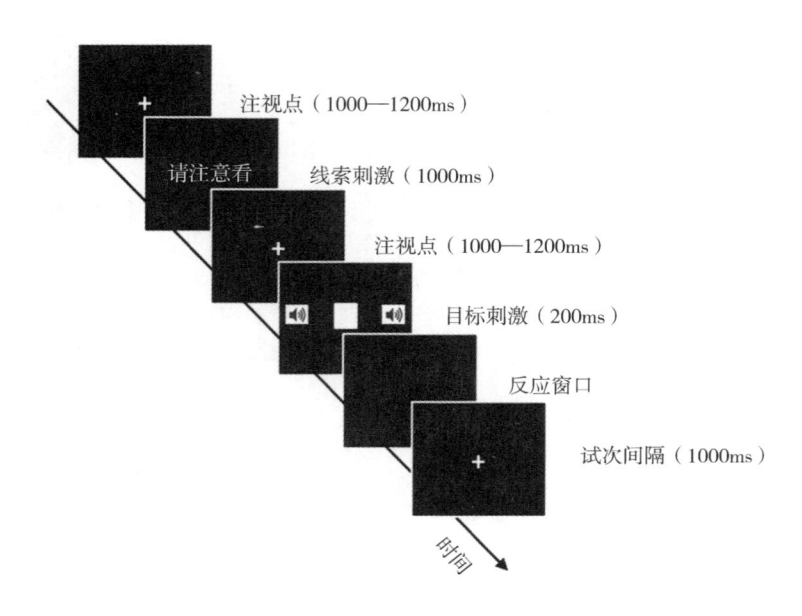

图 5-4 实验 2：注意视觉时呈现双通道目标的试次流程

根据线索的要求，实验设置以下十种试次类型：注意视觉—单通道视觉目标；注意视觉—语义一致双通道目标中的视觉成分；注意视觉—语义不一致双通道目标中的视觉成分；注意听觉—单通道听觉目标；注意听觉—语义一致双通道目标中的听觉成分；注意听觉—语义不一致双通道目标中的听觉成分；注意视听—单通道视觉目标；注意视听—单通道听觉目标；注意视听—语义一致的双通道目标；注意视听—语义不一致的双通道目标。其中，当线索为"请注意看"和"请注意听"时，该试次为选择性注意条件；当线索为"请注意看和听"时，该试次为分配性注意条件。

实验采用2（注意条件：分配性注意、选择性注意）×3（目标刺激类型：单通道视觉目标、单通道听觉目标、双通道目标）的被试内设计。实验中，每个试次持续约5s。实验共有330个试次，整个实验约持续27.5分钟。在正式实验之前有36个试次作为练习部分。在正式实验中每60个试次可进行短暂休息，被试按空格键可以继续进行实验。

（四）结果

对数据进行初步处理：删除反应错误的、反应时小于200ms和大于1000ms的以及反应时超出平均反应时3个标准差的数据。初步处理后删除的数据约占总数据的5.64%。所有被试的数据均有效，因此并没有剔除被试，最终被试人数为26人。对正确率和反应时（见表5-2）进行分析。

表5-2　　实验2：不同注意条件下对四种类型目标的正确率和反应时（N=26）

目标刺激类型	正确率（%）		反应时（ms）	
	选择性注意	分配性注意	选择性注意	分配性注意
单通道听觉目标	95.88 (0.83)	95.77 (1.01)	464.47 (65.53)	490.83 (64.26)
单通道视觉目标	96.92 (1.04)	97.68 (0.55)	438.78 (61.68)	458.55 (63.44)
视听语义一致目标	96.85 (0.67)	97.17 (0.66)	454.80 (59.71)	427.73 (56.94)
视听语义不一致目标	93.01 (1.19)	90.25 (1.40)	452.18 (65.48)	476.75 (66.88)

注：括号中为标准差。

首先，对视听语义一致的双通道目标与单通道目标的正确率和反应时进行分析。

在正确率方面，重复测量方差分析发现，无任何显著效应，

$ps > 0.05$。

在反应时方面,重复测量方差分析发现,目标刺激类型主效应显著,$F(2, 50) = 29.94$,$p < 0.001$,$\eta^2 = 0.55$;注意条件与目标刺激类型交互作用显著(见图 5-5),$F(2, 50) = 31.62$,$p < 0.001$,$\eta^2 = 0.56$。进一步分析发现,在分配性注意条件下,被试对语义一致的双通道目标的反应时显著短于对单通道视觉目标和单通道听觉目标的反应时,单通道视觉目标的反应时显著短于单通道听觉目标的反应时,$ps < 0.001$。即,被试对语义一致的双通道目标反应最快,产生冗余信号效应,而对单通道听觉目标刺激的反应最慢。在选择性注意条件下,被试对单通道视觉目标的反应时显著小于对语义一致的双通道目标的反应时($p < 0.05$)和单通道听觉目标($p < 0.05$)的反应时;双通道目标与单通道听觉目标的反应时之间无显著差异,$p > 0.05$。

其次,对视听语义不一致的双通道目标和单通道目标进行分析。

在正确率方面,重复测量方差分析发现,目标刺激类型主效应显著,$F(2, 50) = 23.05$,$p < 0.001$,$\eta^2 = 0.48$。注意条件与目标刺激类型交互作用显著,$F(2, 50) = 4.14$,$p < 0.05$,$\eta^2 = 0.14$。简单效应检验发现,在分配性注意条件下,语义不一致双通道目标的正确率显著小于单通道听觉目标和单通道视觉目标,$ps < 0.001$;单通道听觉目标正确率边缘显著小于单通道视觉目标,$p = 0.07$。在选择性注意条件下,语义不一致双通道目标的正确率显著小于单通道听觉目标,$p < 0.01$;小于单通道视觉目标,$p < 0.001$;后两者之间差异不显著,$p > 0.1$。

在反应时方面,重复测量方差分析发现,注意条件主效应显著,$F(1, 25) = 30.04$,$p < 0.001$,$\eta^2 = 0.55$,被试在分配性注意条件下的反应时($M = 475.38 \text{ms}$,$SD = 12.17$)显著长于在选择性注意条

件下的反应时（$M = 451.81\text{ms}$，$SD = 12.18$）。目标刺激类型主效应显著，$F(2, 50) = 14.82$，$p < 0.001$，$\eta^2 = 0.37$。比较发现，被试对单通道视觉目标的反应时（$M = 448.66\text{ms}$，$SD = 11.92$）显著短于对语义不一致双通道目标（$M = 464.47\text{ms}$，$SD = 12.72$）的反应时，$p < 0.01$；小于单通道听觉目标（$M = 477.65\text{ms}$，$SD = 12.45$）的反应时，$p < 0.001$；语义不一致的双通道目标的反应时显著短于对单通道听觉目标的反应时，$p < 0.05$；注意条件与目标通道交互作用不显著，$p > 0.05$。上述结果表明，被试对语义不一致的双通道目标的反应不具有加工优势。

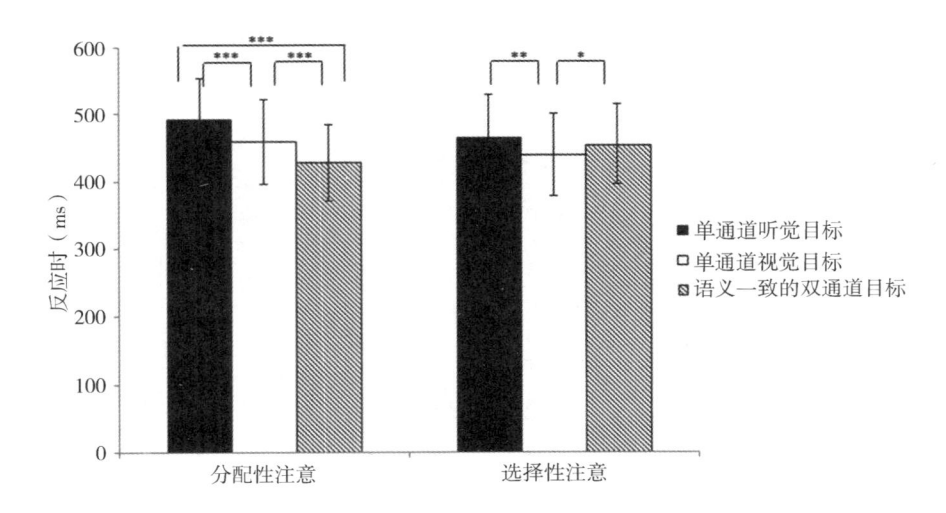

图 5-5 实验 2：不同注意条件下对三种类型目标的反应时

对实验 2 的反应时数据进行竞争模型分析（见图 5-6）。同样，由于只有在分配性注意条件下表现出冗余信号效应，因此只对分配性注意条件下的反应时数据进行竞争模型分析。计算反应时的累积量分布函数单通道视觉 $P(RT_v < t)$、单通道听觉 $P(RT_a < t)$ 和语义一致的多通道 $P(RT_{av\text{语义一致}} < t)$，然后按照实验 1 的方法计算出竞争模型预测值。

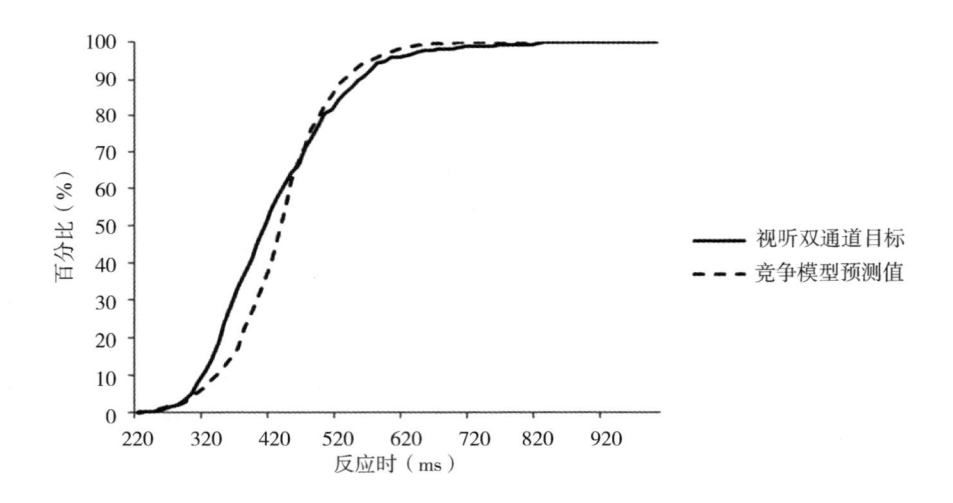

为考察在反应时数据上表现出的冗余信号效应是否源自语义一致双通道目标中视觉和听觉成分的整合，将实验值和竞争模型预测值进行比较，即在每 10% 的时间点上将语义一致的多通道 P（$RT_{av语义一致} < t$）与竞争模型预测值进行配对 t 检验。结果发现，在 340—410ms 之间，语义一致的多通道 P（$RT_{av语义一致} < t$）显著大于竞争模型预测值（340ms，$t = 2.69$，$p = 0.01$；350ms，$t = 3.00$，$p = 0.01$；360ms，$t = 3.68$，$p = 0.001$；370ms，$t = 3.18$，$p < 0.01$；380ms，$t = 2.78$，$p = 0.01$；390ms，$t = 2.42$，$p < 0.05$；400ms，$t = 2.18$，$p < 0.05$；410ms，$t = 2.19$，$p < 0.05$），$ps < 0.05$，即，此结果违背竞争模型。这表明，本实验中出现的冗余信号效应来自语义一致的视听双通道目标刺激的视觉成分和听觉成分的整合。

图 5-6　实验 2：分配性注意条件下的竞争模型分析

（五）讨论

本研究通过线索刺激将被试的注意指向不同的感觉通道，同时，调整实验 1 中的听觉刺激材料，以简单图形作为视觉刺激，以人声读出的单字词作为听觉刺激，在视觉刺激和听觉刺激之间形成一定的语义联结，考察了在不同注意条件（选择性注意和分配性注意）下的视听言语整合加工是否存在差异。实验2结果发现，在反应时方面的分配性注意条件下，被试对语义一致的双通道目标刺激的反应最快，即，在语义一致的视听双通道目标刺激上产生了冗余信号效应。通过竞争模型分析发现，这种冗余信号效应源自语义一致的视听目标刺激的视觉成分和听觉成分的整合加工。而对于语义不一致的双通道目标，被试对其的反应并不快于对任意一个单通道目标的反应，这表明，尽管这种语义不一致视听刺激的视觉成分和听觉成分同时同地呈现，但二者之间由于语义不一致而造成其无法整合，因此其不具有加工优势。在选择性注意条件下，不论视听双通道目标刺激的视觉成分和听觉成分之间是否存在语义一致性，视听双通道目标均不具有加工优势，也就是说，在选择性注意条件下，即便视听双通道刺激的视觉成分和听觉成分同时同地呈现，并且具有一定的语义联结（视听语义一致），仍然不能产生视听整合加工。

有研究者认为，大脑在处理信息时，倾向于将内容上匹配的刺激当作相同资源处理，或者说，当两种刺激在内容上相匹配（如，语义一致）时，大脑更倾向于认为它们来源于同一资源，这样更有益于我们的知觉系统将其整合成统一的知觉[1]。一些以视听言语知觉为考察对象的研究结果与这种视听语义一致信息的加工优势基本一致。比如，有研究发现，与视听不匹配的刺激对相比，当被试听到的声音与看到的面孔在性别上一致[2]，或者当被试听到的词语与

---

[1] Su Y. H., Content Congruency and Its Interplay with Temporal Synchrony Modulate Integration between Rhythmic Audiovisual Streams, *Frontiers in Integrative Neuroscience*, No. 8, February 2014, p. 92.
[2] Vatakis A. & Spence C., Crossmodal Binding: Evaluating the "Unity Assumption" Using Audiovisual Speech Stimuli, *Percept. Psychophys*, Vol. 69, No. 5, July 2007, pp. 744–756.

看到的嘴唇运动相一致时,双通道刺激均被优先整合①。由此可见,视听刺激之间语义一致对于双通道信息的整合有一定的促进作用。但是在实验2中,尽管视听双通道刺激的视觉成分和听觉成分之间存在一定的语义联结,它们只在分配性注意条件下才会产生视听整合加工,而在选择性注意条件下没有产生视听整合加工。

这可能仍然与不同注意条件下的皮层激活情况有关。有研究发现,当个体只注意来自一个感觉通道的信息时,被忽略通道所在皮层的活性会被抑制②③,从而导致在被忽视的皮层中,用于产生多感觉整合的信息减少。同时,已有研究发现,在选择性注意一个感觉通道的刺激时,被试会尝试过滤掉不相关的信息。④ 即便视觉和听觉成分之间存在一定的语义联结,这种语义联结仍不能使被试加工来自被忽略的感觉通道的信息,这样,即使视听语义一致,在选择性注意条件下仍然没有产生视听整合加工。

相对于这种语义一致视听刺激对多感觉整合的促进作用,语义不一致的视听刺激是否会对多感觉整合或者被试的反应产生阻碍作用?实验2发现,无论是分配性注意条件还是选择性注意条件,与单通道视觉、单通道听觉和语义一致的视听刺激相比,语义不一致视听刺激的反应时并不是最大的。或者说,视听刺激之间的语义不

---

① Ten Oever S., Sack A. T., Wheat K. L., Bien N. & Van Atteveldt N., Audio-visual Onset Differences are Used to Determine Syllable Identity for Ambiguous Audio-visual Stimulus Pairs, *Frontiers in Psychology*, No. 4, June 2013, p. 331.

② Farb N. A., Segal Z. V. & Anderson A. K., Attentional Modulation of Primary Interoceptive and Exteroceptive Cortices, *Cerebral Cortex*, Vol. 23, No. 1, January 2013, pp. 114 – 126.

③ Alho K., Rinne T., Herron T. J. & Woods D. L., Stimulus-dependent Activations and Attention-related Modulations in the Auditory Cortex: A Meta-analysis of FMRI Studies, *Hearing Research*, Vol. 307, January 2014, pp. 29 – 41.

④ Talsma D. & Woldorff M. G., Selective Attention and Multisensory Integration: Multiple Phases of Effects on the Evoked Brain Activity, *Journal of Cognitive Neuroscience*, Vol. 17, No. 7, July 2005, pp. 1098 – 1114.

一致并没有完全阻碍被试的反应。这可能是由于本研究中视听刺激之间并不具有明显的语义冲突。比如，视觉刺激采用圆形和方形，在视听语义不一致条件下的听觉刺激采用的是"嘀"声；而当听觉刺激采用人声读出的"圆"和"方"时，在视听语义不一致条件下的视觉刺激采用的是三角形。未来研究可以采用具有语义冲突的刺激对作为实验材料，进一步考察这种冲突刺激是否会对二者关系产生调节作用。

在正确率方面，本研究发现，被试对视听语义不一致的双通道刺激反应正确率最低，这表明，被试对语义不一致的双通道刺激反应最为困难。预测编码模型（predictive coding model）认为，大脑会产生对环境的贝叶斯估计[1]，因此大脑中可能存在对环境估计的随机模型，它们基于当下个体加工的感觉信息而不断更新。这些随机模型能用来调整对正在进行的感觉输入的预测。如果在预测和实际感觉输入之间存在强烈的不匹配，可能会导致内部模型更大的更新。从这个角度看，当输入的视听刺激之间存在不一致甚至冲突的语义联结时，大脑的预测与实际输入之间存在较大差别导致内部模型的较大更新，因此造成对此类信息的加工困难[2]。

（六）小结

实验 2 的结果发现，对于语义一致的视听双通道目标来说，在同时注意视觉和听觉通道（分配性注意）时，对其加工最快，即产生冗余信号效应。竞争模型分析发现，这种加工优势源自语义一致双通道目标中视觉和听觉成分的整合。在只注意视觉通道或听觉通道（选择性注意）时，并没有视听整合产生。

---

[1] Friston K., The Free-energy Principle: A Unified Brain Theory, *Nature Reviews Neuroscience*, Vol. 11, No. 2, January 2010, pp. 127–138.

[2] Talsma D., Predictive Coding and Multisensory Integration: An Attentional Account of the Multisensory Mind, *Frontiers in Integrative Neuroscience*, Vol. 26, No. 6, March 2015.

对于语义不一致的视听双通道目标来说，不论在选择性注意条件还是分配性注意条件下，均没有视听整合产生。

第二节 分配性注意条件下注意负荷对视听言语整合加工的影响

上述研究发现，只有在分配性注意条件下才会产生视听整合加工。实验2在实验1的基础之上调整了听觉刺激，使之与视觉刺激形成一定的语义联结。发现只有语义一致的视听双通道刺激在分配性注意条件下才会产生整合加工。但是在上述研究中，我们假设注意资源量保持不变，因此上述实验结论适用于注意资源恒定的环境中。有研究发现，个体注意资源的减少会影响其认知加工过程。[①②]那么注意资源的减少是否能减弱视听整合加工？

Alsius等人对此问题进行了考察。[③] 发现当注意资源减少时，视听整合程度会减弱。但他们的实验存在以下问题：一是实验中利用了重复呈现的刺激，这本身就会消耗一定认知资源；二是实验中因变量的指标是McGurk效应百分比，可能存在一定的主观性。

基于上述考虑，研究二将采用已有研究中的双任务范式，在实验2的基础上，分别在实验3和实验4中考察视觉注意负荷和听觉注意负荷对视听言语整合加工的影响。

---

① Alsius A., Navarra J., Campbell R. & Soto-Faraco S., Audiovisual Integration of Speech Falters under High Attention Demands, *Current Biology*, Vol. 15, No. 9, May 2005, pp. 839–843.

② Alsius A., Navarra J. & Soto-Faraco S., Attention to Touch Weakens Audiovisual Speech Integration, *Experimental Brain Research*, Vol. 183, No. 3, November 2007, pp. 399–404.

③ Alsius A., Navarra J., Campbell R. & Soto-Faraco S., Audiovisual Integration of Speech Falters under High Attention Demands, *Current Biology*, Vol. 15, No. 9, May 2005, pp. 839–843.

一 实验3：分配性注意条件下视觉注意负荷对视听言语整合加工的影响

（一）目的

在实验2的基础上，以语义刺激为材料，只选取语义一致的视听双通道目标和两种单通道目标，采用双任务范式，对50%的刺激施加视觉负荷，考察在分配性注意条件下，视觉注意负荷对于视听言语整合加工的影响。

（二）假设

在没有视觉负荷时，分配性注意条件可产生视听整合，而在施加视觉负荷之后，分配性注意条件无法产生视听整合加工。

（三）方法

1. 被试

从天津市某高校随机选取25名在校大学生（男生14人，女生11人）作为被试，这些被试并没有参与过实验1和实验2，其平均年龄为20岁。所有被试的视力或矫正视力正常，听力正常，均为右利手，身体健康，无精神系统疾病，没有脑部损伤史。每位被试在完成实验后会得到一个小礼物作为报酬。

2. 实验材料和程序

本实验的材料与实验2基本一致，即采用具有语义联结的视觉和听觉刺激。由于在实验2中，只有在分配性注意条件下，语义一致的视听双通道目标才会产生视听整合加工，因此在实验3中，只选取了语义一致的视听刺激，并且仅在分配性注意条件下考察视觉负荷对视听言语整合加工的影响。视觉负荷刺激为呈现在圆形或正方形中的两个阿拉伯数字。

本实验的程序与实验2基本一致。在每个试次中，首先在黑色屏幕上呈现白色十字注视点，呈现时间在1000—1200ms之间随机。随后注视点消失，在屏幕中央呈现线索1000ms。线索刺激与实验2

不同。在实验3中，为强调同时注意视觉和听觉通道，线索刺激只有"请注意看和听"。线索刺激消失后，白色十字注视点出现在屏幕中央，呈现时间为1000—1200ms之间的随机时间。注视点消失后，呈现目标刺激。视觉目标刺激、听觉目标刺激、视听刺激和视觉负荷刺激均呈现200ms，被试需要在3000ms的时间窗口内做出反应。被试的主要任务是同时注意视觉通道和听觉通道，并按要求对目标刺激进行按键反应：当看到圆形、听到"圆"或看到的圆形和听到的"圆"同时呈现时，按F键；当看到正方形、听到"方"或者看到正方形和听到"方"同时呈现时，按J键。如果超过3000ms不做反应，该试次记为错误。

实验中一半试次伴随视觉负荷刺激。视觉负荷刺激为两个呈现在屏幕中央的红色数字，数字从0—9中随机选取。在对目标刺激进行判断之后，被试需要判断这两个数字之和是奇数还是偶数，奇数按"D"键，偶数按"K"键。按键后是试次间隔1000ms，随后进入下一个试次。实验中人声读出的"圆""方"分别与圆形和正方形形成语义一致的刺激对，即，在双通道目标刺激中，人声读出的"圆"始终与圆形同时呈现，人声读出的"方"始终与正方形同时呈现。在整个实验过程中，要求被试双眼注视屏幕正中央，同时注意视觉和听觉，既快又准确地做出反应。实验流程见图5-7。

实验3采用2（视觉负荷条件：有注意负荷、无注意负荷）×3（目标刺激类型：单通道视觉目标、单通道听觉目标、双通道目标）的被试内设计。实验中，无视觉负荷的试次约持续5s，有视觉负荷的试次约持续5.5s。实验共有336个试次，有无视觉负荷的试次各占一半。整个实验约持续58.8分钟。在正式实验之前有48个试次作为练习部分。在正式实验中每24个试次可进行短暂休息，被试按Q键可以继续进行实验。

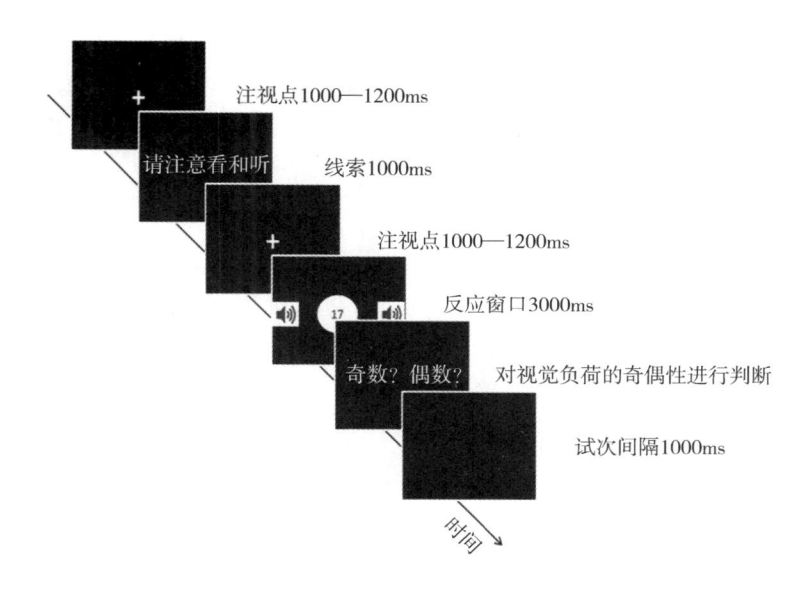

第五章 注意影响视听整合加工的实验研究 ◇ 97

图 5-7 实验 3：视觉负荷条件下呈现双通道目标的试次流程

（四）结果

对数据进行初步处理：删除反应错误的、反应时小于 200ms 和大于 1000ms 的以及反应时超出平均反应时 3 个标准差的数据。初步处理后删除的数据约占总数据的 7.98%。1 名被试因错误率较高（大于 30%）而被剔除，剩余有效被试为 24 人。结果见表 5-3。

表 5-3   有、无注意负荷条件下对三种目标的正确率和反应时（N=24）

目标刺激类型	正确率（%）		反应时（ms）	
	无负荷条件	有负荷条件	无负荷条件	有负荷条件
单通道听觉目标	96.18（1.00）	94.57（1.29）	537.80（66.91）	634.28（86.21）
单通道视觉目标	95.49（1.12）	97.46（0.78）	509.57（74.63）	594.73（62.00）
视听双通道目标	97.22（1.08）	96.53（1.11）	460.02（63.92）	592.10（93.59）

注：括号中为标准差。

对正确率数据进行 2（视觉负荷条件：有注意负荷、无注意负荷)×3(目标刺激类型:单通道视觉目标、单通道听觉目标、视听双通道目标)的重复测量方差分析,任何效应均不显著,$ps > 0.1$。

对反应时数据进行2(视觉负荷条件:有注意负荷、无注意负荷)×3(目标刺激类型:单通道视觉目标、单通道听觉目标、视听双通道目标)的重复测量方差分析。结果发现,视觉负荷条件主效应显著,$F(1, 23) = 68.50$,$p < 0.001$,$\eta^2 = 0.75$。目标刺激类型主效应显著,$F(2, 46) = 8.13$,$p < 0.01$,$\eta^2 = 0.26$。视觉负荷与目标刺激类型交互作用(见图5-8)显著,$F(2, 46) = 2.98$,$p = 0.05$,$\eta^2 = 0.12$。简单效应检验发现,在视觉负荷条件下,被试对单通道听觉、单通道视觉和视听双通道目标的反应时之间无显著差异,$ps > 0.1$。在无视觉负荷条件下,被试对视听双通道目标的反应时显著短于对单通道视觉目标和单通道听觉目标的反应时,$ps < 0.001$;对单通道视觉目标的反应时显著短于对单通道听觉目标的反应时,$p = 0.01$。也就是说,在无视觉负荷条件下被试对视听双通道目标的加工最快,表现出冗余信号效应。

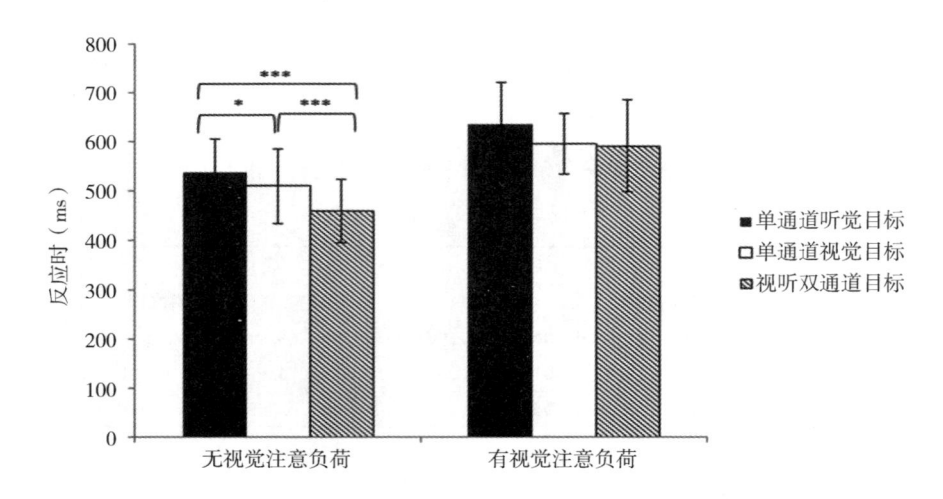

图5-8 实验3:有、无视觉注意负荷条件下三种目标的反应时

为考察上述在无视觉负荷条件下的冗余信号效应是否源自双通道刺激的视觉和听觉成分之间的整合加工，对无视觉负荷条件下的反应时进行竞争模型分析（见图5-9）。分析步骤同实验1。结果发现，在240—430ms上双通道$P(RT_{av} < t)$显著大于竞争模型预测值（240ms，$t = -2.36$，$p < 0.05$；250ms，$t = -3.31$，$p < 0.02$；260ms，$t = -3.84$，$p = 0.001$；270ms，$t = -4.08$，$p < 0.001$；280ms，$t = -4.24$，$p < 0.001$；290ms，$t = -5.85$，$p < 0.001$；300ms，$t = -6.29$，$p < 0.001$；310ms，$t = -6.50$，$p < 0.001$；320ms，$t = -7.00$，$p < 0.001$；330ms，$t = -6.91$，$p < 0.001$；340ms，$t = -6.95$，$p < 0.001$；350ms，$t = -6.87$，$p < 0.001$；360ms，$t = -7.28$，$p < 0.001$；370ms，$t = -7.12$，$p < 0.001$；380ms，$t = -7.41$，$p < 0.001$；390ms，$t = -6.28$，$p < 0.001$；400ms，$t = -4.49$，$p < 0.001$；410ms，$t = -3.58$，$p = 0.001$；420ms，$t = -3.06$，$p < 0.01$；430ms，$t = -2.38$，$p < 0.05$），即，此结果违背竞争模型。这表明，在无负荷条件下，当被试同时注意视觉和听觉时，在反应时中出现的冗余信号效应源自双通道刺激中视觉和听觉成分的整合。

（五）讨论

实验3采用双任务范式，在实验2的结论基础上，进一步考察了视觉注意负荷对视听言语整合加工的影响。结果发现，在视觉注意负荷条件下，被试的平均反应时显著长于无视觉负荷条件下的反应时。这表明，实验3的视觉注意负荷是有效的。

更为重要的是，实验3发现，视觉注意负荷的确对视听言语整合加工存在一定的调制作用，表现为在有视觉注意负荷条件下，被试对视听双通道目标、单通道视觉目标和单通道听觉目标的反应时之间不存在显著差异，即，在视觉注意负荷条件下不存在对语义一致的视听双通道目标的加工优势。而在无视觉负荷条件下，其反应

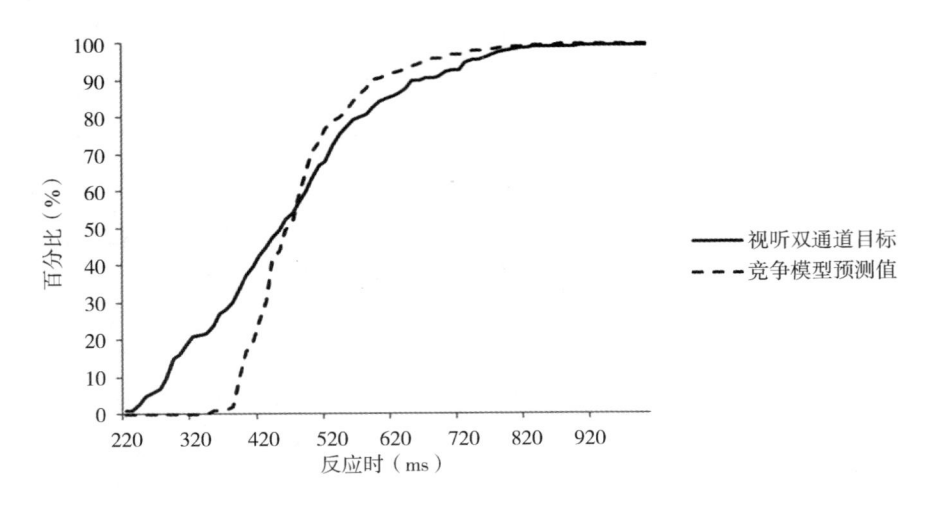

图 5-9　实验 3：无视觉注意负荷条件下的竞争模型分析

时结果与实验 2 基本一致，被试对视听双通道目标的反应时最快，存在对其的加工优势，即产生冗余信号效应。进一步对竞争模型分析发现，在无视觉注意负荷条件下反应时数据的冗余信号效应源自视听双通道目标的视觉成分和听觉成分的整合。

上述结果可能是由于在视觉注意负荷条件下，被试分出一部分注意资源用于做出对视觉负荷刺激的判断，因此减少了总的注意资源量，使用于产生多感觉整合的资源显著减少，造成了在视觉注意负荷条件下并没有产生视听整合加工的结果。本研究结果在一定程度上扩大了有关注意能够影响多感觉整合的研究成果。但是，实验 3 只涉及视觉注意负荷，只能表明视觉注意负荷对于视听整合加工的调制作用，而对于听觉注意负荷是否具有这样的调制作用，或者说视觉和听觉注意负荷在影响视听整合加工时是否具有对称性尚无法得出结论。这些问题将在下面的实验中进行探讨。

（六）小结

实验 3 的结果表明，视觉注意负荷能够影响视听言语整合加工，表现为在有视觉注意负荷条件下，视听双通道目标不具有加工优势；而在无视觉注意负荷条件下，被试对视听双通道目标的反应最快，产生冗余信号效应。进一步对竞争模型分析发现，这种无视觉注意负荷条件下反应时的冗余信号效应源自视听双通道目标的视觉成分和听觉成分的整合。简言之，视觉注意负荷能够对视听言语整合加工产生调制作用，即，只有在无负荷条件下才会产生视听言语整合加工。

二 实验4：分配性注意条件下听觉注意负荷对视听言语整合加工的影响

（一）目的

在实验2的基础上，以语义刺激为材料，只选取语义一致的视听双通道目标和两种单通道目标，采用双任务范式，对50%的刺激施加听觉注意负荷，考察在分配性注意条件下，听觉注意负荷对于视听言语整合加工的影响。

（二）假设

在没有施加听觉负荷时，分配性注意条件可产生视听整合加工，而在施加听觉负荷之后，分配性注意条件无法产生视听整合加工。

（三）方法

1. 被试

从天津市某高校随机选取28名在校大学生（男生14人，女生14人）作为被试，这些被试并没有参与过前面三个实验，其平均年龄为20岁。所有被试的视力或矫正视力正常，听力正常，均为右利手，身体健康，无精神系统疾病，没有脑部损伤史。每位被试在完成实验后会得到一个小礼物作为报酬。

2. 实验材料和程序

本实验的材料与实验 2 基本一致，即采用具有语义联结的视觉和听觉刺激。由于在实验 2 中，只有在分配性注意条件下，语义一致的视听双通道目标才会产生视听整合加工，因此在实验 4 中，同样只选取了语义一致的视听刺激，并且仅在分配性注意条件下考察听觉负荷对视听言语整合加工的影响。听觉负荷刺激为高低短音。

本实验的程序与实验 3 基本一致。在每个试次中，首先在黑色屏幕上呈现白色十字注视点，呈现时间为 1000—1200ms 之间的随机时间。随后注视点消失，在屏幕中央呈现线索。同样，在实验 4 中，由于要强调同时注意视觉和听觉通道，线索刺激只有"请注意看和听"。因此在每个试次中，此线索均会呈现 1000ms。随后白色十字注视点出现在屏幕中央，呈现时间为 1000—1200ms 之间的随机时间。注视点消失后，呈现目标刺激。视觉目标刺激、听觉目标刺激、视听刺激和听觉负荷刺激均呈现 200ms，被试需要在 3000ms 的时间窗口内做出反应。被试的主要任务是同时注意视觉通道和听觉通道，并按要求对目标刺激进行按键反应：当看到圆形、听到"圆"或看到的圆形和听到的"圆"同时呈现时，按 F 键；当看到正方形、听到"方"或者看到正方形和听到"方"同时呈现时，按 J 键。如果超过 3000ms 不做反应，该试次记为错误。

实验中一半试次伴随听觉负荷刺激，听觉负荷刺激为 1200Hz 的高音和 400Hz 的低音，其呈现时间与目标刺激的呈现时间一致。在对目标刺激进行判断之后，被试需要判断与目标刺激同时呈现的短音是高音还是低音。高音按"D"键，低音按"K"键。按键后试次间隔 1000ms，随后进入下一个试次。实验中人声读出的"圆""方"分别与圆形和正方形形成语义一致的刺激对，即，在双通道目标刺激中，人声读出的"圆"始终与圆形同时呈现，人声读出的"方"始终与正方形同时呈现。在整个实验过程中，要求被试双眼注视屏幕正中央，同时注意视觉和听觉，既快又准确地做出反应。实验流程见图 5 – 10。

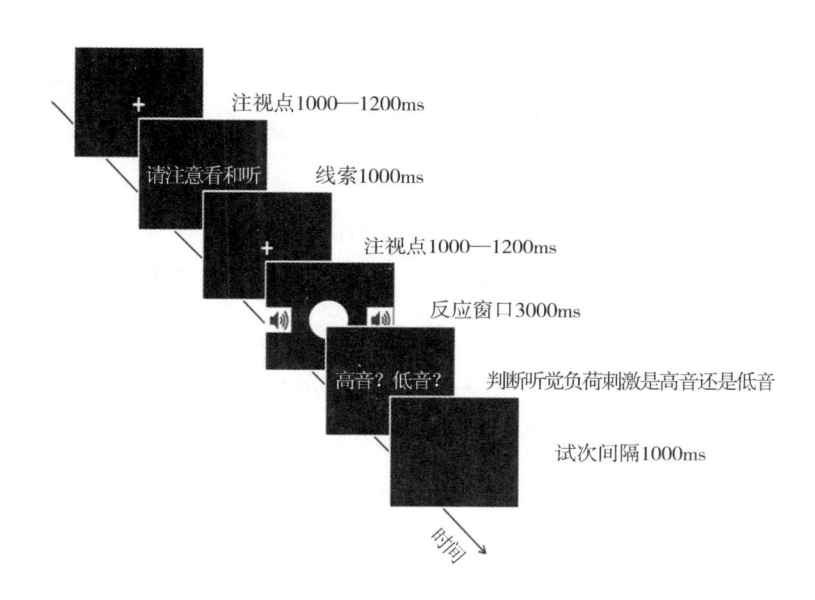

图 5 – 10　实验 4：听觉负荷条件下呈现双通道目标的试次流程

（四）结果

对数据进行初步处理：删除反应错误的、反应时小于 200ms 和大于 1000ms 的以及反应时超出平均反应时 3 个标准差的数据。初步处理后删除的数据约占总数据的 6.41%。一名女性被试因正确率过低（小于 70%）而被删除。最终剩余有效被试 27 人。

对正确率数据（见表 5 – 4）进行 2（听觉负荷条件：有注意负荷、无注意负荷）×3（目标刺激类型：单通道听觉目标、单通道视觉目标、视听双通道目标）的重复测量方差分析，任何效应均不显著，$ps > 0.1$。

表 5-4　有、无注意负荷条件下对三种类型的目标的正确率和反应时（N=27）

目标刺激类型	正确率（%）		反应时（ms）	
	无负荷条件	有负荷条件	无负荷条件	有负荷条件
单通道听觉目标	92.97（1.52）	92.32（1.54）	523.24（55.66）	534.53（76.32）
单通道视觉目标	94.88（1.00）	92.32（1.44）	497.90（62.25）	507.75（66.59）
视听双通道目标	95.52（1.02）	94.14（1.65）	445.37（80.81）	485.02（86.91）

注：括号中为标准差。

对反应时数据（见表 5-4）进行 2（听觉负荷条件：有注意负荷、无注意负荷）×3（目标刺激类型：单通道听觉目标、单通道视觉目标、视听双通道目标）的重复测量方差分析。结果发现，听觉负荷条件主效应显著，$F(1, 26) = 8.76$，$p < 0.01$，$\eta^2 = 0.25$。无负荷条件下的反应时显著短于有负荷条件下的反应时。目标刺激类型主效应显著，$F(2, 52) = 28.05$，$p < 0.001$，$\eta^2 = 0.52$。被试对单通道听觉目标的反应时显著长于对单通道视觉目标（$p < 0.05$）和视听双通道目标（$p < 0.001$）的反应时；对单通道视觉目标的反应时显著长于对视听双通道目标的反应时，$p < 0.001$。听觉负荷条件与目标刺激类型交互作用不显著，$p > 0.1$。也就是说，无论是否呈现听觉负荷刺激，被试均对视听双通道目标的反应最快，产生冗余信号效应。

为考察上述在有、无听觉负荷条件下的冗余信号效应是否源自双通道刺激的视觉和听觉成分之间的整合加工，对有、无听觉负荷条件下的反应时均进行竞争模型分析（见图 5-11、图 5-12）。分析步骤同实验 1。

首先，对于无负荷条件下反应时的分析发现，在 240—390ms 上双通道 $P(RT_{av} < t)$ 显著大于竞争模型预测值（240ms，$t = -2.42$，$p < 0.05$；250ms，$t = -3.29$，$p < 0.01$；260ms，$t = -4.09$，$p <$

0.001；270ms，$t = -4.18$，$p < 0.001$；280ms，$t = -3.91$，$p = 0.001$；290ms，$t = -5.09$，$p < 0.001$；300ms，$t = -6.25$，$p < 0.001$；310ms，$t = -6.57$，$p < 0.001$；320ms，$t = -7.78$，$p < 0.001$；330ms，$t = -7.66$，$p < 0.001$；340ms，$t = -6.23$，$p < 0.001$；350ms，$t = -6.37$，$p < 0.001$；360ms，$t = -4.74$，$p < 0.001$；370ms，$t = -4.31$，$p < 0.001$；380ms，$t = -4.53$，$p < 0.001$；390ms，$t = -3.60$，$p = 0.001$），即：此结果违背竞争模型。这表明，在无负荷条件下，当被试同时注意视觉和听觉通道时，在反应时中出现的冗余信号效应源自双通道刺激中视觉和听觉成分的整合。

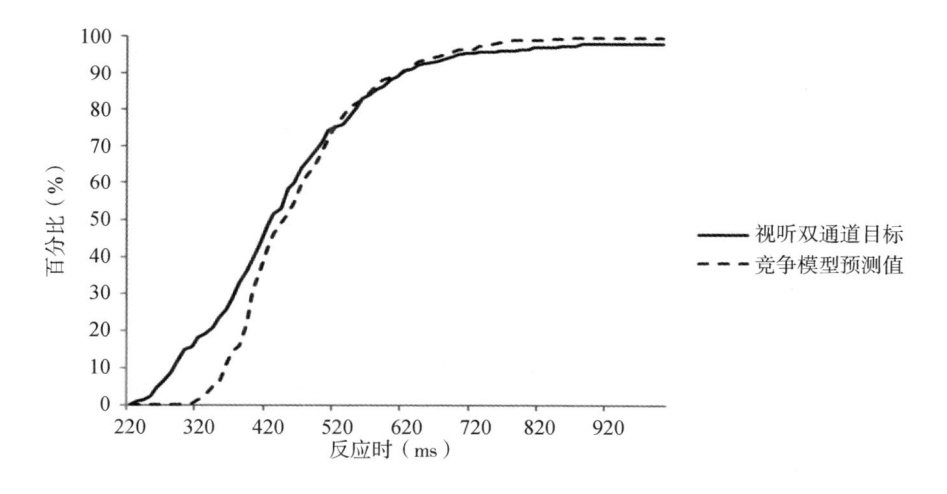

图 5-11 实验 4：无听觉负荷条件下的竞争模型分析

其次，对于有负荷条件下反应时的分析发现，在 280—340ms 上双通道 $P(RT_{av} < t)$ 显著大于竞争模型预测值（280ms，$t = -2.65$，$p < 0.05$；290ms，$t = -2.70$，$p < 0.05$；300ms，$t = -2.60$，$p < 0.05$；310ms，$t = -2.55$，$p < 0.05$；320ms，$t = -2.21$，$p < 0.05$；330ms，$t = -2.37$，$p < 0.05$；340ms，$t = -2.15$，$p < 0.05$），即，此结果违背竞争模型。这表明，在有负荷

条件下，当被试同时注意视觉和听觉时，在反应时中出现的冗余信号效应源自双通道刺激中视觉和听觉成分的整合。

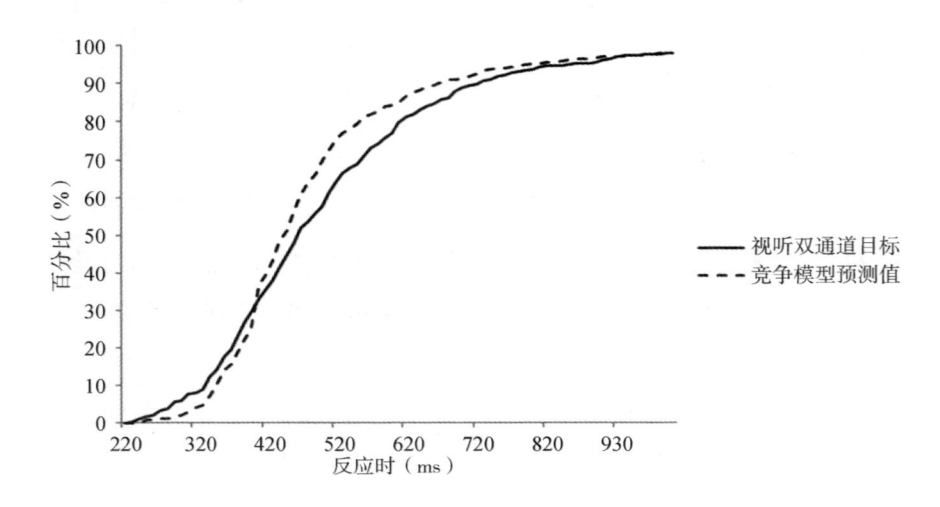

图 5-12　实验 4：有听觉负荷条件下的竞争模型分析

（五）讨论

实验 4 采用双任务范式，在实验 2 的结论基础上，进一步考察了听觉注意负荷对视听言语整合加工的影响。实验结果发现，首先，被试在听觉注意负荷条件下的平均反应时显著长于在无听觉注意负荷条件下的反应时，这表明实验 4 中对于注意资源量的控制是有效的。

其次，实验 4 发现，在无听觉注意负荷条件下，被试对视听双通道目标的反应时最短，即产生冗余信号效应。进一步对竞争模型分析发现，无听觉注意负荷条件下反应时的冗余信号效应均源自视听双通道目标的视觉成分和听觉成分的整合加工。这与实验 2 的结果基本一致。

值得注意的是，实验 4 还发现，在有听觉注意负荷条件下，被试对视听双通道目标的反应时也是最短的，即产生冗余信号效应。

这与实验假设不一致。进一步对竞争模型分析发现，听觉注意负荷条件下反应时的冗余信号效应均源自视听双通道目标的视觉成分和听觉成分的整合加工。也就是说，即便被试在减少听觉注意资源量的条件下仍然产生了视听整合加工。

综观实验3和实验4，不难发现，视觉注意负荷和听觉注意负荷在影响视听言语整合加工时并不具有对称性。表现为视觉注意负荷能够调制视听言语整合加工，而听觉注意负荷不能对视听整合加工产生影响。产生这种不对称性的原因可能是视觉优势效应导致的。有研究者发现，视觉学习具有较强的编码力度和激活水平，对视觉项目的学习能进行精细加工且记忆保持得较好。[1][2] 可以说，视觉在加工程度上比听觉更深一些。这样就使听觉负荷刺激并没有占用被试过多的注意资源，从而产生冗余信号效应。

（六）小结

实验4的结果发现，听觉注意负荷不能影响视听言语整合加工，表现为不论有、无听觉注意负荷，被试对视听双通道目标的反应均是最快的，即产生冗余信号效应。进一步对竞争模型分析发现，在有、无听觉注意负荷条件下，反应时的冗余信号效应源自视听双通道目标的视觉成分和听觉成分的整合。

第三节　分配性注意条件下的注意起伏对视听言语整合加工的影响及其神经机制

稳定性是一种重要的注意品质，它在很大程度上决定着我们的

---

[1]　毛伟宾：《跨视听通道的相继错误记忆效应》，《心理科学》2012年第3期。
[2]　毛伟宾、朱永泽：《跨视听通道的错误记忆ERP新旧效应研究》，《心理与行为研究》2013年第2期。

学习和工作效率。但是，人的感受性并不能长久地保持在稳定状态，而是有规律地增强和减弱。这种现象叫作注意的起伏。注意的起伏现象时刻发生在我们日常的注意活动中。比如，在看注意的双关图时，有时感觉图形向前凸起，有时又感觉似乎向后凹进去；再如，课堂学习中我们有时能够认真听讲，但有时也会开小差，这都是注意起伏现象的体现。有研究发现，注意起伏除了与内部的感觉器官适应性有关之外，还受到外部时间规律的调制。[①②] 一些研究者利用动态注意理论来解释此现象。[③④] 这个理论认为，注意并不是平均分布在各个时间段内的，而是依赖于内部的"动态震荡器"进行周期性变化。这些震荡器决定个体注意的节奏，并决定个体对外部事件的期待或者加工的速度是否处于注意节奏的峰值。更为重要的是，外部事件的节奏化与时间进程可能会通过使内部震荡器与外部事件同步而自动地吸引个体的注意。

Escoffier、Sheng 和 Schirmer 考察了不被注意的音乐节奏对视觉加工的影响。[⑤] 在他们的实验中，节奏化条件是在一小段音乐节奏的最后一拍中呈现一张图片，非节奏化条件是呈现的图片在最后一拍之前 250ms。被试的任务是忽视音乐节奏，同时判断这张图片是正立还是倒立的。结果发现，与非节奏化条件相比，当图片与音乐

---

① Grahn J. A. & Rowe J. B., Finding and Feeling the Musical Beat: Striatal Dissociations between Detection and Prediction of Regularity, *Cerebral Cortex*, Vol. 23, No. 4, April 2012, pp. 913 – 921.

② Nozaradan S., Peretz I., Missal M. & Mouraux A., Tagging Theneuronal Entrainment to Beat and Meter, *Journal of Neuroscience*, Vol. 31, No. 28, July 2011, pp. 10234 – 10240.

③ Escoffier N., Sheng D. Y. J. & Schirmer A., Unattended Musical Beats Enhance Visual Processing, *Acta Psychologica*, Vol. 135, No. 1, September 2010, pp. 12 – 16.

④ Brochard R., Tassin M. & Zagar D., Got Rhythm…for Better and for Worse. Cross – modal Effects of Auditory Rhythm on Visual Word Recognition, *Cognition*, Vol. 127, No. 2, May 2013, pp. 214 – 219.

⑤ Escoffier N., Sheng D. Y. J. & Schirmer A., Unattended Musical Beats Enhance Visual Processing, *Acta Psychologica*, Vol. 135, No. 1, September 2010, pp. 12 – 16.

节奏合拍时，即图片恰好与音乐节奏的最后一拍同时呈现，被试对图片的判断速度最快。也就是说，不被注意的音乐节奏促进的视觉加工是跨通道的。根据 DAT 理论，这可能是由于图片所处的位置恰好位于动态注意的峰值。个体对任何与注意峰值同相位的知觉事件更为期待，因此分配给这些事件更多资源，这些事件也就被更好地加工。[①] 那么，当双通道事件恰好处于动态注意的峰值时，是否能促进双通道事件中视听成分的整合？研究三的实验 5 拟采用节奏化的视听线索，在实验 2 的基础上，进一步考察注意的起伏对视听整合加工的影响。

从已有研究中可以推测，与节奏化线索合拍的目标刺激可能会产生多感觉整合。但是，这种整合在何时产生仍是悬而未决的问题。其主要原因在于，已有的行为研究所依托的反应时等指标只能反映心理加工的综合结果，对于发生在加工早期的感觉整合过程很难进行有效的观察与测量，因而无法揭示感觉整合在何时产生这一动态的过程及其机制。由于事件相关电位具有很高的时间分辨率能够对认知神经活动特征提供即时的评价，从加工的初始就可以对单个的认知过程进行识别和分离[②]，因此，研究三的实验 6 将采用事件相关电位技术考察注意的起伏影响多感觉整合的时间进程及其机制。

---

① Brochard R., Tassin M. & Zagar D., Got Rhythm…for Better and for Worse. Cross–modal Effects of Auditory Rhythm on Visual Word Recognition, *Cognition*, Vol. 127, No. 2, May 2013, pp. 214–219.

② Rhodes S. M. & Donaldson D. I., Association and Not Semantic Relationships Elicit the N400 Effect: Electrophysiological Evidence from an Explicit Language Comprehension Task, *Psychophysiology*, Vol. 45, No. 1, January 2008, pp. 50–59.

一 实验5：分配性注意条件下的注意起伏对视听言语整合加工的影响

（一）目的

通过在目标刺激呈现之前设置具有节律性和非节律性的线索，考察注意的起伏对视听言语整合加工的影响。

（二）假设

当目标刺激恰好呈现在注意的峰值时，能够产生视听整合加工；当目标刺激没有呈现在注意峰值时，不会产生视听整合。

（三）方法

1. 被试

从天津市某高校随机选取25名在校大学生（男生14人，女生11人）作为被试，这些被试并没有参与过前面四个实验，其平均年龄为20岁。所有被试的视力或矫正视力正常，听力正常，均为右利手，身体健康，无精神系统疾病，没有脑部损伤史。每位被试在完成实验后会得到一个小礼物作为报酬。

2. 实验材料和程序

实验刺激通过E-prime 1.1软件编制的实验程序控制。视觉刺激通过17英寸液晶显示器呈现，屏幕分辨率为1024×768，屏幕背景为黑色，被试正对屏幕中心约50cm。听觉刺激通过入耳式耳机呈现，响度调整至被试感觉舒适为宜。

单通道视觉刺激为从互联网上搜索的高清图片（如，汽车、床、灯等），图片视角为5.25°×6.05°。图片包括8张动物图片（龟、鸡、猫、羊、鹰、鱼、猪、鸭）和8张日常用品图片（车、床、灯、门、花、盆、油、针）。

单通道听觉刺激采用Goldwave软件制作和处理，为同一女声读出的单字词（如"车""床""灯"等）和400Hz短音，音量大小调节至被试觉得合适的程度。单字词均选择一声和二声的字，保证在录制时能够在 200ms 内呈现完整个字。

视听双通道刺激为单通道视觉和单通道听觉刺激同时呈现。视听刺激均为语义一致，即，在视听双通道目标中，当图片是猫时，被试听到的也是"猫"；当图片是车时，被试听到的也是"车"。视听双通道刺激不包括语义冲突的情况。同时设置填充刺激。填充刺激为图片与 400Hz 短音同时呈现，或者白色正方形与单字词同时呈现。被试不需要对填充刺激进行反应。

实验中的节奏刺激（见图 5-13）来源于已有研究中采用过的音乐节奏材料。节奏刺激为一个四拍的小节，约持续 2250ms。第一拍为低音鼓，第二拍为小军鼓，第三拍前后为小军鼓，第四拍的鼓声通过声音处理软件抹掉，用于呈现目标刺激。也就是说，第四拍没有鼓声。由于前三拍的影响，可以使被试知觉到第四拍。

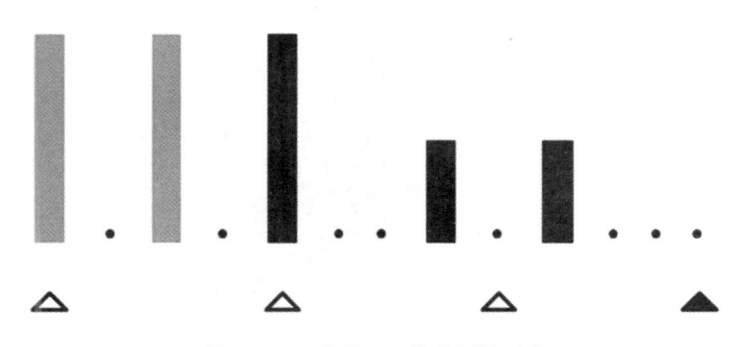

图 5-13　实验 5：节奏刺激示意

注：图中表示的是一个四拍的小节。其中，灰色矩形代表低音鼓，黑色矩形代表小军鼓，矩形长短代表鼓声长短。黑边白色三角形分别代表前三拍的位置，黑色三角形代表应该出现但没有出现的鼓声，即第四拍的位置，并且在此处呈现目标刺激。

实验流程如图 5-14 所示。在合拍和不合拍条件下，十字注视点均与鼓点共同呈现，也就是说，每一个鼓声都伴随一个注视点，注视点伴随鼓声闪烁。采用这种方式呈现线索刺激是为了使被试能够同时注意视觉和听觉。在合拍条件下，节奏刺激之后呈现目标刺激200ms；在不合拍条件下，节奏刺激结束之后300—500ms出现随机空屏，之后呈现目标刺激200ms。合拍和不合拍条件下的节奏均呈现2250ms。在无声条件下，首先呈现2250ms的空屏，之后呈现目标刺激200ms。被试的任务是在2000ms的反应窗口内判断所呈现的目标刺激是不是动物，是动物按"F"键，不是动物按"J"键。按键后自动进入下一试次。如果超过2000ms不做反应，该试次记为错误，自动进入下一试次。按键顺序在被试间进行平衡。反应之后为1000ms的试次间隔。

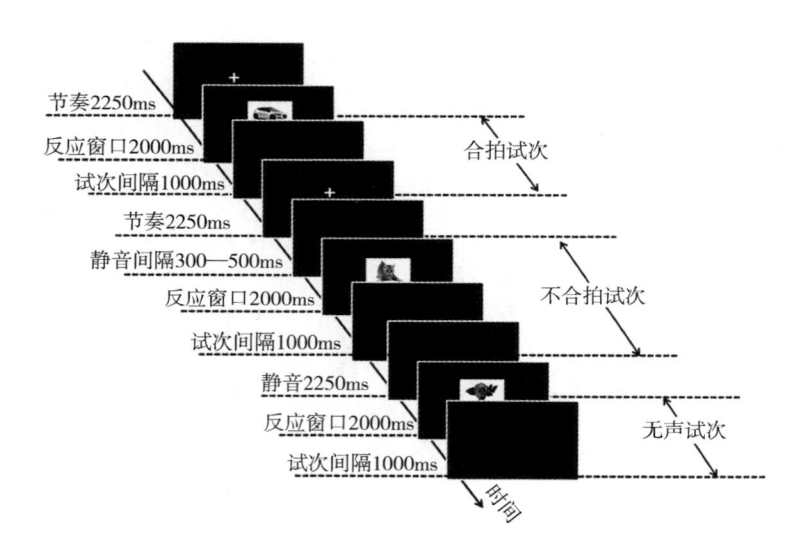

图 5-14　实验 5：在不同目标刺激呈现方式下的视觉目标试次流程

由于目标刺激呈现方式分为与视听节奏合拍、不合拍以及无视听节奏条件，同时，目标刺激分为单通道视觉目标、单通道听觉目标和视听双通道目标，因此，实验包括9种试次类型，分别为：合拍条件—单通道听觉目标；合拍条件—单通道视觉目标；合拍条件—视听双通道目标；无声条件—单通道听觉目标；无声条件—单通道视觉目标；无声条件—视听双通道目标；不合拍条件—单通道听觉目标；不合拍条件—单通道视觉目标；不合拍条件—视听双通道目标。每种类型的试次为 40 个，另有 30 个填充刺激，实验共有 390 个试次。每种条件的试次随机呈现。合拍条件和无声条件下每个试次约为 4.25s，不合拍条件下每个试次约为 4.75s。加上填充刺激以及练习部分，整合实验约持续 60 分钟。

为防止被试疲劳，在实验中设置休息环节。在正式实验之前有 48 个试次作为练习，练习部分的刺激不参与正式实验，并且提供反应时和正确率的反馈。在正式实验中，被试每完成 130 个试次可以进行短暂休息，之后按 Q 键继续进行实验。在正式实验开始之前，首先让被试通过幻灯片观看实验刺激图片，并播放实验中采用的听觉单字词，使之熟悉图片内容。同时，使被试熟悉视听节奏，达到能跟随节奏打拍子的程度。确保被试熟悉实验材料之后再开始正式实验。

表 5-5　不同目标呈现方式条件下对三种类型的目标的正确率和反应时（N=23）

目标刺激类型	正确率（%）			反应时（ms）		
	合拍条件	无声条件	不合拍条件	合拍条件	无声条件	不合拍条件
单通道听觉目标	97.83 (0.84)	98.75 (0.69)	97.50 (1.24)	573.86 (63.17)	608.19 (71.54)	585.59 (51.20)
单通道视觉目标	97.08 (0.13)	96.09 (1.31)	92.29 (2.33)	507.18 (72.27)	513.54 (41.67)	508.03 (62.81)
视听双通道目标	99.56 (0.42)	99.00 (1.00)	98.75 (0.69)	483.83 (50.47)	515.52 (60.97)	502.15 (71.64)

注：括号中为标准差。

（四）结果

对数据进行初步处理：删除反应错误的、反应时小于 200ms 和大于 1000ms 的以及反应时超出平均反应时 3 个标准差的数据。初步处理后删除的数据约占总数据的 8.71%。2 名被试因正确率过低（小于 70%）而被删除。最终剩余有效被试 23 人。

在正确率方面，将单通道目标和视听双通道目标的反应正确率进行 3（目标刺激呈现方式：合拍、无声、不合拍）×3（目标刺激类型：单通道听觉目标、单通道视觉目标、视听双通道目标）的重复测量方差分析。结果发现，目标刺激呈现方式主效应显著，$F(2, 44) = 5.45$，$p < 0.01$，$\eta^2 = 0.20$。进一步分析发现，不合拍条件下目标的正确率（$M = 96.01\%$，$SD = 1.05$）显著低于合拍条件下的目标正确率（$M = 98.08\%$，$SD = 0.60$），$p < 0.05$；低于无声条件下的正确率（$M = 98.20\%$，$SD = 0.56$），$p = 0.057$；无声与合拍条件的正确率无显著差异，$p > 0.1$。目标刺激类型主效应显著，$F(2, 44) = 8.35$，$p = 0.001$，$\eta^2 = 0.28$，被试对单通道听觉目标反应正确率（$M = 94.94\%$，$SD = 1.35$）显著低于对单通道视觉目标（$M = 97.94\%$，$SD = 0.75$）和视听双通道目标的正确率（$M = 99.41\%$，$SD = 0.27$），$ps < 0.05$，后两者之间无显著差异，$p > 0.1$。节奏和目标刺激类型交互作用不显著，$p > 0.1$。

在反应时方面，将单通道目标和视听双通道目标的反应时进行 3（目标刺激呈现方式：合拍、无声、不合拍）×3（目标刺激类型：单通道听觉目标、单通道视觉目标、视听双通道目标）的重复测量方差分析。结果发现，目标刺激呈现方式主效应显著，$F(2, 44) = 38.77$，$p < 0.001$，$\eta^2 = 0.64$。目标刺激类型主效应显著，$F(2, 44) = 56.12$，$p < 0.001$，$\eta^2 = 0.72$。目标刺激呈现方式与目标刺激类型交互作用（见图 5-15）显著，$F(4, 88) = 2.73$，$p < 0.05$，$\eta^2 = 0.11$。简单效应检验发现，在目标刺激的出现与节奏合拍时，被试对视听双通道目标的反应时显著小于对单通道视觉目标（$p < 0.05$）和单通道听觉目标的反应时（$p < 0.001$）；对单通

道视觉目标的反应时显著小于对单通道听觉目标的反应时，$p < 0.001$；在无声条件下，被试对视听双通道目标的反应时与对单通道视觉目标的反应时之间无显著差异，$ps > 0.1$，均小于对单通道听觉目标的反应时，$ps < 0.001$；在不合拍条件下，被试对视听双通道目标的反应时与对单通道视觉目标的反应时之间无显著差异，$ps > 0.1$，均小于对单通道听觉目标的反应时，$ps < 0.001$。这表明，只有当目标刺激的出现与节奏合拍时才会产生冗余信号效应。

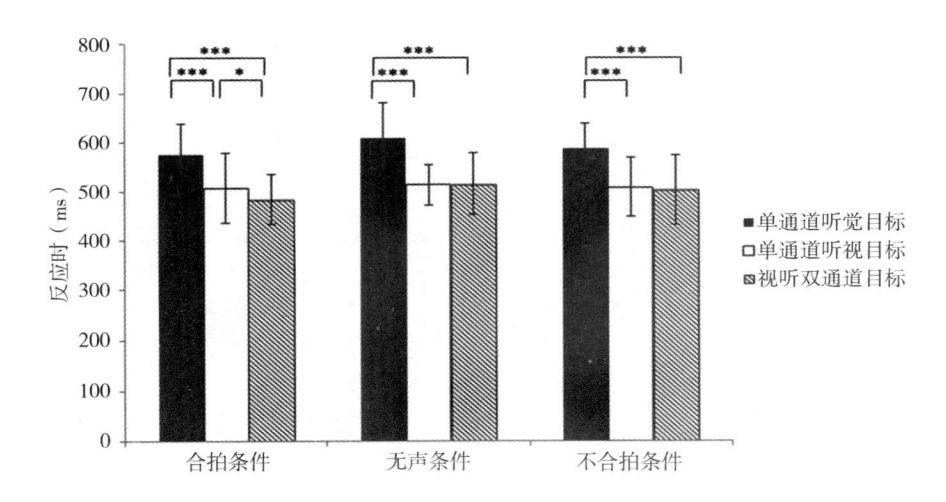

图 5-15　实验 5：不同目标刺激呈现方式下对三种目标的反应时

对合拍条件下的反应时进行竞争模型分析（见图 5-16）。首先，计算反应时的累积量分布函数单通道视觉 $P(RTv < t)$、单通道听觉 $P(RTa < t)$ 和多通道 $P(RTav < t)$。其次，根据已有研究计算出竞争模型预测值 $[P(RTv < t) + P(RTa < t)] - [P(RTv < t) \times P(RTa < t)]$。为考察实验值与竞争模型预测值之间是否存在显著差异，在每 10% 的时间点上将多通道 $P(RTav < t)$ 与竞争模型预测值进行配对 t 检验。结果发现，在 310—490ms 上多通道 $P(RTav < t)$ 显著大于竞争模型预测值（370ms，$t = 2.43$，$p < 0.05$；380ms，$t =$

2.68，$p=0.01$；390ms，$t=2.60$，$p<0.05$；400ms，$t=2.81$，$p<0.05$；410ms，$t=2.47$，$p<0.05$；420ms，$t=2.74$，$p<0.05$；430ms，$t=2.80$，$p=0.01$；440ms，$t=2.38$，$p<0.001$；450ms，$t=4.26$，$p<0.001$；460ms，$t=4.49$，$p<0.001$；470ms，$t=2.46$，$p<0.05$；480ms，$t=3.73$，$p=0.001$），即此结果违背竞争模型。这表明在反应时中出现的冗余信号效应源自双通道刺激中视觉成分和听觉成分的整合。

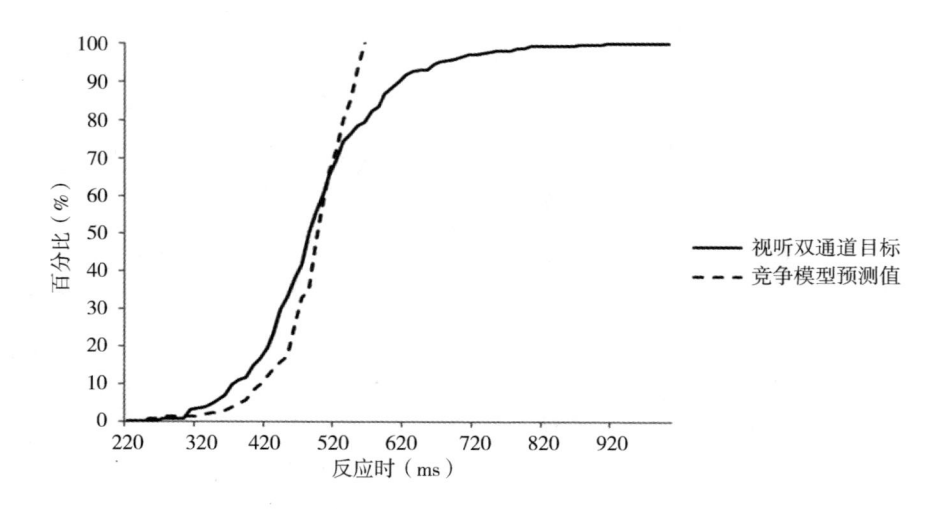

图 5-16 实验5：合拍条件下的竞争模型分析

（五）讨论

实验5通过控制目标刺激在节奏中呈现的位置，形成与视听节奏合拍和不合拍两种条件，同时，将节奏调整为静音以形成基线条件，考察了注意的起伏对视听言语整合加工的影响。结果发现，当目标刺激的出现符合视听节拍时，被试对视听双通道目标的反应最快，即产生冗余信号效应。在对冗余信号效应进行竞争模型分析后发现，这种冗余信号效应的产生源自视听双通道刺激的视觉成分和听觉成分的整合。简言之，只有在目标刺激呈现与音乐节奏合拍时

（处于注意的峰值时），视听双通道刺激才会产生多感觉整合。由于在合拍条件下的反应时均小于不合拍和无声条件下对目标的反应时，表明这种对合拍的双通道目标的加工是对双通道目标的促进作用，而非对不合拍目标的阻碍作用。这种对合拍目标的促进加工效应与已有研究基本一致。比如，早期一些基于单通道刺激的研究发现，视觉节奏能调节对视觉目标的动态化注意。[1] 最近的跨通道研究也证明了这一点，比如，Escoffier、Sheng 和 Schirmer 发现，与非节奏化条件相比，当图片与音乐节奏合拍时，即图片恰好与音乐节奏的最后一拍同时呈现，被试对图片的判断速度最快。[2]

Escoffier、Sheng 和 Schirmer 在其研究中提出，这种节奏化线索之后呈现目标的方式可能是一种时间期待对认知加工的影响。有研究者认为，这种时间上的期待可能涉及准备阶段效应（foreperiod effects）。准备阶段是指线索和目标之间的时间间隔。当准备阶段大于 70ms 且恒定不变时，准备阶段越短，对目标的反应时越短。在实验 5 中，目标出现之前最后一个鼓声与目标之间可以看作是准备阶段，不论合拍还是不合拍条件，准备阶段均大于 70ms。不合拍条件是在节奏的第四拍之前的 200ms 呈现。也就是说，不合拍条件比合拍条件的准备阶段短 200ms。按照准备阶段效应的观点，不合拍条件下的反应时应该小于合拍条件下的反应时。但这与实验 5 的结果恰好相反，这就排除了实验 5 中发现的合拍条件下的优势加工来自准备阶段效应的可能性。

事实上，包括实验 5 结果在内，上述研究均可以用动态注意理论（DAT 理论）解释。DAT 理论认为，注意并非一成不变，而是

---

[1] Correa A. & Nobre A. C., Neural Modulation by Regularity and Passage of Time, *Journal of Neurophysiology*, Vol. 100, No. 3, September 2008, pp. 1649-1655.

[2] Escoffier N., Sheng D. Y. J. & Schirmer A., Unattended Musical Beats Enhance Visual Processing, *Acta Psychologica*, Vol. 135, No. 1, September 2010, pp. 12-16.

存在一定的节奏性。当外部事件恰好处于注意的峰值时，个体会更为期待与注意峰值同相位的知觉事件，这种知觉事件也会被分配给更多的注意资源，因此得到更好地加工。在实验 5 中，节奏中的每一个拍子都恰好处于注意节奏的峰值，与峰值同步的刺激能被更好地加工。具体而言，由于合拍条件下目标刺激恰好处于第四拍的位置上，即恰好呈现在注意的峰值上，这样目标刺激被赋予更多的注意资源，因此对其加工更为深入，表现为在合拍条件下对目标刺激的反应时最短。

但是，并非所有合拍条件下的目标刺激均能得到优势加工。在实验 5 中，与视觉和听觉单通道目标刺激相比，被试对视听双通道目标刺激的反应最快。这种对双通道目标的优势加工源自双通道刺激的视觉和听觉成分之间产生的整合加工。一些研究者认为，这是由于人在感知外界环境时，当两个或两个以上的感官通道在同一时间接收到的线索来源于相同的空间位置时，通常会认为它们是来自同一个物体或事件，因此比单一感官通道输入条件下更容易被检测到。[1][2]

从整体上看，被试对单通道视觉目标的反应时均小于对单通道听觉目标的反应时。也就是说，与听觉刺激相比，视听节奏更能促进对视觉刺激的加工。这可能是由于：一方面，可能是由于生理唤醒水平的改变。已有研究表明，节奏刺激能促进生理唤醒，这反过

---

[1] Frassinetti F., Bolognini N. & Ladavas E., Enhancement of Visual Perception by Crossmodal Visuo-auditory Interaction, *Experimental Brain Research*, Vol. 147, No. 3, December 2002, pp. 332–343.

[2] Calvert G. A. & Thesen T., Multisensory Integration: Methodological Approaches and Emerging Principles in the Human Brain, *Journal of Physiology Paris*, Vol. 98, No. 1–3, June 2004, pp. 191–205.

来能增强注意。另一方面，节奏的介入激活了注意分配规则的改变[1]。注意资源来自一个用量有限的资源库。分配给一个任务的注意资源是增加还是减少取决于同时完成的任务所需要的注意资源。在这个模型的背景下，注意被节奏的调节可以表达为注意资源的分配在一段时间内的改变。当个体需要（期待事件发生）时，注意资源就会被分配得更多，当个体不需要（不期待事件发生）时，注意资源被分配得更少一些。一些考察神经震荡与注意的关系的电生理研究支持这个解释。这些研究将注意控制与 β 波的震荡活性相连接，表明这种震荡活性可以被听觉刺激系列促进[2]。而且，有研究发现，当被试想象听觉刺激系列呈现在节奏的位置上时，一个系列中的听觉事件能够诱发更强的 β 反应[3]。本研究中听觉节奏对视觉目标的促进加工也可能来源于听觉加工区域激活视觉加工区域的神经活性[4]。

此外，本研究中听觉目标刺激的反应时不论在任何条件下均是最大的。也就是说，视听节奏并没有促进对听觉目标的反应。这与最近一项研究的结果相似。Alexander 的研究考察了节奏化线索对认知加工的影响。研究中设置了四种线索—目标条件，分别是视觉线索—视觉目标、视觉线索—听觉目标、听觉线索—听觉目标、听觉线索—视觉目标。结果发现，一个通道内节奏化的线索能影响另一个通道内的时间期待，表明由节奏产生的期待是跨通道的，而非

---

[1] Escoffier N., Sheng D. Y. J. & Schirmer A., Unattended Musical Beats Enhance Visual Processing, *Acta Psychologica*, Vol. 135, No. 1, September 2010, pp. 12 – 16.

[2] Fujioka T., Trainor L. J., Large E. W. & Ross B., Beta and Gamma Rhythms in Human Auditory Cortex during Musical Beat Processing, *Ann N Y Acad Sci*, July 2009, pp. 89 – 92.

[3] Iversen J. R., Repp B. H. & Patel A. D., Top – down Control of Rhythm Perception Modulates Early Auditory Responses, *Ann N Y Acad Sci*, July 2009, No. 1169, pp. 58 – 73.

[4] Lakatos P., Chen C. M., O'Connell M. N., Mills A. & Schroeder C. E., Neuronal Oscillations and Multisensory Interaction in Primary Auditory Cortex, *Neuron*, Vol. 53, No. 2, January 2007, pp. 279 – 292.

通道特异性的。也就是说，Alexander 的研究并没有发现听觉节奏化线索促进听觉目标加工，这与本研究一致。但是，Alexander 的研究所采用的是空间注意，而本研究并未涉及空间注意。至于本研究为何出现这样的结果，有待于未来研究给出答案。

（六）小结

实验 5 的结果发现，只有当目标刺激处于注意的峰值时，被试对双通道目标刺激的反应最快，即产生冗余信号效应。进一步对竞争模型分析发现，这种条件下的冗余信号效应源自视听双通道目标的视觉成分和听觉成分的整合。简言之，只有当目标刺激处于注意峰值时，才会产生视听言语整合加工。

二 实验6：分配性注意条件下的注意起伏影响视听言语整合加工的神经机制

（一）目的

在实验 5 的基础上，考察注意的起伏影响视听言语整合加工的神经机制。

（二）假设

（1）枕部 P1、N1 是与单通道视觉目标刺激相关的电生理成分；全头分布的 N1 是与单通道听觉目标刺激相关的电生理成分。这些成分的波幅在不同的目标刺激呈现方式（合拍条件、无声条件）下会存在差异。

（2）当目标刺激处于注意峰值（合拍条件）时，视听双通道目标引发的 ERP 成分与两个单通道目标引发的 ERP 成分的波幅之和在加工早期出现差异，即在合拍条件下，视听整合加工在对目标刺激加工的早期出现。

（三）方法

1. 被试

从天津市某高校随机选取 20 名在校大学生（男性 9 名，女性 11 名）作为被试，这些被试并没有参与过前面五个实验，其平均年龄为 20 岁。所有被试的视力或矫正视力正常，听力正常，均为右利手，身体健康，无精神系统疾病，没有脑部损伤史。

2. 实验材料和程序

实验材料与实验 5 部分相同。实验 5 发现，只有在目标刺激与节奏合拍时才会产生多感觉整合加工，而在无声和不合拍条件下均没有产生多感觉整合效应，并且无声和不合拍条件下的反应时无显著差异。因此在本实验中，只选取了实验 5 中合拍和无声条件，对比了合拍和无声条件下被试对目标刺激的反应及其认知神经机制。

实验刺激通过 E-prime 1.1 软件编制的实验程序控制。视觉刺激通过 17 英寸液晶显示器呈现，屏幕分辨率为 1024×768，屏幕背景为黑色，被试正对屏幕中心约 50cm。听觉刺激通过入耳式耳机呈现，响度调整至被试感觉舒服为宜。

单通道视觉刺激为从互联网上搜索的高清图片（如，汽车、床、灯等），图片视角为 5.25°×6.05°。图片包括 8 张动物图片（龟、鸡、猫、羊、鹰、鱼、猪、鸭）和 8 张日常用品图片（车、床、灯、门、花、盆、油、针）。

单通道听觉刺激采用 Goldwave 软件制作和处理，为同一女声读出的单字词（如"车""床""灯"等）和 400Hz 短音，音量大小调节至被试觉得合适的程度。单字词均选择一声和二声的字，保证在录制时能够在 200ms 内呈现完整个字。

视听双通道刺激为单通道视觉和单通道听觉刺激同时呈现。视听刺激的语义内容一致，且属于一类。比如，在视听双通道目标中，当图片是猫时，被试同时听到的也是"猫"；当图片是车时，被试同时听到的也是"车"。视听双通道刺激不包括语义冲突的情况。同时设置填充刺激。填充刺激为图片与400Hz短音同时呈现，或者白色正方形与单通道听觉刺激同时呈现。被试不需要对填充刺激进行反应。

实验中的节奏刺激来源于已有研究中采用过的音乐节奏材料[①]。节奏刺激为一个四拍的小节，约持续2250ms。第一拍为低音鼓，第二拍为小军鼓，第三拍前后为小军鼓，第四拍的鼓声通过声音处理软件抹掉，用于呈现目标刺激。也就是说，第四拍没有鼓声。由于前三拍的影响，可以使被试知觉到第四拍。

实验流程如图5-17所示。在合拍条件下，十字注视点均与鼓点共同呈现，也就是说，每一个鼓声都伴随一个注视点，注视点伴随鼓声闪烁。采用这种方式呈现线索刺激是为了使被试能够同时注意视觉和听觉。在合拍条件下，节奏刺激之后呈现目标刺激200ms；在无声条件下，首先呈现2250ms的空屏，之后呈现目标刺激200ms。被试的任务是在2000ms的反应窗口内判断所呈现的目标刺激是不是动物，是动物按"F"键，不是动物按"J"键。按键后自动进入下一试次。如果超过2000ms不做反应，该试次记为错误，自动进入下一试次。按键顺序在被试间进行平衡。反应之后为1000ms的试次间隔。

由于目标刺激呈现方式分为与视听节奏合拍以及无视听节奏条件，同时，目标刺激分为单通道视觉目标、单通道听觉目标和视听双通道目标，因此，实验包括6种试次类型，分别为：合拍条件—单通道听觉目标；合拍条件—单通道视觉目标；合拍条件—视听双通道目标；无声条件—单通道听觉目标；无声条件—单通道视觉目

---

① Escoffier N., Sheng D. Y. J. & Schirmer A., Unattended Musical Beats Enhance Visual Processing, *Acta Psychologica*, Vol. 135, No. 1, September 2010, pp. 12–16.

标；无声条件—视听双通道目标。为保证后期脑电数据叠加次数，每种类型的试次为 70 个，另有 60 个填充刺激，实验共有 480 个试次。合拍和无声条件下每个试次约为 4s。填充刺激不需要被试反应，每个试次约为 5.25s。加上前期准备工作以及练习部分，正式实验共需要约 1 小时。

为防止被试疲劳，在实验中设置休息环节。在正式实验之前有 70 个试次作为练习，其中，每种条件下 10 个试次，另有 10 个填充刺激。练习部分的刺激不参与正式实验，并且提供反应时和正确率的反馈。在正式实验中，被试每完成 120 个试次可以进行短暂休息，之后按"Q"键继续进行实验。在正式实验开始之前，首先让被试通过幻灯片观看实验刺激图片，并播放实验中采用的听觉单字词，使之熟悉图片内容。同时，播放节奏刺激，让被试跟着节奏打拍子，直到被试能够熟悉实验中所使用的节奏。确保被试熟悉实验材料之后再开始正式实验。

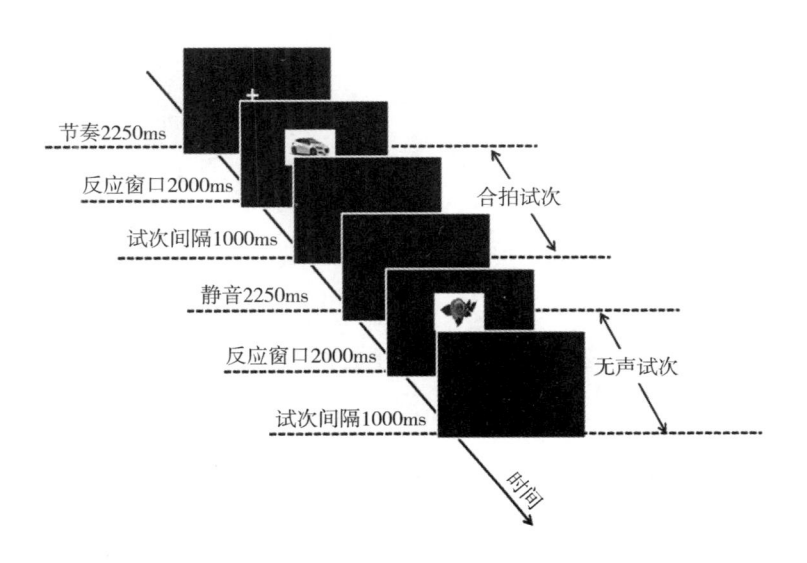

图 5-17 实验 6：合拍和无声条件下视觉目标的试次流程

3. EEG 数据记录和分析

采用 NeuroScan 公司生产的 ERP 系统采集和处理脑电数据，按照国际 10—20 系统扩展的 64 导电极帽记录 EEG。记录时以左耳乳突为参考电极，在离线数据处理时转换为左右两耳乳突的平均电位作为参考。双眼外侧 1.5cm 处放置测量水平眼电（HEOG）的电极，左眼上下各 1.5cm 处放置测量垂直眼电（VEOG）的电极。在正式实验过程中，确保每个电极处的头皮电阻小于 5kΩ。滤波带通为 0.05—100Hz，采样频率为 1000Hz/导。离线滤波的低通为 30Hz（24dB/oct），剔除波幅大于 ±100μV 的伪迹。根据已有研究设置分析窗口。对于单通道视觉目标和听觉目标诱发的 ERP，分析窗口为目标刺激呈现前 200ms 至目标刺激呈现后 800ms，以刺激呈现前 200ms 为基线。对于视听整合效应的考察，分析窗口为目标刺激呈现前 200ms 至目标刺激呈现后 500ms，以刺激呈现前 200ms 为基线。

4. 数据处理与统计分析

（1）有效被试的筛选与数据处理

4 名被试由于伪迹太多被剔除，最后剩余 16 名被试（9 名女性，7 名男性）的数据。

（2）脑电数据处理

对于单通道视觉目标和单通道听觉目标，选择目标刺激呈现之前 200ms 到目标刺激呈现之后 800ms 作为脑电数据处理的时间窗口，并以目标刺激呈现之前 200ms 作为基线，按照目标刺激的出现是否与节奏合拍（合拍/无声）以及目标刺激类型（单通道听觉目标/单通道视觉目标/视听双通道目标）叠加出各条件下的 ERP。对于单通道视觉和单通道听觉目标所诱发的 ERP 成分，采用其波峰幅值作为分析的因变量。对于视听整合效应，根据已有文献中的分析方法，在目标刺激呈现到呈现后 500ms 内采用特定时间窗口内的平均波幅（每20ms的ERP平均波幅）作为因变量。

对于听觉目标，各实验条件在头皮各处均引发了峰位于155ms左右的负波（听觉N1）和峰位于235ms左右的正波（听觉P2）。根据相关参考文献与总平均图，将听觉N1成分的波幅分析窗口设定为100—200ms，将听觉P2成分的平均波幅分析窗口设定为200—300ms。选择F3/FZ/F4、C3/CZ/C4、P3/PZ/P4作为听觉N1、P2成分的参考电极。对于视觉目标，各实验条件在枕区诱发了峰位于84ms左右的正波（视觉P1），以及峰位于145ms左右的负波（枕区视觉N1），在额中区诱发了峰位于100ms左右的负波（额区视觉N1）。根据相关参考文献与总平均图，将枕区视觉P1的波幅分析窗口设定为60—110ms，选择PO7/O1/O2/PO8作为其参考电极；将枕区视觉N1的波幅分析窗口设定为100—200ms，选择PO7/O1/O2/PO8作为其参考电极；将额区视觉N1的波幅分析窗口设定为60—120ms，选择F3/FZ/F4、FC3/FCZ/FC4、C3/CZ/C4九个电极点作为额区视觉N1的参考电极；将额区视觉P2的波幅分析窗口设定为100—250ms，选择F3/FZ/F4、FC3/FCZ/FC4、C3/CZ/C4九个电极点作为枕区视觉P2的参考电极。

采用SPSS16.0统计软件分别对视觉ERP和听觉ERP进行2（目标刺激呈现方式：合拍、无声）×3（电极左右位置：左侧、中线、右侧）×3（电极前后位置：前部、中央、后部）的重复测量方差分析。

为比较两种目标刺激呈现方式条件下视听整合在时间进程上的差异，分别将两种条件下的视觉和听觉ERP相加（A+V），在不同实验条件下与视听双通道目标诱发的ERP（AV）相比较，即在不同时间段内进行2（目标刺激呈现方式：合拍、无声）×2（整合效应：A+V，AV）×3（脑区：额区、额中区、中央区）×3（电极左右位置：左侧、中线、右侧）的四因素重复测量方差分析。

记录电极头皮分布及纳入统计分析的电极名称及位置详见图 5–18。

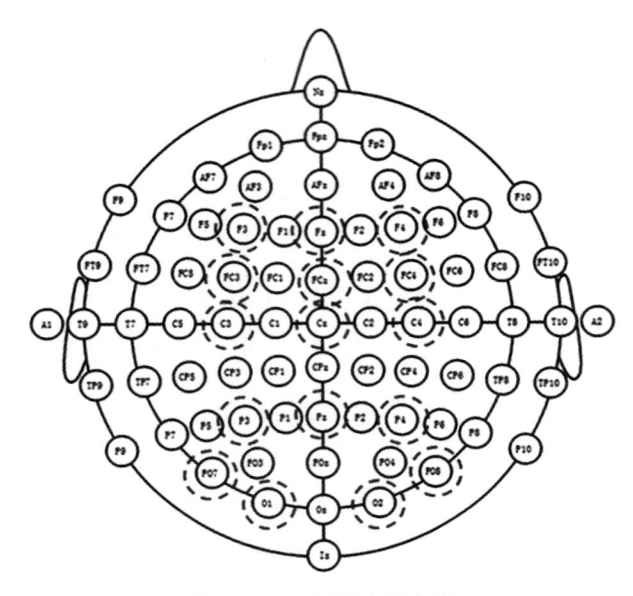

图 5–18　记录电极分布

注：圈中者为参与统计分析的电极。

对数据进行初步处理：删除反应错误的、反应时小于 200ms 和大于 1000ms 的以及反应时超出平均反应时 3 个标准差的数据。初步处理后删除的数据约占总数据的 3.3%。各实验条件下被试的平均反应时和反应正确率见表 5–6。

对于反应正确率，进行 2（目标刺激呈现方式：合拍、无声）× 3（目标刺激类型：单通道听觉目标、单通道视觉目标、视听双通道目标）的两因素重复测量方差分析。结果发现，目标刺激类型主效应显著，$F(2, 30) = 6.97$，$p < 0.01$，$\eta^2 = 0.32$。进一步分析发现，被试对单通道听觉目标的反应正确率（$M = 98.20\%$，$SD = 0.51$）与单通道视觉目标的反应正确率（$M = 99.64\%$，$SD = 0.15$）无显著差异，但显著小于对视听双通道目标的反应正确率（$M = 99.60\%$，

$SD = 0.20$),$p < 0.05$;后两者之间无显著差异,$p > 0.1$。其他主效应与交互作用均不显著,$ps > 0.1$。

对于反应时数据,进行2(目标刺激呈现方式:合拍、无声)×3(目标刺激类型:单通道听觉目标、单通道视觉目标、视听双通道目标)的两因素重复测量方差分析。结果发现,目标刺激呈现方式主效应显著,$F(1,15) = 66.32$,$p < 0.001$,$\eta^2 = 0.82$。目标刺激类型主效应显著,$F(2,30) = 104.77$,$p < 0.001$,$\eta^2 = 0.88$。目标刺激呈现方式与目标刺激类型交互作用(见图5-19)显著,$F(2,30) = 4.38$,$p < 0.05$,$\eta^2 = 0.23$。简单效应分析发现,在当目标刺激的呈现与节奏合拍时,被试对视听双通道目标的反应时显著短于对单通道听觉目标($p < 0.001$),边缘显著短于单通道视觉目标($p = 0.56$),对单通道视觉目标的反应时显著短于对单通道听觉目标的反应时($p < 0.001$)。而在无声条件下,被试对单通道听觉目标的反应时最长,而对单通道视觉目标和视听双通道目标的反应时之间无显著差异,$p > 0.1$。

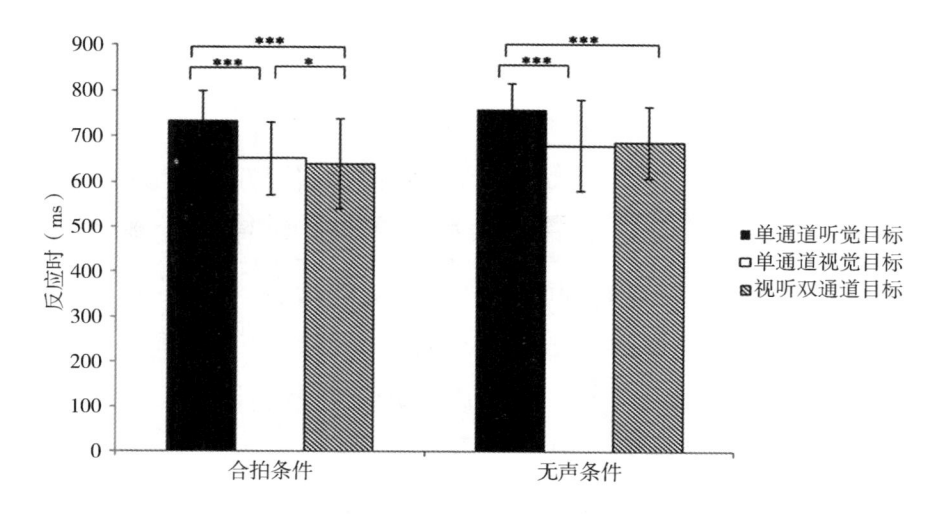

图5-19 实验6:不同目标刺激呈现方式下对三种目标的反应时

表 5-6 两种实验条件下被试对三种类型目标刺激的正确率和
反应时（N = 16）

目标刺激类型	正确率（%）		反应时（ms）	
	合拍条件	无声条件	合拍条件	无声条件
单通道听觉目标	98.18（0.55）	98.23（0.56）	733.83（75.97）	760.23（57.08）
单通道视觉目标	99.82（0.12）	99.46（0.22）	651.44（80.37）	680.55（99.87）
视听双通道目标	99.73（0.14）	99.46（0.32）	639.41（79.15）	687.31（78.81）

注：括号中为标准差。

（3）ERP 数据结果

①听觉目标

图 5-20 为听觉目标在合拍和无声条件下的总平均波形图。

N1

对听觉目标的 N1 波幅进行 2（目标刺激呈现方式：合拍、无声）×3（电极左右位置：左侧、中线、右侧）×3（电极前后位置：前部、中央、后部）的三因素重复测量方差分析。结果发现，目标刺激呈现方式主效应显著，$F(1, 15) = 6.55$，$p < 0.05$，$\eta^2 = 0.30$。电极前后位置主效应显著，$F(2, 30) = 4.74$，$p < 0.05$，$\eta^2 = 0.24$。目标刺激呈现方式与前后位置交互作用显著，$F(2, 30) = 5.54$，$p < 0.01$，$\eta^2 = 0.27$。简单效应检验发现，在额区，合拍条件下的波幅（$M = -7.64\mu V$，$SD = 0.85$）显著大于无声条件下的波幅（$M = -6.44\mu V$，$SD = 0.73$），$p < 0.05$；中央区合拍条件下的波幅（$M = -9.67\mu V$，$SD = 0.95$）显著大于无声条件下的波幅（$M = -7.71\mu V$，$SD = 0.88$），$p < 0.01$；枕区合拍条件下的波幅（$M = -7.58\mu V$，$SD = 0.97$）与无声条件下的波幅（$M = -6.93\mu V$，$SD = 1.14$）无显著差异，$p > 0.1$。

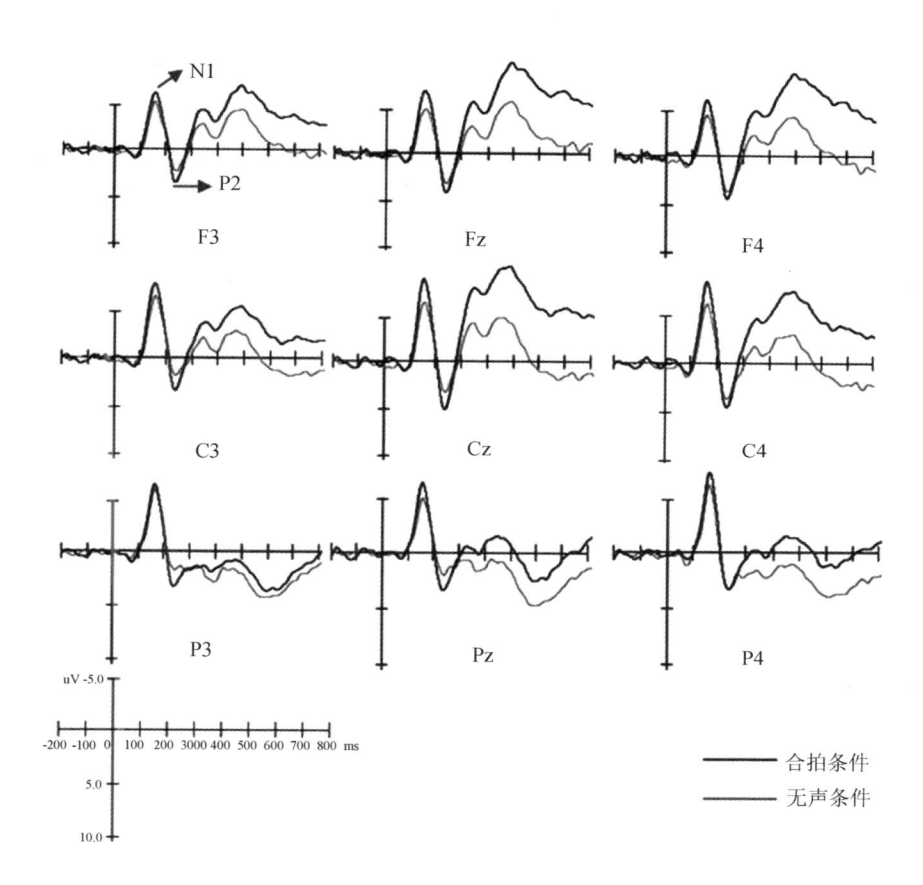

图 5-20 合拍和无声条件下的听觉目标 ERP 波形图

目标刺激呈现方式和电极左右位置交互作用显著，$F(2, 30) = 15.02$，$p<0.001$，$\eta^2 =0.50$。简单效应分析发现，在左侧电极处合拍条件下 N1 波幅（$M = -7.83\mu V$，$SD =0.86$）与无声条件下的 N1 波幅（$M = -7.07\mu V$，$SD =0.87$）之间无显著差异，$p >0.1$；在中线电极处合拍条件下的 N1 波幅（$M = -8.86\mu V$，$SD =0.91$）显著大于无声条件下 N1 波幅（$M = -7.06\mu V$，$SD =0.85$），$p <0.01$；在右侧电极处合拍条件下的 N1 波幅（$M = -8.21\mu V$，$SD =0.84$）显著大于无声条件下 N1 波幅（$M = -6.95\mu V$，$SD =0.90$），$p <0.01$。其他主效应与交互作

用均不显著，$ps > 0.1$。潜伏期统计未见显著差异。

P2

对听觉 P2 波幅进行 2（目标刺激呈现方式：合拍、无声）×3（电极前后位置：前、中、后）×3（电极左右位置：左、中、右）的三因素重复测量方差分析。结果发现，电极左右位置主效应显著，$F(2, 30) = 3.72$，$p < 0.05$，$\eta^2 = 0.20$。前后位置与左右位置交互作用显著，$F(4, 60) = 3.37$，$p < 0.05$，$\eta^2 = 0.18$。

目标刺激呈现方式、电极前后位置和电极左右位置三者交互作用显著，$F(4, 60) = 5.33$，$p < 0.01$，$\eta^2 = 0.26$。简单效应检验发现，在头皮前部，左侧电极处的合拍条件下 P2 波幅（$M = 4.34\mu V$，$SD = 0.81$）与无声条件下的 P2 波幅（$M = 3.18\mu V$，$SD = 0.82$）之间无显著差异，$p > 0.09$；中线处合拍条件下的 P2 波幅（$M = 5.10\mu V$，$SD = 0.85$）与无声条件下的 P2 波幅（$M = 4.07\mu V$，$SD = 0.95$）之间无显著差异；右侧合拍条件下的 P2 波幅（$M = 5.32\mu V$，$SD = 1.09$）与无声条件下的 P2 波幅（$M = 4.23\mu V$，$SD = 0.98$）之间无显著差异。在头皮中央区，左侧电极处的合拍条件下 P2 波幅（$M = 4.11\mu V$，$SD = 0.96$）与无声条件下的 P2 波幅（$M = 3.03\mu V$，$SD = 0.79$）之间无显著差异；中线处合拍条件下的 P2 波幅（$M = 6.14\mu V$，$SD = 1.29$）与无声条件下的 P2 波幅（$M = 4.65\mu V$，$SD = 1.15$）之间无显著差异；右侧合拍条件下的 P2 波幅（$M = 5.51\mu V$，$SD = 1.07$）与无声条件下的 P2 波幅（$M = 4.57\mu V$，$SD = 0.96$）之间无显著差异，$ps > 0.1$。在枕区，左侧电极处合拍条件下的 P2 波幅（$M = 4.54\mu V$，$SD = 0.97$）边缘显著大于无声条件下的 P2 波幅（$M = 3.35\mu V$，$SD = 0.80$），$p = 0.078$；中线电极处合拍条件下的 P2 波幅（$M = 4.97\mu V$，$SD = 1.18$）边缘显著大于无声条件下的 P2 波幅（$M = 3.72\mu V$，$SD = 1.09$），$p =$

0.08;右侧电极处合拍条件下的 P2 波幅（$M = 4.53\mu V$，$SD = 1.07$）与无声条件下的 P2 波幅（$M = 4.85\mu V$，$SD = 0.94$）之间无显著差异，$p > 0.1$。潜伏期统计未见显著差异。

②视觉目标

图 5-21、图 5-22 为视觉目标在合拍和无声条件下的总平均波形图。

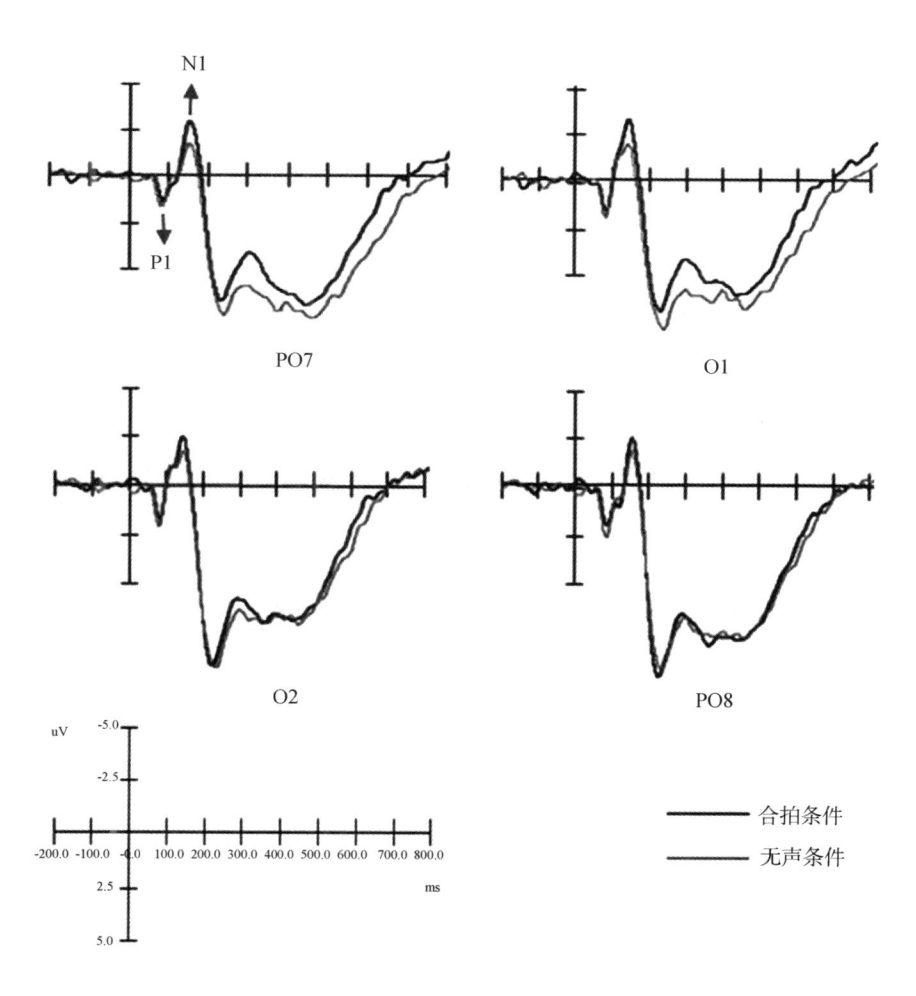

图 5-21 后部 P1、N1 波形图

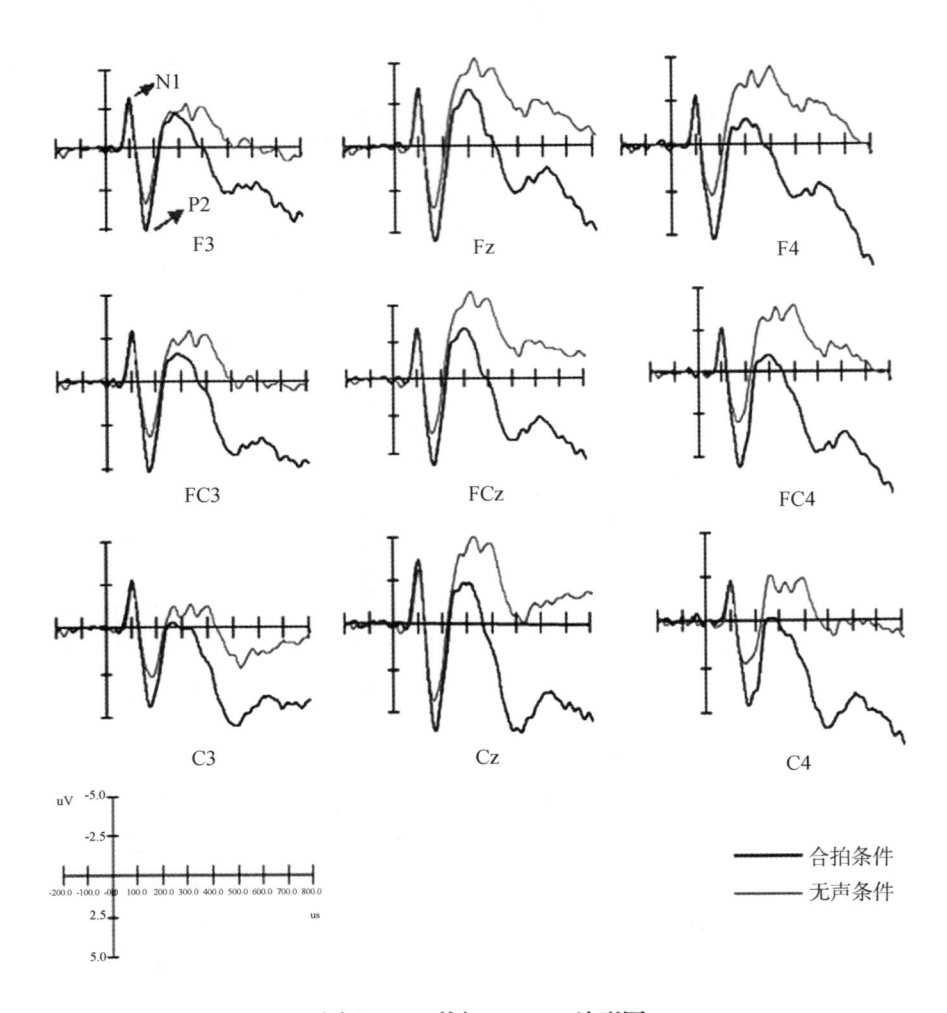

图 5–22　前部 N1、P2 波形图

后部 P1

对后部视觉 P1 的平均波幅进行 2（目标刺激呈现方式：合拍、无声）×2（电极左右位置：左、右）的重复测量方差分析。结果发现，任何主效应和交互作用均不显著，$ps > 0.1$。潜伏期统计未见显著差异。

后部 N1

对后部视觉 N1 的平均波幅进行 2（目标刺激呈现方式：合拍、无声）×2（电极左右位置：左、右）的重复测量方差分析。结果发现，目标刺激呈现方式主效应显著，$F(1, 15) = 4.95$，$p < 0.05$，$\eta^2 = 0.24$。合拍条件下的 N1 波幅（$M = -5.20\mu V$，$SD = 0.60$）显著大于无声条件下的 N1 波幅（$M = -3.91\mu V$，$SD = 0.71$）。其他主效应和交互作用均不显著，$ps > 0.1$。潜伏期统计未见显著差异。

前部 N1

对前部视觉 N1 的平均波幅进行 2（目标刺激呈现方式：合拍、无声）×3（脑区：额区、额中区、中央区）×3（左右位置：左、中、右）的重复测量方差分析。目标刺激呈现方式主效应显著，$F(1, 15) = 4.71$，$p < 0.05$，$\eta^2 = 0.24$。合拍条件下的 N1 波幅（$M = -2.85\mu V$，$SD = 0.60$）显著大于无声条件下的 N1 波幅（$M = -1.97\mu V$，$SD = 0.53$）。电极左右位置主效应显著，$F(2, 30) = 5.32$，$p < 0.05$，$\eta^2 = 0.26$。进一步分析发现，中线区波幅（$M = -2.80\mu V$，$SD = 0.64$）显著大于左侧（$M = -2.37\mu V$，$SD = 0.54$）和右侧（$M = -2.07\mu V$，$SD = 0.44$）的 N1 波幅，后两者波幅之间无显著差异，$ps > 0.1$。目标刺激呈现方式主效应及二者交互作用均不显著，$ps > 0.1$。潜伏期统计未见显著差异。

前部 P2

对前部视觉 P2 的平均波幅进行 2（目标刺激呈现方式：合拍、无声）×3（脑区：额区、额中区、中央区）×3（左右位置：左、中、右）的重复测量方差分析。结果发现，目标刺激呈现方式主效应显著，$F(1, 15) = 4.99$，$p < 0.05$，$\eta^2 = 0.25$。左右位置主效应显著，$F(2, 30) = 8.88$，$p = 0.001$，$\eta^2 = 0.37$。电极前后位置与左右位置交互作用显著，$F(4, 60) = 2.82$，$p < 0.05$，$\eta^2 = 0.16$。目标刺激呈现方式、脑区和左右位置三因素交互作用显著，$F(4, 60) = 2.62$，$p < 0.05$，$\eta^2 = 0.15$。简单效应检验发现，在额区，左侧电极处合拍条件下P2波幅（$M = 4.50\mu V$，$SD = 0.75$）显著大于无声条件下的P2波幅（$M = 3.17\mu V$，$SD = 0.61$），$p < 0.05$；中线电极处合拍条件下的P2波幅（$M = 5.25\mu V$，$SD = 0.81$）边缘显著大于无声条件下的P2波幅（$M = 3.91\mu V$，$SD = 0.87$），$p = 0.057$；右侧电极处合拍条件下P2波幅（$M = 5.71\mu V$，$SD = 0.95$）显著大于无声条件下的P2波幅（$M = 4.16\mu V$，$SD = 0.89$），$p < 0.05$。在额中区，左侧合拍条件下的P2波幅（$M = 4.58\mu V$，$SD = 0.86$）与无声条件下的P2波幅（$M = 3.41\mu V$，$SD = 0.68$）之间无显著差异；中线合拍条件下的P2波幅（$M = 6.10\mu V$，$SD = 1.01$）与无声条件下的P2波幅（$M = 4.60\mu V$，$SD = 0.94$）之间无显著差异，$ps > 0.1$；右侧合拍条件下的P2波幅（$M = 6.61\mu V$，$SD = 1.28$）显著大于无声条件下的P2波幅（$M = 4.52\mu V$，$SD = 1.05$），$p < 0.05$。在枕区，左侧电极处合拍条件下P2波幅（$M = 4.46\mu V$，$SD = 0.84$）与无声条件下的P2波幅（$M = 3.23\mu V$，$SD = 0.59$）之间无显著差异；中线合拍条件下的P2波幅（$M = 6.47\mu V$，$SD = 1.19$）与无声条件下的P2波幅（$M = 4.73\mu V$，$SD = 0.93$）之间无显著差异；右侧电极处合拍条件下的P2波幅（$M = 5.86\mu V$，$SD = 0.94$）与无声条件下的P2波幅（$M = 4.45\mu V$，$SD = 0.86$）之间无显著差异，$ps > 0.1$。潜伏期统计未见显著差异。

（4）注意的起伏与视听整合加工的关系

根据已有研究中对多感觉整合ERP的分析方法，将单通道听觉目标（A）的ERP和单通道视觉目标（V）的ERP相加，即A + V，然后将A + V与视听双通道目标（AV）的ERP相比。如果

AV > A + V，那么表明产生了视听整合加工。已有研究发现，颞上沟是产生视听整合的重要脑区。[1] 同时根据已有研究中所选取的分析电极，选取 F3/Fz/F4，FC3/FCz/FC4，C3/Cz/C4 作为分析电极。[2][3][4]

根据已有相关研究中采用的分析方法，对视听整合加工的 ERP 进行分析。已有研究均发现，多感觉整合效应发生在信息加工的早期阶段（0—500ms）[5][6]，因此，选取 0—500ms 作为数据分析的时间窗口。在此窗口内，对每 20ms 的 ERP 波幅数据进行 2（目标刺激呈现方式：合拍、无声）×2（整合效应：A + V，AV）×3（脑区：额区、额中区、中央区）×3（左右位置：左侧脑区、中线脑区、右侧脑区）的四因素重复测量方差分析。由于本研究关注的是目标刺激的呈现是否与节奏相符（是否处于注意峰值）对多感觉整合的影响有无差异，因此在此结果部分只关注包含目标刺激呈现方式与整合效应的交互作用的结果，其他结果只做描述，不再做进一

---

[1] Barraclough N. E., Xiao D. K., Baker C. I., Oram M. W. & Perrett D. I., Integration of Visual and Auditory Information by Superior Temporal Sulcus Neurons Responsive to the Sight of Actions, *Journal of Cognitive Neuroscience*, Vol. 17, No. 3, March 2005, pp. 377 – 391.

[2] Talsma D. & Woldorff M. G., Selective Attention and Multisensory Integration: Multiple Phases of Effects on the Evoked Brain Activity, *Journal of Cognitive Neuroscience*, Vol. 17, No. 7, July 2005, pp. 1098 – 1114.

[3] Talsma D., Doty T. J. & Woldorff M. G., Selective Attention and Audiovisual Integration: Is Attending to Both Modalities a Prerequisite for Early Integration, *Cerebral Cortex*, Vol. 17, No. 3, March 2007, pp. 679 – 690.

[4] Yang W., Yang J., Gao Y., Tang X., Ren Y., Takahashi S., et al, Effects of SoundFrequency on Audiovisual Integration: An EventRelated Potential Study, *PLoS ONE*, Vol. 10, No. 9, September 2015, e0138296.

[5] Talsma D. & Woldorff M. G., Selective Attention and Multisensory Integration: Multiple Phases of Effects on the Evoked Brain Activity, *Journal of Cognitive Neuroscience*, Vol. 17, No. 7, July 2005, pp. 1098 – 1114.

[6] Yang W., Yang J., Gao Y., Tang X., Ren Y., Takahashi S., et al, Effects of SoundFrequency on Audiovisual Integration: An EventRelated Potential Study, *PLoS ONE*, Vol. 10, No. 9, September 2015, e0138296.

步分析。方差分析结果如下：

0—20ms：任何主效应与交互作用均不显著，$ps > 0.1$。

21—40ms：整合效应与脑区交互作用显著，$F(2,30) = 4.02$，$p < 0.05$，$\eta^2 = 0.21$。其他主效应与交互作用均不显著，$ps > 0.1$。

41—60ms：任何主效应与交互作用均不显著，$ps > 0.1$。

61—80ms：脑区主效应显著，$F(2,30) = 3.41$，$p < 0.05$，$\eta^2 = 0.19$。目标刺激呈现方式与左右位置交互作用显著，$F(2,30) = 3.39$，$p < 0.05$，$\eta^2 = 0.18$。其他主效应与交互作用均不显著，$ps > 0.1$。

81—100ms：脑区主效应显著，$F(2,30) = 4.56$，< 0.05，$\eta^2 = 0.23$。左右位置主效应显著，$F(2,30) = 5.11$，$p < 0.05$，$\eta^2 = 0.25$。脑区与左右位置交互作用显著，$F(4,60) = 2.90$，$p < 0.05$，$\eta^2 = 0.16$。其他主效应与交互作用均不显著，$ps > 0.1$。

101—120ms：左右位置主效应显著，$F(2,30) = 12.65$，$p < 0.001$，$\eta^2 = 0.46$。其他主效应和交互作用均不显著，$ps > 0.1$。

121—140ms：目标刺激呈现方式主效应显著，$F(1,15) = 11.84$，$p < 0.01$，$\eta^2 = 0.44$。脑区主效应显著，$F(2,30) = 7.73$，$p < 0.01$，$\eta^2 = 0.34$。左右位置主效应显著，$F(2,30) = 12.09$，$p < 0.001$，$\eta^2 = 0.45$。目标刺激呈现方式与脑区交互作用显著，$F(2,30) = 5.46$，$p = 0.01$，$\eta^2 = 0.27$。简单效应分析发现，在额区，合拍条件下波幅（$M = -3.14\mu V$，$SD = 0.66$）显著大于无声条件下波幅（$M = -1.73\mu V$，$SD = 0.72$），$p < 0.05$；在额中区，合拍条件下波幅（$M = -4.43\mu V$，$SD = 0.82$）显著大于无声条件下波幅（$M = -2.43\mu V$，$SD = 0.77$），$p < 0.01$；在中央区，合拍条件下波幅（$M = -4.60\mu V$，$SD = 0.90$）显著大于无声条件下波幅（$M = -2.66\mu V$，$SD = 0.76$），$p = 0.001$。整合效应与

左右位置交互作用显著，$F(2, 30) = 15.65$，$p < 0.001$，$\eta^2 = 0.51$。目标刺激呈现方式、整合效应与左右位置三因素交互作用显著，$F(2, 30) = 6.44$，$p < 0.01$，$\eta^2 = 0.30$。简单效应分析发现，只有在合拍条件下，右侧脑区的 A + V 波幅（$M = -2.21\mu V$，$SD = 0.90$）显著小于 AV 波幅（$M = -4.34\mu V$，$SD = 0.69$），$p = 0.001$。其他条件下的 A + V 与 AV 波幅之间均无显著差异，$ps > 0.1$。其他主效应与交互作用均不显著，$ps > 0.1$。也就是说，在此时间段内，只有在合拍条件下的右侧脑区产生了超加性效应，即在合拍条件下的右侧脑区产生了多感觉整合。

141—160ms：目标刺激呈现方式主效应显著，$F(1, 15) = 33.42$，$p < 0.001$，$\eta^2 = 0.69$。脑区主效应显著，$F(2, 30) = 4.35$，$p < 0.05$，$\eta^2 = 0.23$。目标刺激呈现方式与脑区交互作用显著，$F(2, 30) = 5.41$，$p = 0.01$，$\eta^2 = 0.27$。目标刺激呈现方式与脑区交互作用显著，$F(2, 30) = 18.18$，$p < 0.001$，$\eta^2 = 0.55$。目标刺激呈现方式与左右位置交互作用显著，$F(2, 30) = 6.76$，$p < 0.01$，$\eta^2 = 0.31$。简单效应分析发现，在左侧、中线和右侧脑区，合拍条件下的波幅均显著大于无声条件下的波幅，$ps < 0.001$。目标刺激呈现方式、整合效应和脑区的三因素交互作用显著，$F(2, 30) = 22.44$，$p < 0.001$，$\eta^2 = 0.60$。简单效应检验发现，只有在合拍条件下，脑中央区的 A + V 波幅（$M = -3.48\mu V$，$SD = 1.16$）显著小于 AV 波幅（$M = -5.49\mu V$，$SD = 0.94$），$p < 0.01$，在额区和额中区处二者之间均无差异，$ps > 0.1$。在无声条件下，三部分脑区的 A + V 和 AV 之间均无显著差异，$ps > 0.1$。这表明，在 141—160ms 内，只有在合拍条件下的中央脑区产生了超加性效应，即在合拍条件下的中央脑区产生了多感觉整合。

161—180ms：目标刺激呈现方式主效应显著，$F(1, 15) =$

57.49，$p<0.001$，$\eta^2=0.79$。目标刺激呈现方式与脑区交互作用显著，$F(2,30)=6.02$，$p<0.01$，$\eta^2=0.29$。整合效应和脑区交互作用显著，$F(2,30)=10.96$，$p<0.001$，$\eta^2=0.42$。目标刺激呈现方式、整合效应和左右位置三因素交互作用显著，$F(2,30)=4.22$，$p<0.05$，$\eta^2=0.22$。脑区与左右位置交互作用显著，$F(4,60)=7.28$，$p<0.001$，$\eta^2=0.33$。脑区、整合效应和左右位置交互作用显著，$F(4,60)=3.30$，$p<0.05$，$\eta^2=0.18$。目标刺激呈现方式、整合效应、左右位置和脑区四因素交互作用显著，$F(4,60)=7.03$，$p<0.001$，$\eta^2=0.32$。进一步分析发现，只有在合拍条件下，额区左侧 A+V 波幅（$M=-1.92\mu V$，$SD=1.32$）边缘显著小于 AV 波幅（$M=-3.48\mu V$，$SD=0.97$），$p>0.05$。在其他脑区和条件下，A+V 和 AV 之间均无显著差异，$ps>0.1$。

181—200ms：目标刺激呈现方式主效应显著，$F(1,15)=6.57$，$p<0.05$，$\eta^2=0.31$。目标刺激呈现方式与脑区交互作用显著，$F(2,30)=4.76$，$p<0.05$，$\eta^2=0.24$。整合效应与脑区交互作用显著，$F(2,30)=5.15$，$p<0.05$，$\eta^2=0.26$。目标刺激呈现方式与左右位置交互作用显著，$F(2,30)=3.75$，$p<0.05$，$\eta^2=0.20$。目标刺激呈现方式、脑区与左右位置三因素交互作用显著，$F(4,60)=3.76$，$p<0.05$，$\eta^2=0.20$。其他主效应与交互作用均不显著，$ps>0.1$。

201—220ms：左右位置主效应显著，$F(2,30)=4.96$，$p<0.05$，$\eta^2=0.25$。目标刺激呈现方式与左右位置交互作用显著，$F(2,30)=8.28$，$p=0.001$，$\eta^2=0.36$。目标刺激呈现方式、脑区和左右位置三因素交互作用显著，$F(4,60)=3.46$，$p<0.05$，$\eta^2=0.19$。其他主效应与交互作用均不显著，$ps>0.1$。

221—240ms：左右位置主效应显著，$F(2,30)=3.36$，$p=$

0.048，$\eta^2 = 0.18$。目标刺激呈现方式与左右位置交互作用显著，$F(2, 30) = 4.12$，$p < 0.05$，$\eta^2 = 0.22$。目标刺激呈现方式、脑区和左右位置三因素交互作用显著，$F(4, 60) = 3.04$，$p < 0.05$，$\eta^2 = 0.17$。其他主效应与交互作用均不显著，$ps > 0.1$。

241—260ms：左右位置主效应显著，$F(2, 30) = 3.78$，$p < 0.05$，$\eta^2 = 0.20$。目标刺激呈现方式与脑区交互作用显著，$F(2, 30) = 9.80$，$p = 0.001$，$\eta^2 = 0.40$。整合效应和脑区交互作用显著，$F(2, 30) = 12.44$，$p < 0.001$，$\eta^2 = 0.45$。目标刺激呈现方式、整合效应和脑区三因素交互作用显著，$F(2, 30) = 15.91$，$p < 0.001$，$\eta^2 = 0.52$。目标刺激呈现方式与左右位置交互作用显著，$F(2, 30) = 4.52$，$p = 0.019$，$\eta^2 = 0.23$。整合效应和左右位置交互作用显著，$F(2, 30) = 11.85$，$p < 0.001$，$\eta^2 = 0.44$。目标刺激呈现方式、整合效应和左右位置三因素交互作用显著，$F(2, 30) = 7.21$，$p < 0.01$，$\eta^2 = 0.33$。脑区与左右位置交互作用显著，$F(4, 60) = 10.09$，$p < 0.001$，$\eta^2 = 0.40$。目标刺激、脑区和左右位置三因素交互作用显著，$F(4, 60) = 15.87$，$p < 0.001$，$\eta^2 = 0.51$。整合效应、脑区和左右位置三因素交互作用显著，$F(4, 60) = 20.44$，$p < 0.001$，$\eta^2 = 0.58$。目标刺激呈现方式、整合效应、脑区和左右位置四因素交互作用显著，$F(4, 60) = 16.44$，$p < 0.001$，$\eta^2 = 0.52$。进一步分析发现，只有在合拍条件下，在额中区中线处（FCz 电极处）A + V 波幅（$M = -8.20\mu V$，$SD = 1.67$）显著大于 AV 波幅（$M = 0.94\mu V$，$SD = 1.02$），$p < 0.001$，而在其他条件和脑区，A + V 和 AV 波幅之间无显著差异，$ps > 0.1$。

261—280ms：目标刺激呈现方式与左右位置交互作用显著，$F(2, 30) = 4.24$，$p < 0.05$，$\eta^2 = 0.22$。其他主效应与交互作用均不显著，$ps > 0.1$。

281—300ms：目标刺激呈现方式主效应显著，$F(1, 15) =$

6.78，$p<0.05$，$\eta^2=0.31$。整合效应主效应显著，$F(1,15)=10.17$，$p<0.01$，$\eta^2=0.40$。脑区主效应显著，$F(2,30)=3.60$，$p=0.04$，$\eta^2=0.19$。左右位置主效应显著，$F(2,30)=6.09$，$p<0.01$，$\eta^2=0.29$。目标刺激呈现方式与左右位置交互作用显著，$F(2,30)=3.96$，$p<0.05$，$\eta^2=0.21$。整合效应与左右位置交互作用显著，$F(2,30)=5.06$，$p<0.05$，$\eta^2=0.25$。其他主效应与交互作用均不显著，$ps>0.1$。

301—320ms：目标刺激呈现方式主效应显著，$F(1,15)=9.66$，$p<0.01$，$\eta^2=0.39$。整合效应主效应显著，$F(1,15)=14.76$，$p<0.01$，$\eta^2=0.50$。脑区主效应显著，$F(2,30)=7.78$，$p<0.01$，$\eta^2=0.34$。左右位置主效应显著，$F(2,30)=12.25$，$p<0.001$，$\eta^2=0.45$。目标刺激呈现方式与左右位置交互作用显著，$F(2,30)=4.55$，$p<0.05$，$\eta^2=0.23$。整合效应与左右位置交互作用显著，$F(2,30)=6.14$，$p<0.05$，$\eta^2=0.29$。脑区与左右位置交互作用显著，$F(4,60)=5.06$，$p<0.001$，$\eta^2=0.31$。其他主效应与交互作用均不显著，$ps>0.1$。

321—340ms：左右位置主效应显著，$F(2,30)=4.96$，$p<0.05$，$\eta^2=0.25$。目标刺激呈现方式与左右位置交互作用显著，$F(2,30)=8.28$，$p=0.001$，$\eta^2=0.36$。目标刺激呈现方式、脑区和左右位置三因素交互作用显著，$F(4,60)=3.46$，$p<0.05$，$\eta^2=0.19$。其他主效应与交互作用均不显著，$ps>0.1$。

341—360ms：目标刺激呈现方式主效应显著，$F(1,15)=27.83$，$p<0.001$，$\eta^2=0.65$。整合效应主效应显著，$F(1,15)=22.02$，$p<0.001$，$\eta^2=0.60$。左右位置主效应显著，$F(2,30)=13.14$，$p<0.001$，$\eta^2=0.47$。目标刺激呈现方式与整合效应交互作用显著，$F(1,15)=5.04$，$p<0.05$，$\eta^2=0.25$。目标刺激呈现方

式与脑区交互作用显著，$F(2, 30) = 5.24$，$p < 0.05$，$\eta^2 = 0.26$。目标刺激呈现方式与左右位置交互作用显著，$F(2, 30) = 5.64$，$p < 0.01$，$\eta^2 = 0.27$。整合效应和左右位置交互作用显著，$F(2, 30) = 5.30$，$p < 0.05$，$\eta^2 = 0.26$。脑区与左右位置交互作用显著，$F(4, 60) = 5.87$，$p = 0.001$，$\eta^2 = 0.28$。目标刺激呈现方式、脑区和左右位置交互作用显著，$F(4, 60) = 5.77$，$p = 0.001$，$\eta^2 = 0.28$。整合效应、脑区和左右位置交互作用显著，$F(4, 60) = 2.79$，$p < 0.05$，$\eta^2 = 0.16$。其他主效应与交互作用均不显著，$ps > 0.1$。

361—380ms：目标刺激呈现方式主效应显著，$F(1, 15) = 42.02$，$p < 0.001$，$\eta^2 = 0.74$。整合效应主效应显著，$F(1, 15) = 11.05$，$p < 0.01$，$\eta^2 = 0.42$。左右位置主效应显著，$F(2, 30) = 10.95$，$p < 0.001$，$\eta^2 = 0.42$。目标刺激呈现方式与整合效应交互作用显著，$F(1, 15) = 11.28$，$p < 0.01$，$\eta^2 = 0.43$。简单效应分析发现，在合拍条件下，A+V波幅（$M = -7.99\mu V$，$SD = 1.35$）显著大于AV波幅（$M = -4.28\mu V$，$SD = 0.86$），$p = 0.001$；在无声条件下，A+V波幅（$M = -1.85\mu V$，$SD = 1.48$）与AV波幅（$M = -0.89\mu V$，$SD = 1.08$）之间无显著差异，$p > 0.1$。目标刺激呈现方式与脑区交互作用显著，$F(2, 30) = 7.15$，$p < 0.01$，$\eta^2 = 0.32$。目标刺激呈现方式与左右位置交互作用显著，$F(2, 30) = 6.98$，$p < 0.01$，$\eta^2 = 0.32$。脑区与左右位置交互作用显著，$F(4, 60) = 5.51$，$p = 0.001$，$\eta^2 = 0.27$。目标刺激呈现方式、脑区与左右位置三因素交互作用显著，$F(4, 60) = 6.00$，$p < 0.001$，$\eta^2 = 0.29$。整合效应、脑区和左右位置三因素交互作用显著，$F(4, 60) = 2.92$，$p < 0.05$，$\eta^2 = 0.16$。其他主效应与交互作用均不显著，$ps > 0.1$。

381—400ms：目标刺激呈现方式主效应显著，$F(1, 15) =$

61.80，$p<0.001$，$\eta^2=0.81$。整合效应主效应显著，$F(1, 15)=5.02$，$p<0.05$，$\eta^2=0.25$。左右位置主效应显著，$F(2, 30)=12.02$，$p<0.001$，$\eta^2=0.45$。目标刺激呈现方式与整合效应交互作用显著，$F(1, 15)=16.12$，$p=0.001$，$\eta^2=0.52$。目标刺激呈现方式与脑区交互作用显著，$F(2, 30)=13.03$，$p<0.001$，$\eta^2=0.47$。整合效应与脑区交互作用显著，$F(2, 30)=5.17$，$p<0.05$，$\eta^2=0.26$。目标刺激呈现方式、整合效应与脑区三因素交互作用显著，$F(2, 30)=5.88$，$p<0.01$，$\eta^2=0.28$。目标刺激呈现方式与左右位置交互作用显著，$F(2, 30)=5.88$，$p<0.05$，$\eta^2=0.28$。整合效应与左右位置交互作用显著，$F(2, 30)=6.66$，$p<0.01$，$\eta^2=0.31$。脑区与左右位置交互作用显著，$F(4, 60)=7.60$，$p<0.001$，$\eta^2=0.34$。目标刺激呈现方式、脑区和左右位置三因素交互作用显著，$F(4, 60)=2.96$，$p<0.05$，$\eta^2=0.17$。整合效应、脑区和左右位置三因素交互作用显著，$F(4, 60)=6.15$，$p<0.001$，$\eta^2=0.29$。目标刺激呈现方式、整合效应、脑区和左右位置四因素交互作用显著，$F(4, 60)=3.30$，$p<0.05$，$\eta^2=0.18$。进一步分析发现，在合拍条件下，额区左侧 A+V 波幅（$M=-5.56\mu V$，$SD=1.18$）显著大于 AV 波幅（$M=-3.34\mu V$，$SD=0.88$），$p<0.05$，中线 A+V 波幅（$M=-8.88\mu V$，$SD=1.38$）显著大于 AV 波幅（$M=-4.86\mu V$，$SD=090$），$p=0.001$，右侧 A+V 波幅（$M=-8.45\mu V$，$SD=1.59$）显著大于 AV 波幅（$M=-4.79\mu V$，$SD=1.08$），$p<0.05$；额中区左侧 A+V 波幅（$M=-6.81\mu V$，$SD=1.20$）显著大于 AV 波幅（$M=-3.82\mu V$，$SD=0.90$），$p=0.001$，中线 A+V 波幅（$M=-12.02\mu V$，$SD=1.57$）显著大于 AV 波幅（$M=-6.44\mu V$，$SD=1.13$），$p<0.001$，右侧 A+V 波幅（$M=-9.07\mu V$，$SD=1.64$）显著大于 AV 波幅（$M=-4.59\mu V$，$SD=1.00$），$p<0.01$；中央区左侧 A+V 波幅（$M=-4.02\mu V$，$SD=1.16$）与 AV 波幅（$M=$

$-2.26\mu V$, $SD=1.08$) 之间无显著差异，$p>0.1$，中线 A+V 波幅 ($M=-12.02\mu V$, $SD=2.18$) 显著大于 AV 波幅 ($M=-6.48\mu V$, $SD=1.67$)，$p<0.001$，右侧 A+V 波幅 ($M=-6.94\mu V$, $SD=1.60$) 显著大于 AV 波幅 ($M=-3.60\mu V$, $SD=1.10$)，$p<0.01$；对于无声条件下，三个脑区的不同位置上 A+V 波幅与 AV 波幅之间均无显著差异，$ps>0.1$。

401—420ms：目标刺激呈现方式主效应显著，$F(1, 15)=86.73$，$p<0.001$，$\eta^2=0.85$。整合效应主效应显著，$F(1, 15)=4.84$，$p<0.05$，$\eta^2=0.24$。左右位置主效应显著，$F(2, 30)=8.51$，$p=0.001$，$\eta^2=0.36$。目标刺激呈现方式与整合效应交互作用显著，$F(1, 15)=10.44$，$p<0.05$，$\eta^2=0.41$。目标刺激呈现方式与脑区交互作用显著，$F(2, 30)=7.09$，$p<0.01$，$\eta^2=0.32$。整合效应与脑区交互作用显著，$F(2, 30)=4.05$，$p<0.05$，$\eta^2=0.21$。目标刺激呈现方式、脑区和左右位置三因素交互作用显著，$F(4, 60)=3.57$，$p<0.05$，$\eta^2=0.19$。整合效应、脑区和左右位置三因素交互作用显著，$F(4, 60)=2.55$，$p<0.05$，$\eta^2=0.15$。目标刺激呈现方式、整合效应与脑区三因素交互作用显著，$F(2, 30)=5.03$，$p<0.05$，$\eta^2=0.25$。简单简单效应检验发现，对于合拍条件，额区 A+V 波幅 ($M=-8.47\mu V$, $SD=1.23$) 显著大于 AV 波幅 ($M=-5.21\mu V$, $SD=0.88$)，$p<0.01$，额中区 A+V 波幅 ($M=-10.14\mu V$, $SD=1.34$) 显著大于 AV 波幅 ($M=-5.69\mu V$, $SD=0.97$)，$p=0.001$，中央区 A+V 波幅 ($M=-7.69\mu V$, $SD=1.68$) 显著大于 AV 波幅 ($M=-4.46\mu V$, $SD=1.20$)，$p<0.01$；在无声条件下，无论哪个脑区，A+V 波幅与 AV 波幅之间均无显著差异，$ps>0.1$。目标刺激呈现方式与左右位置交互作用显著，$F(2, 30)=7.35$，$p<0.01$，$\eta^2=0.33$。目标刺激呈现方式、整合效应和

左右位置三因素交互作用显著，$F(2, 30) = 3.70$，$p < 0.05$，$\eta^2 = 0.20$。简单简单效应检验发现，在合拍条件下，左侧 A + V 波幅（$M = -6.04\mu V$，$SD = 1.19$）显著大于 AV 波幅（$M = -3.80\mu V$，$SD = 0.89$），$p < 0.05$，中线 A + V 波幅（$M = -11.25\mu V$，$SD = 1.43$）显著大于 AV 波幅（$M = -6.49\mu V$，$SD = 1.13$），$p = 0.001$，右侧 A + V 波幅（$M = -9.01\mu V$，$SD = 1.59$）显著大于 AV 波幅（$M = -5.07\mu V$，$SD = 0.98$），$p < 0.01$；在无声条件下，无论哪个位置，A + V 波幅与 AV 波幅之间均无显著差异，$ps > 0.1$。其他主效应与交互作用均不显著，$ps > 0.1$。

421—440ms：目标刺激呈现方式主效应显著，$F(1, 15) = 98.97$，$p < 0.001$，$\eta^2 = 0.87$。整合效应主效应显著，$F(1, 15) = 11.30$，$p < 0.01$，$\eta^2 = 0.43$。脑区主效应显著，$F(2, 30) = 4.83$，$p < 0.05$，$\eta^2 = 0.24$。左右位置主效应显著，$F(2, 30) = 9.45$，$p = 0.001$，$\eta^2 = 0.39$。目标刺激呈现方式与整合效应交互作用显著，$F(1, 15) = 9.06$，$p < 0.01$，$\eta^2 = 0.38$。目标刺激呈现方式与脑区交互作用显著，$F(2, 30) = 7.24$，$p < 0.01$，$\eta^2 = 0.33$。目标刺激呈现方式、整合效应和脑区三因素交互作用显著，$F(2, 30) = 5.55$，$p < 0.01$，$\eta^2 = 0.27$。简单简单效应检验发现，对于合拍条件，额区 A + V 波幅（$M = -9.13\mu V$，$SD = 1.29$）显著大于 AV 波幅（$M = -5.72\mu V$，$SD = 1.00$），$p < 0.01$，额中区 A + V 波幅（$M = -10.59\mu V$，$SD = 1.41$）显著大于 AV 波幅（$M = -6.05\mu V$，$SD = 1.08$），$p < 0.001$，中央区 A + V 波幅（$M = -8.22\mu V$，$SD = 1.73$）显著大于 AV 波幅（$M = -4.52\mu V$，$SD = 1.21$），$p < 0.01$；在无声条件下，无论哪个脑区，A + V 波幅与 AV 波幅之间均无显著差异，$ps > 0.1$。目标刺激呈现方式和左右位置交互作用显著，$F(2, 30) = 8.96$，$p = 0.001$，$\eta^2 = 0.37$。整

合效应和左右位置交互作用显著，$F(2, 30) = 6.00$，$p < 0.01$，$\eta^2 = 0.29$。目标刺激呈现方式、整合效应和左右位置三因素交互作用显著，$F(2, 30) = 3.61$，$p < 0.05$，$\eta^2 = 0.19$。简单简单效应检验发现，左侧 A+V 波幅（$M = -6.46\mu V$，$SD = 1.20$）显著大于 AV 波幅（$M = -4.10\mu V$，$SD = 0.97$），$p < 0.05$，中线 A+V 波幅（$M = -12.26\mu V$，$SD = 1.55$）显著大于 AV 波幅（$M = -6.82\mu V$，$SD = 1.25$），$p < 0.001$，右侧 A+V 波幅（$M = -9.22\mu V$，$SD = 1.59$）显著大于 AV 波幅（$M = -5.38\mu V$，$SD = 1.05$），$p < 0.01$；在无声条件下，无论哪个位置，A+V 波幅与 AV 波幅之间均无显著差异，$ps > 0.1$。脑区和左右位置交互作用显著，$F(4, 60) = 2.69$，$p < 0.05$，$\eta^2 = 0.15$。目标刺激呈现方式、脑区和左右位置三因素交互作用显著，$F(4, 60) = 6.03$，$p < 0.001$，$\eta^2 = 0.29$。整合效应、脑区和左右位置三因素交互作用显著，$F(4, 60) = 4.84$，$p < 0.01$，$\eta^2 = 0.24$。其他主效应与交互作用均不显著，$ps > 0.1$。

441—460ms：目标刺激呈现方式主效应显著，$F(1, 15) = 106.61$，$p < 0.001$，$\eta^2 = 0.88$。整合效应主效应显著，$F(2, 30) = 17.50$，$p = 0.001$，$\eta^2 = 0.54$。脑区主效应显著，$F(2, 30) = 9.15$，$p = 0.001$，$\eta^2 = 0.38$。左右位置主效应显著，$F(2, 30) = 8.06$，$p < 0.01$，$\eta^2 = 0.35$。目标刺激呈现方式与整合效应交互作用显著，$F(1, 15) = 8.68$，$p = 0.01$，$\eta^2 = 0.37$。目标刺激呈现方式与脑区交互作用显著，$F(2, 30) = 8.09$，$p < 0.01$，$\eta^2 = 0.35$。整合效应和脑区交互作用显著，$F(2, 30) = 5.31$，$p < 0.05$，$\eta^2 = 0.26$。目标刺激呈现方式、整合效应和脑区三因素交互作用显著，$F(2, 30) = 4.27$，$p < 0.05$，$\eta^2 = 0.22$。简单简单效应检验发现，对于合拍条件，额区 A+V 波幅（$M = -9.63\mu V$，$SD = 1.27$）显著大于 AV 波幅（$M = -5.74\mu V$，$SD = 0.98$），$p < 0.001$，额中区 A+V 波幅（$M = -10.68\mu V$，$SD = 1.40$）显著大于 AV 波幅（$M = -5.81\mu V$，

$SD = 1.08$），$p < 0.001$，中央区 A + V 波幅（$M = -7.56 \mu V$，$SD = 1.63$）显著大于 AV 波幅（$M = -4.00 \mu V$，$SD = 1.18$），$p < 0.01$；在无声条件下，无论哪个脑区，A + V 波幅与 AV 波幅之间均无显著差异，$ps > 0.1$。目标刺激呈现方式与左右位置交互作用显著，$F(2, 30) = 8.16$，$p = 0.001$，$\eta^2 = 0.35$。整合效应与左右位置交互作用显著，$F(2, 30) = 4.40$，$p < 0.05$，$\eta^2 = 0.23$。目标刺激呈现方式、脑区与左右位置交互作用显著，$F(4, 60) = 4.80$，$p < 0.01$，$\eta^2 = 0.24$。其他主效应与交互作用均不显著，$ps > 0.1$。

461—480 ms：目标刺激呈现方式主效应显著，$F(1, 15) = 151.78$，$p < 0.001$，$\eta^2 = 0.91$。整合效应主效应显著，$F(1, 15) = 29.92$，$p < 0.001$，$\eta^2 = 0.67$。脑区主效应显著，$F(2, 30) = 9.48$，$p = 0.001$，$\eta^2 = 0.39$。左右位置主效应显著，$F(2, 30) = 7.13$，$p < 0.01$，$\eta^2 = 0.32$。目标刺激呈现方式与整合效应交互作用显著，$F(1, 15) = 7.58$，$p < 0.05$，$\eta^2 = 0.34$。目标刺激呈现方式与脑区交互作用显著，$F(2, 30) = 5.26$，$p < 0.05$，$\eta^2 = 0.26$。目标刺激呈现方式、整合效应和脑区三因素交互作用显著，$F(2, 30) = 3.44$，$p < 0.05$，$\eta^2 = 0.19$。简单简单效应检验发现，在合拍条件下，额区 A + V 波幅（$M = -10.18 \mu V$，$SD = 1.27$）显著大于 AV 波幅（$M = -5.67 \mu V$，$SD = 0.92$），$p < 0.001$，额中区 A + V 波幅（$M = -10.82 \mu V$，$SD = 1.39$）显著大于 AV 波幅（$M = -5.39 \mu V$，$SD = 1.04$），$p < 0.001$，中央区 A + V 波幅（$M = -7.53 \mu V$，$SD = 1.79$）显著大于 AV 波幅（$M = -3.31 \mu V$，$SD = 1.16$），$p = 0.001$；在无声条件下，无论哪个脑区，A + V 波幅与 AV 波幅之间均无显著差异，$ps > 0.1$。目标刺激呈现方式与左右位置交互作用显著，$F(2, 30) = 9.71$，$p = 0.001$，$\eta^2 = 0.39$。整合效应与左右位置交互作用显著，$F(2, 30) = 4.74$，$p < 0.05$，

$\eta^2 = 0.24$。目标刺激呈现方式、整合效应和左右位置三因素交互作用显著,$F(2, 30) = 3.64$,$p < 0.05$,$\eta^2 = 0.20$。简单简单效应检验发现,左侧 A + V 波幅($M = -6.67\mu V$,$SD = 1.19$)显著大于 AV 波幅($M = -3.59\mu V$,$SD = 0.94$),$p < 0.001$,中线 A + V 波幅($M = -12.30\mu V$,$SD = 1.53$)显著大于 AV 波幅($M = -6.10\mu V$,$SD = 1.20$),$p < 0.001$,右侧 A + V 波幅($M = -9.56\mu V$,$SD = 1.64$)显著大于 AV 波幅($M = -4.68\mu V$,$SD = 0.98$),$p = 0.001$;在无声条件下,无论哪个位置,A + V 波幅与 AV 波幅之间均无显著差异,$ps > 0.1$。目标刺激呈现方式、脑区和左右位置三因素交互作用显著,$F(4, 60) = 6.93$,$p < 0.001$,$\eta^2 = 0.32$。

481—500ms:目标刺激呈现方式主效应显著,$F(1, 15) = 104.49$,$p < 0.001$,$\eta^2 = 0.87$。整合效应主效应显著,$F(1, 15) = 25.30$,$p < 0.001$,$\eta^2 = 0.63$。脑区主效应显著,$F(2, 30) = 9.85$,$p = 0.001$,$\eta^2 = 0.40$。左右位置主效应显著,$F(2, 30) = 7.01$,$p < 0.01$,$\eta^2 = 0.32$。目标刺激呈现方式与整合效应交互作用显著,$F(1, 15) = 9.68$,$p < 0.01$,$\eta^2 = 0.39$。目标刺激呈现方式与脑区交互作用显著,$F(2, 30) = 4.83$,$p < 0.01$,$\eta^2 = 0.24$。整合效应与脑区交互作用显著,$F(2, 30) = 4.43$,$p < 0.05$,$\eta^2 = 0.23$。目标刺激呈现方式、整合效应和脑区三因素交互作用显著,$F(2, 30) = 6.90$,$p < 0.01$,$\eta^2 = 0.32$。简单简单效应检验发现,在合拍条件下,额区 A + V 波幅($M = -10.26\mu V$,$SD = 1.27$)显著大于 AV 波幅($M = -5.52\mu V$,$SD = 0.91$),$p < 0.001$,额中区 A + V 波幅($M = -10.63\mu V$,$SD = 1.46$)显著大于 AV 波幅($M = -5.09\mu V$,$SD = 1.09$),$p < 0.001$,中央区 A + V 波幅($M = -7.18\mu V$,$SD = 1.92$)显著大于 AV 波幅($M = -2.92\mu V$,$SD = 1.23$),$p = 0.001$;在无声条件下,无论哪个脑区,A + V 波幅与 AV 波幅之间均无显著差异,$ps > 0.1$。目标刺激

呈现方式与左右位置交互作用显著，$F(2, 30) = 9.22$，$p = 0.001$，$\eta^2 = 0.38$。整合效应和左右位置交互作用显著，$F(2, 30) = 4.79$，$p < 0.05$，$\eta^2 = 0.24$。目标刺激呈现方式、整合效应和左右位置三因素交互作用显著，$F(2, 30) = 4.64$，$p < 0.05$，$\eta^2 = 0.24$。简单简单效应检验发现，左侧 A+V 波幅（$M = -6.35 \mu V$，$SD = 1.28$）显著大于 AV 波幅（$M = -3.36 \mu V$，$SD = 1.01$），$p < 0.001$，中线 A+V 波幅（$M = -12.17 \mu V$，$SD = 1.62$）显著大于 AV 波幅（$M = -5.72 \mu V$，$SD = 1.23$），$p < 0.001$，右侧 A+V 波幅（$M = -9.55 \mu V$，$SD = 1.63$）显著大于 AV 波幅（$M = -4.45 \mu V$，$SD = 0.97$），$p < 0.001$；在无声条件下，无论哪个位置，A+V 波幅与 AV 波幅之间均无显著差异，$ps > 0.1$。目标刺激呈现方式、脑区和左右位置三因素交互作用显著，$F(4, 60) = 5.73$，$p = 0.001$，$\eta^2 = 0.28$。

综合上述结果来看，当目标刺激处于注意峰值（合拍条件）时，在特定电极和特定时间段内产生了超加性效应，即视听双通道目标诱发的 ERP（AV）显著大于单通道视觉和单通道听觉目标诱发的 ERP 之和（A+V）。具体而言，这种超加性效应发生在：121—140ms 内的右侧电极（F4/FC4/C4），141—160ms 内的中央区电极（Fz/FCz/Cz）。而在无声条件下并没有产生超加性效应。总体来说，当目标刺激处于注意峰值时，在头皮的中线区和右侧脑区均产生视听整合加工。但是这种加工并不具有持续性，而是发生在加工的早期阶段（121—160ms）。

（五）讨论

实验 6 在实验 5 结果的基础上，结合 ERP 技术考察了注意的起伏影响视听整合加工的时间进程。由于在实验 5 中发现，合拍条件的反应时显著短于不合拍和无声条件的反应时，因此实验 6 只选取了合拍条件和无声条件，并增加每种条件下的试次数，以获得足够的叠加次数。实验6的行为结果与实验5基本一致,对此不再讨论。同时,本实验根据已有研究,采用特定时间窗口内的波峰幅值作为因变量,在不同类型的目标刺激上考察了当目标刺激处于注意峰值(合拍条件)和基线条件(无声条件)下的波幅是否存在差异。

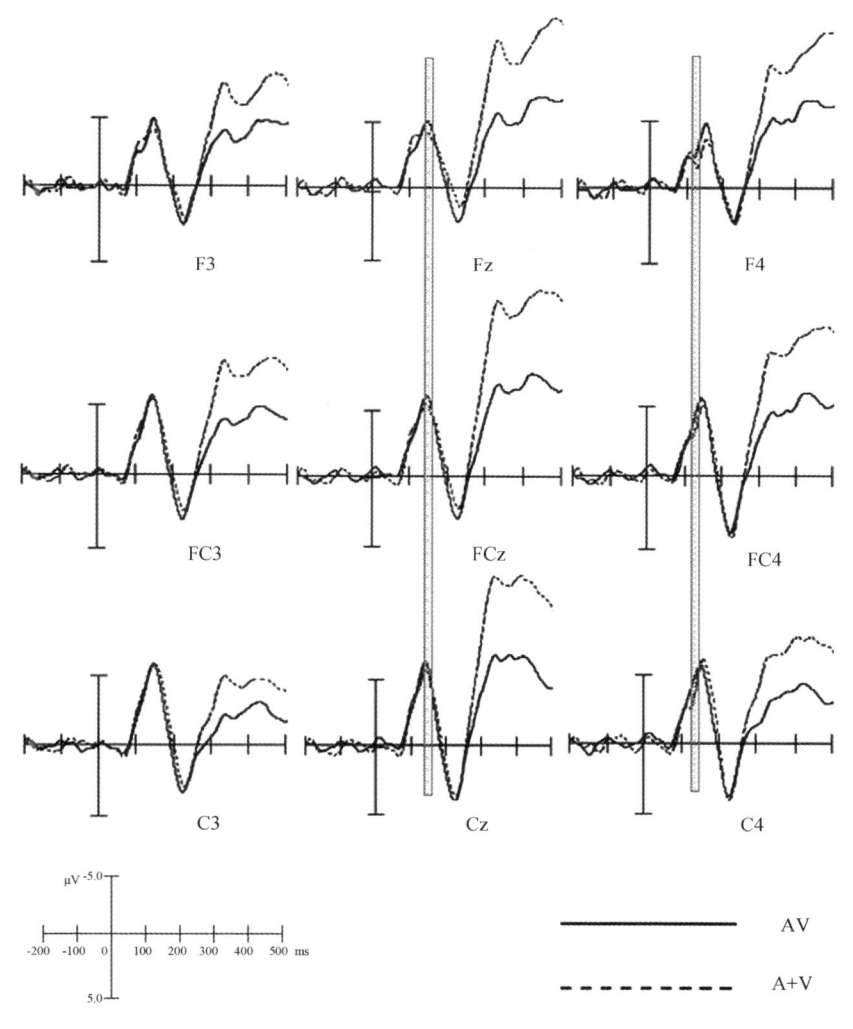

图 5-23 合拍条件下视听双通道目标诱发的 ERP（AV）与两个单通道目标诱发的 ERP 之和（A+V）的比较

注：图中的阴影区域为产生超加性效应的时间段,即产生视听整合加工的时间窗口。

首先，对于听觉目标，本实验发现，合拍和无声条件均诱发了波峰在 155ms 左右并在全头分布的 N1 成分。对其波幅的分析发现，不论头皮分布的左侧还是右侧，合拍条件下的 N1 波幅均显著大于无声条件下的 N1 波幅；同时，不论在合拍还是无声条件，不论头皮分布的左侧、中线或右侧，中央区的 N1 波幅均显著大于前部后部电极的 N1 波幅。此外，本实验还发现，波峰在 237ms 左右出现全头分布的 P2 成分。对其波幅的分析发现，在 P2 和 P3 电极处，合拍条件下的 P2 波幅均显著大于无声条件下的 P2 波幅，而在其他电极处，均未发现合拍和无声条件下波幅的差异。

其次，对于视觉目标，本实验发现，合拍和无声条件均诱发了波峰在 84ms 左右、在枕区出现的 P1 成分。同样在枕区出现了波峰在 150ms 左右的 N1 成分，对二者波幅的分析发现合拍条件下的 N1 波幅显著大于无声条件。在头皮前部，本实验发现了波峰在 100ms 左右的 N1 成分。对其波峰幅值的分析发现，合拍条件下的波峰显著大于无声条件下的波峰，并且中线处的波峰最大。另外，本实验还发现了波峰在 170ms 左右的正波 (P2)。对其波峰的分析发现，在额区和右侧额中区，合拍条件的波幅均显著大于无声条件，而在其他头皮位置两种条件均无显著差异。

1. 注意起伏对单通道目标刺激诱发 ERP 的影响

整合上述结果可以发现，对于听觉目标来说，在全头分布的 N1 成分上合拍条件的波幅更大。早期研究者采用双耳分听的范式考察了注意耳与非注意耳的 ERP 波幅差异。[①] 结果发现，相较于非注意耳，注意耳诱发的 N1 波幅更大，即 N1 注意效应。同时，已有研究均发现，N1 波幅与注意有关，表现为被注意的刺激的 N1 波幅

---

① Hillyard S. A., Hink R. F., Schwent V. L. & Picton T. W., Electrical Signs of Selective Attention in the Human Brain, *Science*, Vol. 182, No. 4108, October 1973, pp. 177–180.

更大。①② 实验6与上述N1注意效应的结果基本一致，表明在合拍条件下，注意随着音乐节奏线索起伏，在目标出现时达到峰值，因此引发了最强烈的注意，表现为N1注意效应。同时，在听觉N1成分上的注意效应也反映了由音乐节奏和注视点引发的注意在早期（知觉阶段）的过滤作用。在听觉P2成分上，同样发现合拍条件下的波幅显著大于无声条件下的波幅。有研究者认为，听觉P2成分可能与刺激分类有关。③ 根据上述观点，本实验中出现的听觉P2成分在两种条件下的波幅差异可以推测为：在合拍条件下，被试对目标刺激的分类更明确，从而能够做出更迅速的判断。

对于视觉目标来说，在枕区N1波幅上出现了两种目标刺激呈现方式上的差异，即合拍条件下的N1波幅显著大于无声条件下的N1波幅。这与听觉N1注意效应类似，也与一些已有研究基本一致。比如，Vogel和Luck认为，视觉N1包括两个子成分：波峰在100ms左右的中线附近出现的前部N1，和在枕区出现的波峰在165ms左右的后部N1④。已有研究对视觉N1成分做出了解释，认为在被注意的位置上N1波幅增大是由于对被注意的位置上的刺激加工增强。⑤ 尽管这种适用于空间注意的研究结论，但仍可推测，

---

① Mangun G. , Neural Mechanisms of Visual Selective Attention, *Psychophysiology*, Vol. 32, No. 1, January 1995, pp. 4 – 18.

② Ritter W. , Simson R. & Vaughan H. , Effects of the Amount of Stimulus Information Processed on Negative Event-related Potentials, *Electroencephalography & Clinical Neurophysiology*, Vol. 28, No. 69, Mar1988, pp. 244 – 258.

③ García-Larrea L. , Lukaszewicz A. C. & Mauguiére F. , Revisiting the Oddball Paradigm. Nontarget Vs Neutral Stimuli and the Evaluation of ERP Attentionaleffects, *Neuropsychologia*, Vol. 30, No. 8, August 1992, pp. 723 – 741.

④ Vogel E. K. & Luck S. J. , The Visual N1 Component as an Index of a Discrimination Process, *Psychophysiology*, No. 37, March 2000, pp. 190 – 203.

⑤ Coull J. , Neural Correlates of Attention and Arousal: Insights from Electrophysiology, Functional Neuroimaging and Psychopharmacology, *Progress in Neurology*, Vol. 55, No. 4, July 1998, pp. 343 – 361.

本研究中合拍条件下枕区 N1 波幅的增大可能与注意加工的增强有关。同时，在视觉目标中还出现了波峰在 170ms 左右的额区 P2 成分。这也与已有一些研究的发现相一致[1][2]。尽管已有研究并没有发现视觉 P2 的注意效应，但仍可以推测，在本研究的实验环境中，合拍条件所带来的注意效应可能会造成 P2 波幅的增大。因此在本研究中，位于枕区的视觉 P2 可能也与注意有关。

综合上述关于视觉和听觉目标的 ERP 成分分析结果，同时结合行为数据结果，可以推测，与无声条件相比，在合拍条件下对目标加工的反应时的减少，可能与在这种条件下对目标刺激的加工增强有关。具体而言，在合拍条件下，注意随着音乐节奏和注视点的闪烁在音乐节奏的最后一拍处达到峰值。根据动态注意理论，个体对于注意峰值同相位的知觉事件更为期待，会被分配给更多的注意资源，因此会被更好地加工，从而表现为与注意有关的 ERP 成分的波幅更大，最终表现为合拍条件下的反应时更短。

2. 注意起伏影响视听言语整合加工的神经机制

实验 6 根据已有研究中考察多感觉整合脑机制的研究方法，通过将不同时间段的单通道听觉和单通道视觉目标引发的 ERP 相加，将二者之和（A + V）与视听双通道目标引发的 ERP（AV）相比较。已有相关研究者认为，如果 AV 大于 A + V，即产生超加性效应，则表明产生多感觉整合。本实验发现，在合拍条件下，121—140ms 的右侧脑区、141—160ms 的中央区均出现 AV 大于 A + V 的超加性效应。这个结果表明，在本研究的实验条件下，当目标刺激

---

[1] Kenemans J. L., Kok A. & Smulders F. T., Event-related Potentials to Conjunctions of Spatial Frequency and Orientation as a Function of Stimulus Parameters and Response Requirements, *Electroencephalography & Clinical Neurophysiology*, Vol. 28, No. 88, Jan-Feb 1993, pp. 51 – 63.

[2] Van der Stelt O., Kok A., Smulders F. T. Y., Snel J. & Gunning B., Cerebral Event-related Potentials Associated with Selective Attention to Color: Developmental Changes from Childhood to Adulthood, *Psychophysiology*, Vol. 35, No. 3, May 1998, pp. 227 – 239.

处于注意的峰值更易产生整合加工，这种由注意的起伏对视听整合加工产生的影响并不是持续的，而是只在加工的早期阶段产生。

有关注意对多感觉整合的影响，已有研究大多涉及空间注意。比如，一些早期的行为研究发现，空间注意并不能影响腹语术效应（多感觉整合的典型代表）的方向或者强度，因此得出注意不能影响多感觉整合的结论。但是也有一些研究认为，注意能够与多通道加工产生交互作用。Talsma 和 Woldorff 在其研究中考察了空间注意对多感觉整合影响的时间进程。① 其研究结果与本研究结果有一定的相似性，比如，Talsma 和 Woldorff 发现，空间注意对多感觉整合的影响也具有一定的阶段性。他们的实验结果表明，在 P50 成分上发现了超加性效应，比本研究的超加性效应更早。这可能是由于，Talsma 和 Woldorff 采用的是简单刺激，并且被试的任务是探测不常出现的偏差刺激。而本研究采用的是语义刺激，刺激本身比 Talsma 和 Woldorff 的研究更为复杂，同时本研究的任务是让被试判断出现的目标是不是动物，即辨别任务。辨别任务本身也比探测任务难度更大，因此在双通道刺激产生整合之前对刺激的知觉可能会更慢一些，所以整合阶段发生得较为靠后。

从产生整合加工的脑区来看，整理本研究的结果可以发现，头皮前部的中线区和右侧区域可能是注意起伏影响视听整合加工的重要脑区。早期一些动物研究发现，许多感觉皮层的激活可能与多感觉整合有关。比如，单细胞记录研究发现了在猫和猴子上丘的外部

---

① Talsma D. & Woldorff M. G., Selective Attention and Multisensory Integration: Multiple Phases of Effects on the Evoked Brain Activity, *Journal of Cognitive Neuroscience*, Vol. 17, No. 7, July 2005, pp. 1098 – 1114.

空间中存在多通道表征①②。这些细胞不仅能够对单通道视觉和听觉刺激产生反应，并且能够产生超加性效应，表现为对同时呈现的双通道刺激的反应强于对单通道刺激的反应之和。以人类作为被试的研究也发现，上丘与顶叶和其他皮层区域之间也存在相互影响的联结，并且在将注意指向空间中某一个特定位置和在不同感觉通道中调节空间上起着重要作用。③ 另有一些研究认为，许多皮层与多通道加工有关。比如，Downar、Grawley、Mikulis 和 Davis 发现左侧和右侧颞顶联合区，右颞中回，左、右下回以及前后脑岛都与多通道加工有密切关系。④ Calvert、Hansen、Iversen 和 Brammers 采用 fMRI 技术考察了视听整合加工，结果发现，除上丘之外，右顶上小叶、右侧顶下沟、右侧顶下岛，以及额区（包括额下回）一些部位均对多通道刺激敏感。⑤ 本研究采用的是具有较高时间分辨率的事件相关电位技术，无法精确定位在本实验条件下产生多感觉整合效应与注意起伏的交互作用的脑区，未来研究可以采用具有更高空间分辨率的技术更为细致地考察这种交互作用的脑内源。

（六）小结

实验 6 采用具有高时间分辨率的 ERP 技术，在实验 5 的研究结果基础上，考察了注意的起伏影响视听整合加工的神经机制。结果发现，当目标刺激处于注意峰值时，在头皮前部的中线区和右侧脑

---

① Wallace M. T., Meredith M. A. & Stein B. E., Multisensory Integration in the Superior Colliculusof the Alert Cat, *Journal of Neurophysiology*, Vol. 80, No. 2, August 1998, pp. 1006 – 1010.

② Wallace M. T. & Stein B. E., Development of Multisensory Neurons and Multisensory Integration Incat Superior Colliculus, *Journal of Neuroscience*, Vol. 17, Apr1997, pp. 2429 – 2444.

③ LaBerge D., *Attentional processing: The brain's artof mindfulness*. Cambridge: Harvard University Press. 1995.

④ Downar J., Grawley A. P., Mikulis D. J. & Davis K. D., A Multimodal Cortical Network for the Detection of Changes in the Sensory Environment, *Nature Neuroscience*, Vol. 3, March 2000, pp. 277 – 283.

⑤ Calvert G. A., Crossmodal Processing in the Human Brain: Insights from Functional Neuroimaging Studies, *Cerebral cortex*, Vol. 11, No. 12, December 2001, pp. 1110 – 1123.

区均产生视听整合加工。但是这种加工并不具有持续性，而是发生在加工的早期阶段（121—160ms）。

第四节　注意与视听整合加工的总讨论

"弄时临溪坐，寻花绕石行。时时闻鸟语，处处是泉声。"白居易的这首《遗爱寺》生动地描绘了春天的盎然生机。不难看出，"小溪""石"是诗人看到的景色，"鸟语""泉声"是诗人听到的声音。不仅仅是诗中的意境，我们的日常生活中时时处处充斥着来自不同感觉通道的信息。通过看、听、触、嗅、味等几大感觉通道，我们随时随地都在感受着这个生动的世界。值得注意的是，我们并非仅仅通过一个个单一的感觉通道感受世界，而是通过两个甚至多个感觉通道的共同作用来加工信息。因此，多通道加工的研究对于人类更好地感受、知觉信息，认识、了解世界具有重要的作用。多感觉整合是多通道加工的重要方面，尤其是注意对多感觉整合的影响，近年来引起许多研究者的关注。通过整理以往研究，发现已有研究的不足之处，本研究以多感觉整合中的视听整合加工为例，在研究一中首先考察了指向不同感觉通道的注意对视听整合加工的影响是否不同；基于研究一的结论，研究二控制了可用的注意资源量，分别考察了视觉注意负荷和听觉注意负荷对视听整合加工的影响；研究三从注意的品质出发，并采用具有高时间分辨率的事件相关电位技术考察了注意的起伏对视听整合加工的影响及其神经机制。

一　选择性注意和分配性注意条件下视听整合加工的差异

一直以来，多感觉整合受到许多研究者的关注。作为多通道加工的重要方面，研究者们采用不同的被试、不同的刺激材料以及不同的研究范式对其特性及其加工方式进行了深入有效的探讨。近年来，注意与多感觉整合的关系逐渐成为多通道加工领域的重要问题。研究者们针对多感觉整合是否受到注意的影响进行争论。早期一些研究者认为多感觉整合是一种自动化加工过程，发生在前注意阶段，因此注意不会影响多感觉整合。然而，另有研究者提出相反的观点，认为只有当被试注意到刺激时，才会产生多感觉整合，这样，多感觉整合的确依赖于注意才会产生，也就是说，注意是多感觉整合产生的重要条件。针对上述产生分歧的实验进行分析，不难发现，上述争论是基于不同的注意条件。认为注意不会影响多感觉整合的研究均基于空间注意，而认为注意能够影响多感觉整合的研究侧重于注意与不注意的区分。众所周知，注意除可以指向空间、客体之外，还可以指向感觉通道。那么，指向感觉通道的不同注意条件能否影响多感觉整合？

　　本研究的研究一通过线索将注意指向不同感觉通道，形成了选择性注意（只注意视觉或者听觉通道）和分配性注意（同时注意视觉和听觉通道）两种注意条件，同时结合竞争模型分析技术，考察了在选择性注意和分配性注意条件下视听整合加工存在的差异。研究一的实验1采用了由几何图形和短纯音构成的简单刺激作为材料，发现只有当被试同时注意视觉和听觉（分配性注意）时才会产生对双通道目标的加工优势（冗余信号效应）。对冗余信号效应的竞争模型分析发现，对双通道目标的加工优势源自双通道目标中视觉成分和听觉成分的整合。也就是说，只有在分配性注意条件下才会产生多感觉整合，而在选择性注意条件下并没有多感觉整合产生。这与实验1的假设相符。由于当个体只注意一个感觉通道时，被忽略的通道所在皮层的活性被抑制①，从而导致在被忽略的皮层中，用于产生多感觉整合的信息减少，因此与分配性注意相比，选择性注意于一个通道内难以产生多感觉整合。而在分配性注意时，两个被注意通道的皮层均被激活，这样就保证了多感觉整合所需的资源量，因此能够产生整合加工。

但是，我们的生活环境并不仅仅由简单刺激构成。在日常生活中，语义信息在社会交往中起着举足轻重的作用。同时，我们生活环境中的刺激除共享时间和空间特征，还共享语义特征②，这就构成了刺激之间的语义联结。同时，已有研究发现，当视觉和听觉刺激在内容上相匹配时，更易产生整合加工。鉴于此，研究一的实验2在实验1的基础上，调整实验1中的听觉刺激材料，使视听刺激之间形成一定的语义联结（视听语义一致和视听语义不一致），考察了在选择性注意和分配性注意条件下的视听言语整合加工是否存在差异。实验结果表明，只有在分配性注意条件下，被试对语义一致的双通道目标反应最快，即产生冗余信号效应，而在选择性注意条件下没有冗余信号效应产生。按照实验1的步骤，同样进行竞争模型分析。结果发现，在分配性条件下，语义一致的双通道目标产生的冗余信号效应是源自其视觉和听觉成分的整合。也就是说，在分配性条件下，语义一致的双通道刺激的视觉成分和听觉成分产生了感觉整合。而对于语义不一致的双通道目标，即使其视觉成分和听觉成分同时呈现，在任何一种注意条件下均没有产生整合。

有研究者认为，大脑在处理信息时，倾向于将内容上匹配的刺

---

① Farb N. A., Segal Z. V. & Anderson A. K., Attentional Modulation of Primary Interoceptive and Exteroceptive Cortices, *Cerebral Cortex*, Vol. 23, No. 1, January 2013, pp. 114–126.

② Laurienti P. J., Kraft R. A., Maldjian J. A., Burdette J. H. & Wallace M. T., Semantic Congruence is a Critical Factor in Multisensory Behavioral Performance, *Experimental Brain Research*, Vol. 158, No. 4, October 2004, pp. 405–414.

激当作相同资源处理,这样更有益于我们的脑将其整合成统一的知觉。[1] 同时,Friston 提出的预测编码模型指出,脑会产生对环境的贝叶斯估计,因而可能存在对环境估计的随机模型。[2] 这些模型基于当下个体加工的感觉信息进行不断更新。这些随机模型能用来调整对当前感觉输入的预测。如果在预测和实际感觉输入之间存在强烈的不匹配,可能会导致内部模型更大的更新。从这个角度看,当输入的视听刺激之间存在不一致甚至冲突的语义联结时,大脑的预测与实际输入之间的较大差别可能导致内部模型的较大更新,因此造成对此类信息的加工更为困难[3],因此难以整合语义不一致的双通道刺激。

通过研究一的两个实验可以看出,指向感觉通道的注意的确能够影响视听整合加工,但是这种注意存在一定的限制,即只有在同时注意视觉和听觉两个感觉通道(分配性注意)时才会产生视听整合加工。这种效应不仅体现在简单刺激的整合加工上,还体现在具有语义一致性的视听刺激上。而对于语义不一致的视听刺激,即便其视觉和听觉成分同时呈现,仍不能产生整合。研究一从简单刺激和语义刺激两种实验材料的角度,较为全面地考察了选择性注意和分配性注意条件下的视听整合加工。但是,这种结论只是基于注意资源不会缺失的前提条件下。当同时注意两个通道时,其中一个感觉通道的注意资源减少,是否能够影响研究一的结论?或者说,注意负荷能否影响视听整合加工?鉴于上述考虑,本研究的研究二在

---

[1] Su Y. H., Content Congruency and Its Interplay with Temporal Synchrony Modulate Integration between Rhythmic Audiovisual Streams, *Frontiers in Integrative Neuroscience*, No. 8, February 2014, p. 92.

[2] Friston K., The Free-energy Principle: A Unified Brain Theory, *Nature Reviews Neuroscience*, Vol. 11, No. 2, January 2010, pp. 127-138.

[3] Talsma D., Predictive Coding and Multisensory Integration: An Attentional Account of the Multi-sensory Mind, *Frontiers in Integrative Neuroscience*, Vol. 26, No. 6, March 2015.

实验2的结论基础上,采用双任务范式,分别考察了视觉注意负荷和听觉注意负荷对于视听整合加工的影响。

二 视觉注意负荷和听觉注意负荷影响视听整合加工的不对称性

研究一的实验2结果表明,在分配性注意条件下,只有视听语义一致的双通道刺激才会产生整合加工,而对于视听语义不一致的双通道刺激,即便其视觉成分和听觉成分同时同地呈现,仍不会产生视听整合。但是,这种结论只是基于注意资源量保持完整的前提下。那么,注意负荷是否会对视听整合产生调制作用?

有研究者针对上述问题进行了探讨。比如,Alsius、Navarra 和 Campbell 在双任务范式中考察了被试对 McGurk 效应的敏感性,被试对注意负荷刺激的任务是探测重复出现的刺激。这就存在一定的局限性。首先,被试需要记住上一次刺激的内容,才能对当前刺激进行判断,在对负荷刺激进行反应时,可能不仅消耗了被试的注意资源,还消耗了一定的记忆资源,这样,难以将注意负荷和记忆负荷对视听整合的影响进行剥离。其次,上述研究中采用的分析指标是 McGurk 效应的百分比。这个指标与竞争模型分析技术相比具有一定的主观性,在行为研究中并不能说明注意负荷的调节作用。因此,研究二的实验3和实验4从注意负荷的角度出发,考察了注意负荷对于视听整合的影响。根据注意负荷研究中的双任务范式,分别加入视觉负荷刺激和听觉负荷刺激。

实验3发现,在视觉负荷条件下,即使是同时呈现的视听语义一致的双通道刺激,仍然无法产生整合,只有在无视觉负荷条件下才会产生整合。后者与实验2的结果相一致。这种结果可能是由于,在视觉注意负荷条件下,被试分出一部分注意资源用于做出对视觉负荷刺激的判断,因此减少了总的注意资源量,使用于产生多感觉整合的资源显著减少,造成了在视觉注意负荷条件下并没有产生视听整合加工的结果。那么，听觉注意负荷是否也会产生与视觉注意负荷同样的效应？

实验4发现，不论是否呈现听觉负荷，被试对视听双通道目标均产生了加工优势，这种冗余信号效应同样是由于双通道刺激的视觉和听觉成分的整合产生的。这表明，视觉注意负荷和听觉注意负荷在影响视听整合加工时具有不对称性，表现为视觉注意负荷能够影响视听整合，而听觉注意负荷不能影响视听整合。产生这种不对称性的原因可能是由于视觉和听觉在影响信息加工时的功效不同，即视觉优势效应导致的。毛伟宾等人发现，视觉学习具有较强的编码力度和激活水平，对视觉项目的学习能进行精细加工且记忆保持得较好。可以说，视觉在加工程度上比听觉更深一些。这样就使听觉负荷刺激并没有占用被试过多的注意资源，从而产生冗余信号效应。但这只是一种推测，对于听觉负荷无法影响视听言语整合的真正原因，还有待于未来研究给出答案。

三 注意的起伏对视听整合加工的影响及其神经机制

稳定性是注意的一项重要品质，它对于人们的日常生活、工作和学习具有重要作用。比如，学生需要持续性地注意老师讲课的内容，才能更好地掌握知识；外科手术医生需要连续几个小时聚精会神地完成工作。然而，注意并不能够始终保持稳定状态，而是有规律地增强和减弱。这种现象叫作注意的起伏。注意的起伏现象时刻发生在我们日常的注意活动中。比如，在看注意的双关图时，有时感觉图形向前凸起，有时又感觉似乎向后凹进去。再如，课堂学习中我们有时能够认真听讲，但有时也会开小差。动态注意理论可以解释注意被外部时间规律调制的特性。根据动态注意理论，如果双通道刺激处于注意的峰值，可能会得到更多的注意资源，也就会受到更强的加工。那么，是否处于注意峰值的双通道刺激更易产生整合呢？鉴于此，研究三的实验 5 在实验 2 的基础上，采用具有节奏性的视听线索，使被试注意视觉和听觉通道，考察了注意的起伏对视听整合加工的影响。结果发现，只有当双通道目标符合视听节奏，即处于注意峰值时，才会产生冗余信号效应。进一步对竞争模型分析发现，冗余信号效应源自视听双通道目标的视觉成分和听觉成分的整合。也就是说，只有当双通道刺激处于注意峰值时才会产生视听整合。而在其他两种条件下，即便视听刺激的视觉和听觉成分同时同地呈现，且语义一致，仍无法产生整合。

上述结果与假设相一致，产生此结果的原因可以从动态注意理论的角度出发来解释。动态注意理论认为，注意并非一成不变，而是存在一定的节奏性。当外部事件恰好处于注意的峰值时，个体会更为期待与注意峰值同相位的知觉事件，这种知觉事件也会被分配给更多的注意资源，因此得到更好的加工。在实验 5 中，节奏中的每一个拍子都恰好处于注意节奏的峰值，与峰值同步的刺激能被更好地加工。具体而言，由于合拍条件下目标刺激恰好处于第四拍的位置上，即恰好呈现在注意的峰值上，这样目标刺激被赋予更多的注意资源，因此对其加工更为深入，表现为在合拍条件下对目标刺激的反应时最短。

这个结果与已有一些跨通道研究相一致。比如，Escoffier、Sheng 和 Schirmer 考察了不被注意的音乐节奏对视觉加工的影响。[1] 结果发现，与非节奏化条件相比，当图片与音乐节奏合拍时，即图片恰好与音乐节奏的最后一拍同时呈现，被试对图片的判断速度最快。也就是说，不被注意的音乐节奏促进的视觉加工是跨通道进行的。

---

[1] Escoffier N., Sheng D. Y. J. & Schirmer A., Unattended Musical Beats Enhance Visual Processing, *Acta Psychologica*, Vol. 135, No. 1, September 2010, pp. 12 – 16.

实验5已经发现，与注意峰值同相位的双通道刺激产生了整合，但是，这种整合在何时产生仍是悬而未决的问题。其主要原因在于已有的行为研究所依托的反应时等指标只能反映心理加工的综合结果，对于发生在加工早期的感觉整合过程很难进行有效的观察与测量，因而无法揭示感觉整合在何时产生这一动态的过程及其机制。由于事件相关电位具有很高的时间分辨率能够对认知神经活动特征提供即时的评价，从加工的初始就可以对单个的认知过程进行识别和分离[1]，因此，研究三的实验6在实验5的基础上，采用事件相关电位技术考察了注意的起伏影响多感觉整合的时间进程及其机制。研究结果分别从不同条件下单通道目标诱发ERP的差异以及视听整合效应的ERP两部分进行了阐述。

研究三首先对单通道目标所诱发的ERP进行分析。结果发现，听觉目标在合拍条件下诱发的N1波幅均显著大于无声条件下的N1波幅，不论在合拍还是无声条件下，不论在头皮分布的左侧、中线还是右侧，中央区的N1波幅均显著大于前部、后部电极的N1波幅。不难看出，当听觉目标刺激与视听节奏相符合时，目标刺激诱发的N1波幅更大。这与早期研究中的N1注意效应类似。比如，Hillyard等人采用双耳分听范式考察了注意耳与非注意耳的ERP波幅差异。[2] 结果发现，注意耳比非注意耳诱发的N1波幅更大，即N1注意效应。同时，已有研究均发现，N1波幅与注意有关，表现

---

[1] Rhodes S. M. & Donaldson D. I., Association and Not Semantic Relationships Elicit the N400 Effect: Electrophysiological Evidence from an Explicit Language Comprehension Task, *Psychophysiology*, Vol. 45, No. 1, January 2008, pp. 50–59.

[2] Hillyard S. A., Hink R. F., Schwent V. L. & Picton T. W., Electrical Signs of Selective Attention in the Human Brain, *Science*, Vol. 182, No. 4108, October 1973, pp. 177–180.

为被注意的刺激的 N1 波幅更大。①② 在本研究中，不同条件下的 N1 波幅可能与目标刺激是否处于注意峰值有关。表明在合拍条件下，注意随着视听节奏线索起伏，在目标出现时达到注意的峰值，从而将更多的注意资源投入处于注意峰值的刺激上，表现为 N1 注意效应。同时，合拍条件下的 P2 波幅均显著大于无声条件下的 P2 波幅。有研究者认为，听觉 P2 成分可能与刺激分类有关。③ 本研究中合拍条件的听觉 P2 波幅更大，可能是在合拍条件下，被试对目标刺激的分类更明确，从而能够做出更迅速的判断。

对于视觉目标来说，在枕区 N1 波幅上出现了两种目标刺激呈现方式的差异，即合拍条件下的 N1 波幅显著大于无声条件下的 N1 波幅。这与听觉 N1 注意效应类似，也与一些已有研究基本一致。比如，在 Vogel 和 Luck 的研究中也出现了类似的结果，④ 这种视觉 N1 成分代表被注意的位置上的刺激本身的加工增强。⑤ 本研究还发现了与已有研究一致的额区 P2 成分。⑥⑦

---

① Mangun G., Neural Mechanisms of Visual Selective Attention, *Psychophysiology*, Vol. 32, No. 1, January 1995, pp. 4 – 18.

② Ritter W., Simson R. & Vaughan H., Effects of the Amount of Stimulus Information Processed on Negative Event-related Potentials, *Electroencephalography & Clinical Neurophysiology*, Vol. 28, No. 69, March 1988, pp. 244 – 258.

③ García-Larrea L., Lukaszewicz A. C. & Mauguiére F., Revisiting the Oddball Paradigm. Nontarget Vs Neutral Stimuli and the Evaluation of ERP Attentional Effects, *Neuropsychologia*, Vol. 30, No. 8, August 1992, pp. 723 – 741.

④ Vogel E. K. & Luck S. J., The Visual N1 Component as an Index of a Discrimination Process, *Psychophysiology*, No. 37, March 2000, pp. 190 – 203.

⑤ Coull J., Neural Correlates of Attention and Arousal: Insights from Electrophysiology, Functional Neuroimaging and Psychopharmacology, *Progress in Neurology*, Vol. 55, No. 4, July 1998, pp. 343 – 361.

⑥ Kenemans J. L., Kok A. & Smulders F. T., Event – related Potentials to Conjunctions of Spatial Frequency and Orientation as a Function of Stimulus Parameters and Response Requirements, *Electroencephalography & Clinical Neurophysiology*, Vol. 28, No. 88, Jan-Feb 1993, pp. 51 – 63.

⑦ Van der Stelt O., Kok A., Smulders F. T. Y., Snel J. & Gunning B., Cerebral Event-related Potentials Associated with Selective Attention to Color: Developmental Changes from Childhood to Adulthood, *Psychophysiology*, Vol. 35, No. 3, May 1998, pp. 227 – 239.

综合上述关于视觉和听觉目标的 ERP 成分分析结果，同时结合行为数据结果，可以推测，与无声条件相比，在合拍条件下对目标加工的反应时减少，可能与在这种条件下对目标刺激的加强有关。具体而言，在合拍条件下，注意随着音乐节奏和注视点的闪烁在音乐节奏的最后一拍达到峰值。根据动态注意理论，个体对于与注意峰值同相位的知觉事件更为期待，会被分配给更多的注意资源，因此会被更好地加工，从而表现为与注意有关的 ERP 成分的波幅更大，最终表现为合拍条件下的反应时更短。

除考察单通道目标刺激诱发的 ERP 之外，本研究还根据已有研究中的分析方法对视听整合加工进行了分析。通过将不同时间段的单通道听觉和单通道视觉目标引发的 ERP 相加（A+V），与视听双通道目标引发的 ERP（AV）相比较，如果 AV 大于 A+V，即产生超加性效应，则表明产生多感觉整合。本研究发现，在合拍条件下，121—140ms 的右侧脑区和 141—160ms 的中央区均出现 AV 大于 A+V 的超加性效应。这个结果表明，在本研究的实验条件下，目标刺激处于注意的峰值更易产生整合，这种由注意的起伏对多感觉整合产生的影响并不是持续的，而是在加工阶段的早期产生。

对于注意起伏影响视听整合的脑区，本研究的结果与已有研究部分一致。早期一些动物研究发现，许多感觉皮层的激活可能与多感觉整合有关。比如，单细胞记录研究发现了在猫和猴子上丘的外部空间中存在多通道表征。[1][2] 这些细胞不仅能够对单通道视觉和听觉刺激产生反应，并且能够产生超加性效应，表现为对同时呈现

---

[1] Wallace M. T., Meredith M. A. & Stein B. E., Multisensory Integration in the Superior Colliculusof the Alert Cat, *Journal of Neurophysiology*, Vol. 80, No. 2, August 1998, pp. 1006 – 1010.

[2] Wallace M. T. & Stein B. E., Development of Multisensory Neurons and Multisensory Integration Incat Superior Colliculus, *Journal of Neuroscience*, Vol. 17, April 1997, pp. 2429 – 2444.

的双通道刺激的反应强于对单通道刺激的反应之和。以人类作为被试的研究也发现，上丘与顶叶和其他皮层区域之间也存在相互影响的联结，并且在将注意指向空间中某一个特定位置和在不同感觉通道中调节空间上起着重要作用。[1] 另有一些研究认为，许多皮层与多通道加工有关。比如，Downar、Grawley、Mikulis 和 Davis 发现左侧和右侧颞顶联合区，右颞中回，左、右下回以及前后脑岛都与多通道加工有密切关系。[2] Calvert、Hansen、Iversen 和 Brammers 采用 fMRI 技术考察了视听整合加工，结果发现，除上丘之外，右顶上小叶、右侧顶下沟、右侧顶下岛，以及额区（包括额下回）一些部位均对多通道刺激敏感。[3]

  研究三的结果首先从行为学的角度出发，发现注意起伏的确能够影响视听整合加工，同时利用认知神经科学的手段，采用较高时间分辨率的 ERP 技术，发现了这种注意起伏对视听整合加工的影响出现在目标刺激呈现之后的 120ms 左右，并持续 40ms，在 160ms 结束，并且这种影响主要发生在头皮前部中线和右侧区域。由于技术手段有限，本研究并不能将这种影响精确至具体位置，但仍可做出推断，头皮前部的中线和右侧区域是注意起伏影响视听整合的重要脑区。未来研究可以尝试采用具有更高空间分辨率的技术设备进一步考察这种效应的脑内源。

---

  [1] LaBerge D., *Attentional processing*: *The brain's art of mindfulness*. Cambridge: Harvard University Press. 1995.

  [2] Downar J., Grawley A. P., Mikulis D. J. & Davis K. D., A Multimodal Cortical Network for the Detection of Changes in the Sensory Environment, *Nature Neuroscience*, Vol. 3, March 2000, pp. 277–283.

  [3] Calvert G. A., Hansen P. C., Iversen S. D. & Brammer M. J., Detection of Audio-visual Integration Sites in Humans by Application of Electrophysiological Criteria to the BOLD Effect, *Neuroimage*, Vol. 14, No. 2, August 2001, pp. 427–438.

四 研究展望

本研究在前人研究的基础上，从指向不同感觉通道的注意入手，首先考察了指向不同感觉通道的注意对视听整合加工的影响。同时，根据动物研究中常用的超加性原则，采用行为研究中较为有效的竞争模型分析技术，对反应时数据中的冗余信号效应进行检验，较为客观地检验了在分配性注意条件下产生视听整合的结果。同时，对这种影响作用的稳定性进行检验，发现了视觉注意负荷以及注意起伏均能够调制这种影响作用。为考察注意的起伏影响视听整合的时间进程，采用具有较高时间分辨率的事件相关电位技术，并结合行为数据进行探讨。研究结果不仅丰富了对注意与多感觉整合的影响中调制因素的认识，并补充了认知神经机制方面的研究成果，而且能够丰富已有的相关研究，为今后注意与多感觉整合的关系研究提供一定的数据支持。

值得指出的是，本研究只是初步地探讨了注意对视听整合的影响，仍存在一些值得商榷和进一步讨论的问题。

第一，本研究只关注了注意对多感觉整合的影响，如若尝试建立注意与多感觉整合的关系模型，还需继续探讨多感觉整合是否能够影响注意的方面。一些研究者对此问题进行了考察，关注的焦点在于多感觉整合是否会影响外源性注意，他们得出的观点也存在差异。比如，有研究者认为，多感觉整合不影响外源性注意。Santangelo、Van der Lubbe、Belardinelli 和 Postma[1] 在实验中设置了三种条件：（1）单通道刺激条件：线索、目标均为视觉刺激；（2）跨通

---

[1] Santangelo V., Van der Lubbe R. H., Belardinelli M. O. & Postma A., Multisensory Integration Affects ERP Components Elicited by Exogenous Cues, *Experimental Brain Research*, Vol. 185, No. 2, February 2008, pp. 269–277.

道刺激条件：线索为听觉刺激，目标为视觉刺激；（3）双通道刺激条件：线索为视听同时呈现的刺激，目标为视觉刺激。根据线索是否与目标刺激在同一位置，将线索分为有效线索（线索与目标在同一位置）和无效线索（线索与目标在相反的位置）。被试的任务是既快又准确地判断目标刺激的朝向，同时记录被试的脑电信号。对行为数据的分析发现，由单通道、跨通道和双通道线索所引发的线索效应无显著差异，也就是说，双通道线索并没有引发明显的空间朝向效应。对由线索引发的 ERP 成分分析发现，与视觉或听觉线索相比，由双通道线索引发的 P1 成分在顶枕区表现出超加性效应，即由视听双通道同时呈现的线索引发的 P1 大于视觉线索和听觉线索引发的 P1 成分之和。这表明，在顶枕区，多感觉整合能够影响由外源性视听线索引发的神经活性。这种与行为数据相反的脑电数据结果表明，由双通道线索引发的多感觉整合并不影响空间朝向，或者说，在 Santangelo 等人的实验中，多感觉整合不会影响外源性空间注意。Santangelo 等人认为导致此结果的原因可能是：首先，在神经机制上，涉及多感觉整合的脑区和涉及空间注意的脑区之间并没有联结；其次，单通道空间非预测性线索已经提供了最大的注意捕获（外源性注意的最大幅度）。因此，双通道线索不会比单通道线索产生更大的效应。

在另外一项研究中，Santangelo 和 Spence 考察了在不同认知负荷条件下，单通道（视觉或听觉）与双通道（视听）空间非预测性外周刺激在捕获视觉空间注意上的能力差异。[①] 他们的实验采用了直角空间线索范式，其中单通道或双通道线索之后会呈现视觉目

---

① Santangelo V. & Spence C., Multisensory Cues Capture Spatial Attention Regardless of Perceptual Load, *Journal of Experimental Psychology: Human Perception and Performance*, Vol. 33, No. 6, December 2007, pp. 1311–1321.

标刺激，被试的任务是判断视觉目标刺激的位置（在屏幕上方或下方）。在认知负荷条件下，被试需要在屏幕中央快速呈现的字母刺激中监控偶尔呈现的数字，并做出反应；在无认知负荷条件下，由注视点代替中央呈现的字母刺激。结果发现，在无认知负荷条件下，单通道视觉、单通道听觉和视听线索均能捕获视觉空间注意。在认知负荷条件下，单通道视觉和听觉线索不能捕获视觉空间注意；相反，视听线索不受认知负荷的影响，仍能捕获视觉空间注意。此结果表明，视听线索在产生整合时不受认知负荷的影响，也就是说，多感觉整合能在空间注意的朝向上起一定的作用。

上述两个研究虽关注了多感觉整合对注意的影响，但由于实验范式和实验材料的不同导致其产生了分歧。未来研究可以在上述研究结论的基础上，进一步对实验范式和环境进行统一，试图找到多感觉整合影响注意的加工机制。

第二，整理已有研究可以发现，当前研究采用的实验范式较为混乱，有研究采用冗余目标范式[1]，有研究采用快速系列视觉呈现范式[2]。实验范式的差异很有可能是同类研究得出不同结论的重要原因。有研究者提出，决定多感觉整合和注意之间相互关系的实质和方向的关键因素是环境的复杂性，尤其是环境中刺激成分之间的竞争水平。比如，在刺激之间的竞争水平较低时，注意对多感觉整合几乎没有影响[3]，而当刺激之间竞争水平较高时，可以得出注意

---

[1] Harrar V., Tammam J., Pérez-Bellido A., Pitt A., Stein J. & Spence C., Multisensory Integration and Attention in Developmental Dyslexia, *Current Biology*, Vol. 24, No. 5, March 2014, pp. 531–535.

[2] Talsma D., Doty T. J. & Woldorff M. G., Selective Attention and Audiovisual Integration: Is Attending to Both Modalities a Prerequisite for Early Integration, *Cerebral Cortex*, Vol. 17, No. 3, March 2007, pp. 679–690.

[3] Bertelson P., Vroomen J., De Gelder B. & Driver J., The Ventriloquist Effect Does Not Depend on the Direction of Deliberate Visual Attention, *Perception and Psychophysics*, Vol. 62, No. 2, February 2000, pp. 321–332.

影响多感觉整合的结论①。因此，有必要发展一个多通道注意范式，在此范式中调节刺激之间的竞争，同时控制个体的注意状态，以构建多感觉整合与注意的关系网络，并对二者关系进行更为详尽的探索。

第三，当前研究多针对正常成年被试，而对于临床被试的考察则更有实践意义。比如，一项研究以发展性阅读障碍个体为被试，考察了多感觉整合与注意的关系。② 结果发现，与正常被试相比，阅读障碍被试在跨通道的注意转移上表现出明显的困难，这种注意转移困难只体现在注意从视觉向听觉通道转移时，而注意从听觉向视觉通道转移时并未发现转移困难。这个结果表明，阅读障碍被试比正常被试更难于分配跨通道的注意，导致其多通道加工模式与正常被试存在差异。笔者认为，在发展性阅读障碍人群的训练中应着重考虑跨通道注意不对称性的转移问题。此外，对半球忽视、精神分裂症③、孤独症④人群的考察能将多感觉整合和注意的关系研究扩展至新的层面，对于解决这些临床人群的认知问题有一定的贡献。

第四，当前关于多感觉整合和注意关系的研究多针对大学生被试，而对于儿童和老年人的研究少之又少。有研究发现，与年轻人

---

① Van Ee R., Van Boxtel J. J., Parker A. L. & Alais D., Multisensory Congruency as a Mechanism for Attentional Control over Perceptual Selection, *The Journal of Neuroscience*, Vol. 29, No. 37, September 2009, pp. 11641－11649.

② Harrar V., Tammam J., Pérez－Bellido A., Pitt A., Stein J. & Spence C., Multisensory Integration and Attention in Developmental Dyslexia, *Current Biology*, Vol. 24, No. 5, March 2014, pp. 531－535.

③ Ross L. A., Saint-Amour D., Leavitt V. M., Javitt D. C. & Foxe J. J., Do You See What I am Saying? Exploring Visual Enhancement of Speech Comprehension in Noisy Environments, *Cerebral Cortex*, Vol. 17, No. 5, May 2007, pp. 1147－1153.

④ Magnée M. J., De Gelder B., Van Engeland H. & Kemner C., Audiovisual Speech Integration in Pervasive Developmental Disorder: Evidence from Event-related Potentials, *Journal of Child Psychology and Psychiatry*, Vol. 49, No. 9, September 2008, pp. 995－1000.

相比，老年人能在更大的程度上整合来自不同通道的刺激。①② 那么，对于老年被试而言，多感觉整合与注意的关系是否会与其他年龄段的被试有差别？未来研究可以从纵向研究的角度，将二者关系的被试年龄向前和向后延伸，在更大的年龄跨度上考察二者关系的毕生发展变化。

第五，本研究采用的事件相关电位技术虽然具有较高的时间分辨率，但在空间分辨率上并不具有优势。尤其是，本研究并未发现与多感觉整合出现密切相关的脑电成分，只是在大致脑区上有一定的发现，因此无法准确定位注意起伏影响视听言语整合加工的脑区。未来研究可以采用具有较高空间分辨率的功能性磁共振技术来更为细致地探讨这一问题。

第六，本研究对于变量的控制大多是对于实验材料的调整，或者说更多的是对认知因素的控制，而忽略了个体本身的因素，比如动机、情绪状态。未来研究可以从个体因素的角度出发，进一步深入探讨在不同的个体状态（如不同动机水平、不同情绪状态）下，是否存在注意影响多感觉整合加工的调节因素。

第七，本研究着重考察的是视听整合，并未涉及对于其他感觉通道的考察。目前，相关领域研究者已将研究的方向延伸至触觉、味觉、嗅觉等领域。③ 因此，未来研究可以从其他感觉通道出发，考察注意对其他感觉通道信息的整合加工是否存在影响。

---

① Laurienti P. J., Burdette J. H., Maldjian J. A. & Wallace M. T., Enhanced Multisensory Integration in Older Adults, *Neurobiology of Aging*, Vol. 27, No. 8, August 2006, pp. 1155 – 1163.

② Poliakoff E., Ashworth S., Lowe C. & Spence C., Vision and Touch in Ageing: Crossmodal Selective Attention and Visuotactile Spatial Interactions, *Neuropsychologia*, Vol. 44, No. 4, February 2006, pp. 507 – 517.

③ Pasqualotto A., Dumitru M. L. & Myachykov A., Editorial: Multisensory Integration: Brain, Body, and World, *Frontiers in Psychology*, Vol. 6, January 2016, p. 1068.

参考文献

一 中文文献

刘强:《多感觉整合的脑机制研究》,博士学位论文,西南大学,2010年。

毛伟宾:《跨视听通道的相继错误记忆效应》,《心理科学》2012年第3期。

孙远路、胡中华、张瑞玲、寻茫茫、刘强、张庆林:《多感觉整合测量范式中存在的影响因素探讨》,《心理学报》2011年第11期。

王苹、潘治辉、张立洁、陈煦海:《动态面孔和语音情绪信息的整合加工及神经生理机制》,《心理科学进展》2015年第7期。

张亮、孙向红、张侃:《情绪信息的多通道整合》,《心理科学进展》2009年第16期。

二 外文文献

Alais D., Newell F. N. & Mamassian P., Multisensory Processing in Review: From Physiology to Behaviour, *Seeing & Perceiving*, Vol. 23, No. 1, 2010.

Alho K., Rinne T., Herron T. J. & Woods D. L., Stimulus-dependent

Activations and Attention-related Modulations in the Auditory Cortex: A Meta-analysis of FMRI Studies, *Hearing Research*, Vol. 307, January 2014.

Aloufy S., Lapidot M. & Myslobodsky M., Differences in Susceptibility to the "Blending Illusion" Among Native Hebrew and English Speakers, *Brain and Language*, Vol. 53, No. 1, April 1996.

Alsius A., Navarra J., Campbell R. & Soto-Faraco S., Audiovisual Integration of Speech Falters under High Attention Demands, *Current Biology*, Vol. 15, No. 9, May 2005.

Alsius A., Navarra J. & Soto-Faraco S., Attention to Touch Weakens Audiovisual Speech Integration, *Experimental Brain Research*, Vol. 183, No. 3, November 2007.

Andersen T. S. & Mamassian P., Audiovisual Integration of Stimulus Transients, *Vision research*, Vol. 48, No. 25, July 2008.

Anne C., Salvador S. F., Alan K. & Charles S., Tactile "Capture" of Audition, *Perception & Psychophysics*, Vol. 64, No. 4, May 2002.

Aschersleben G. & Bertelson P., Temporal Ventriloquism: Crossmodal Interaction on the Time Dimension. Evidence from Sensorimotor Synchronization, *International Journal of Psychophysiology*, Vol. 50, No. 1, October 2003.

Auer E. T. & Jr Bernstein L. E., Enhanced Visual Speech Perception in Individuals with Early-onset Hearing Impairment, *Journal of Speech, Language and Hearing Research*, Vol. 50, No. 5, October 2007.

Bahrick L. E., Intermodal Perception and Selective Attention to Intersensory Redundancy: Implications for Typical Social Developmental and Autism, In *The Wiley-Blackwell Handbook of Infant Development*, 2nd edn. (eds. J. G. Bremner, and T. D. Wachs), 2010, pp. 120 – 166. Wiley-Blackwell, Oxford, UK.

Bahrick L. E. & Todd J. T. , Multisensory Processing in Autism Spectrum Disorders: Intersensory Processing Disturbance as a Basis for Atypical Development, In *The New Handbook of Multisensory Processes* (ed. B. E. Stein), 2012, MIT Press, Cambridge, M. A.

Baier B. , Kleinschmidt A. & Müller N. G. , Cross-modal Processing in Early Visual and Auditory Cortices Depends on Expected Statistical Relationship of Multisensory Information, *The Journal of neuroscience*, Vol. 26, No. 47, November 2006.

Baier R. , Idsardi W. & Lidz J. , Two-month-olds are Sensitive to Lip Rounding in Dynamic and Static Speech Events. Paper Presented in *the International Conference on Auditory-Visual Speech Processing* (AVSP2007), Kasteel Groenendaal, Hilvarenbeek, The Netherlands, 31 August-3 September 2007.

Balconi M. & Carrera A. , Cross-modal Integration of Emotional Face and Voice in Congruous and Incongruous Pairs: The P2 ERP Effect, *Journal of Cognitive Psychology*, Vol. 23, No. 1, 2011.

Baranek G. T. , Autism duringInfancy: A Retrospective Video Analysis of Sensory-motor and Social Behaviors at 9-12 Months of Age, *Journal of Autism and Developmental Disorders*, Vol. 29, No. 3, June 1999.

Barbara A. B. , Lucy J. M. , William J. G. & Patricia L. D. , Multisensory Integration in Children: A Preliminary ERP Study, *Brain Research*, No. 1242, November 2008.

Barker B. A. & Tomblin J. B. , Bimodal Speech Perception in Infant Hearing Aid and Cochlear Implant Users, *Archives of Otolaryngology-Head and Neck Surgery*, Vol. 130, No. 5, May 2004.

Baron-Cohen S. , Ashwin E. , Ashwin C. , Tavassoli T. & Chakrabati B. , Talent in Autism: Hypersystemizing, Hyper-attention to Detail and Sensory Hypersensitivity, *Philosophical Transactions of the Royal Society B: Biological Sciences*, Vol. 364, No. 1522, May 2009.

Barraclough N. E. , Xiao D. K. , Baker C. I. , Oram M. W. & Perrett D. I. , Integration of Visual and Auditory Information by Superior Temporal Sulcus Neurons Responsive to the Sight of Actions, *Journal of Cognitive Neuroscience*, Vol. 17, No. 3, March 2005.

Battaglia P. W. , Jacobs R. A. & Aslin R. N. , Bayesian Integration of Visual and Auditory Signals for Spatial Localization, *Journal of the Optical Society of America A Optics Image Science & Vision*, Vol. 20, No. 7, August 2003.

Beck D. M. & Kastner S. , Top-down and Bottom-up Mechanisms in Biasing Competition in the Human Brain, *Vision research*, Vol. 49, No. 10, June 2009.

Benevento L. A. , Fallon J. , Davis B. J. & Rezak M. , Auditory-Visual Interaction in Single Cells in Cortex of Superior Temporal Sulcus and Orbital Frontal Cortex of Macaque Monkey, *Experimental Neurology*, Vol. 57, No. 3, December 1977.

Bertelson P. & Aschersleben G. , Automatic Visual Bias of Perceived Auditory Location, *Psychonomic Bulletin & Review*, Vol. 5, No. 3, September 1998.

Bernstein L. E. , Auer E. T. Jr. & Tucker P. E. , Enhanced Speechreading in Deaf Adults: Can Shortterm Training/practice Close the Gap for Hearing Adults, *Journal of Speech, Language and Hearing Research*, Vol. 44, No. 1, February 2001.

Bernstein L. E. , Auer E. T. , Wagner M. & Ponton C. W. , Spatiotemporal Dynamics of Audiovisual Speech Processing, *Neuroimage*, Vol. 39, No. 1, January 2008.

Bernstein L. E. , Demorest M. E. & Tucker P. E. , Speech Perception without Hearing, *Perception and Psychophysics*, Vol. 62, No. 2, 2000.

Bertelson P. & Radeau M. , Cross-modal Bias and Perceptual Fusion with Auditory-visual Spatial Discordance, *Percept. Psychophys*, Vol. 29, No. 6, 1981.

Bertelson P. , *Ventriloquism: A case of crossmodal perceptual grouping*. In G. Achersleben, T. Bachman, & J. Musseler (Eds.), Cognitive contributions to the perceptionof spatial and temporal events. Amsterdam: Elsevier. Vol. 129, January 1999.

Bertelson P. , Vroomen J. , De Gelder B. & Driver J. , The Ventriloquist Effect Does Not Depend on the Direction of Deliberate Visual Attention, *Perception and Psychophysics*, Vol. 62, No. 2, February 2000.

Besle J. , Fort A. , Delpuech C. & Giard M. H. , Bimodal Speech: Early Suppressive Visual Effects in Human Auditory Cortex, *European Journal of Neuroscience*, Vol. 20, No. 8, October 2004.

Birch H. G. & Belmont L. , Auditory Visual Integration in Normal and Retarded Readers, *Annals of Dyslexia*, No. 15, 1964.

Birch H. G. & Lefford A. , Visual Differentiation, Intersensory Integration, and Voluntary Motor Control, *Monographs of the Society for Research in Child Development*, No. 32, 1967.

Bizley J. K. , Nodal F. R. , Bajo V. M. , Nelken I. & King A. J. , Physiological and Anatomical Evidence for Multisensory Interactions in Auditory Cortex, *Cerebral Cortex*, Vol. 17, No. 9, September 2007.

Bolognini N. , Frassinetti F. , Serino A. & Ladavas E. , "Acoustical Vision" of Below Threshold Stimuli: Interaction among Spatially Converging Audiovisual Inputs, *Experimental Brain Research*, Vol. 160, No. 3, January 2005.

Bonath B., Noesselt T., Martinez A., Mishra J., Schwiecker K., Heinze H. J. & Hillyard S. A., Neural Basis of the Ventriloquist Illusion, *Current Biology*, Vol. 17, No. 19, October 2007.

Bristow D., Dehaene-Lambertz G., Mattout J., et al., Hearing Faces: How the Infant Brain Matches the Face It Sees with the Speech It Hears, *Journal of Cognitive Neuroscience*, Vol. 21, No. 5, May 2008.

Brochard R., Tassin M. & Zagar D., Got Rhythm…for Better and for Worse. Cross-modal Effects of Auditory Rhythm on Visual Word Recognition, *Cognition*, Vol. 127, No. 2, May 2013.

Bruce C., Desimone R. & Gross C. G., Visual Properties of Neurons in a Polysensory Area in Superior Temporal Sulcus of the Macaque, *Journal of Neurophysiology*, Vol. 46, No. 2, August 1981.

Budinger E., Heil P., Hess A. & Scheich H., Multisensory Processing Via Early Cortical Stages: Connections of the Primary Auditory Cortical Field with Other Sensory Systems, *Neuroscience*, Vol. 143, No. 4, December 2006.

Burr D. & Alais D., Combining Visual and Auditory Information, *Progress in Brain Research*, Vol. 155, 2006.

Burnham D., Visual Recognition of Mother by Young Infants: Facilitation by Speech, *Perception*, Vol. 22, No. 10, 1993.

Burnham D. & Dodd B., Auditory-visual Speech Integration by Pre-linguistic Infants: Perception of an Emergent Consonant in the McGurk Effect, *Developmental Psychobiology*, Vol. 45, No. 4, December 2004.

Bushara K. O., Grafman J. & Hallett M., Neural Correlates of Auditory-visual Stimulus onset Asynchrony Detection, *The Journal of Neuro-

science, Vol. 21, No. 1, January 2001.

Callan D. E., Callan A. M., Kroos C. & Vatikiotis-Bateson E., Multimodal Contribution to Speech Perception Revealed by Independent Component Analysis: A Single-sweep EEG Case Study, *Cognitive Brain Research*, Vol. 10, No. 3, January 2001.

Calvert G. A., Crossmodal Processing in the Human Brain: Insights from Functional Neuroimaging Studies, *Cerebral Cortex*, Vol. 11, No. 12, December 2001.

Calvert G. A., Brammer M. J., Bullmore E. T., Campbell R., Iversen S. D. & David A. S., Response Amplification in Sensory-specific Cortices during Crossmodal Binding, *Neuroreport*, Vol. 10, No. 12, August 1999.

Calvert G. A., Bullmore E. T., Brammer M. J., Campbell R., Williams S. C., McGuire P. K. & David A. S., Activation of Auditory Cortex during Silent Lipreading, *Science*, Vol. 276, No. 5312, April 1997.

Calvert G. A., Campbell R. & Brammer M. J., Evidence from Functional Magnetic Resonance Imaging of Crossmodal Binding in the Human Heteromodalcortex, *Current Biology*, Vol. 10, No. 11, Junuary 2000.

Calvert G. A., Hansen P. C., Iversen S. D. & Brammer M. J., Detection of Audio-visual Integration Sites in Humans by Application of Electrophysiological Criteria to the BOLD Effect, *Neuroimage*, Vol. 14, No. 2, August 2001.

Calvert G. A. & Thesen T., Multisensory Integration: Methodological Approaches and Emerging Principles in the Human Brain, *Journal of Physiology Paris*, Vol. 98, No. 1-3, June 2004.

Campanella S. & Belin P., Integrating Face Andvoice in Person Perception, *Trends in Cognitive Sciences*, Vol. 11, No. 12, December 2007.

Campanella S., Bruyer R., Froidbise S., Rossignol M., Joassin F., Kornreich C., …Verbanck P., Is Two Better than One? A Cross-modal Oddball Paradigm Reveals Greater Sensitivity of the P300 to Emotional Face-voice Associations, *Clinical Neurophysiology*, Vol. 121, No. 11, November 2010.

Campbell R. & MacSweeney M., *Neuroimaging studies of crossmodal plasticity and language processing in deaf people*. In The Handbook of Multisensory Processes (ed. G. A. Calvert, C. Spence, and B. A. Stein), 2004, pp. 773 – 778. MIT Press, Cambridge, M. A.

Chen L. & Vroomen J., Intersensory Binding across Space and Time: A Tutorial Review, *Attention, Perception, & Psychophysics*, Vol. 75, No. 5, July 2013.

Colavita F. B. & Weisberg D., A Further Investigation of Visual Dominance, *Percept Psychophys*, Vol. 25, No. 4, April 1979.

Colby C. L., Duhamel J. R. & Goldberg M. E., Visual, Presaccadic, and Cognitive Activation of Single Neurons in Monkey Lateral Intraparietal Area, *Journal of Neurophysiology*, Vol. 76, No. 5, November 1996.

Colby C. L. & Goldberg M. E., Space and Attention in Parietal Cortex, *Annual Review of Neuroscience*, Vol. 22, No. 1, February 1999.

Collignon O., Girard S., Gosselin F., Roy S., Saint-Amour D., Lassonde M. & Lepore F., Audio-visual Integration of Emotion Expression, *Brain Research*, Vol. 25, No. 1242, November 2008.

Coulon M., Guellai B. & Streri A., Recognition of Unfamiliar Talking Faces at Birth, *International Journal of Behavioral Development*, No. 35, April 2011.

Conrey B. & Pisoni D. B., Auditory-visual Speech Perception and Synchrony Detection for Speech and Nonspeech Signals, *Journal of Acoustical Society of America*, Vol. 119, No. 6, June 2006.

Correa A. & Nobre A. C., Neural Modulation by Regularity and Passage of Time, *Journal of Neurophysiology*, Vol. 100, No. 3, September 2008.

Coull J., Neural Correlates of Attention and Arousal: Insights from Electrophysiology, Functional Neuroimaging and Psychopharmacology, *Progress in Neurology*, Vol. 55, No. 4, July 1998.

Crane L., Goddard L. & Pring L., Sensory Processing in Adults with Autism Spectrum Disorders, *Autism*, Vol. 13, No. 3, May 2009.

Critchley M., *The dyslexic child*. Heinemann, London, 1970.

Dawson G., Osterling J., Meltzoff A. N. & Kuhl P., Case Study of the Development of an Infant with Autism from Birth to 2 Years of Age, *Journal of Applied Developmental Psychology*, Vol. 21, No. 3, May 2000.

De Gelder B. & Bertelson P., Multisensory Integration, Perception and Ecological Validity, *Trends in Cognitive Science*, Vol. 7, No. 10, October 2003.

De Gelder B., Boecker K., Tuomainen J., Hensen M. & Vroomen J., The Combined Perception of Emotion from Voice and Face: Early Interaction Revealed by Human Electric Brain Responses, *Neuroscience Letters*, No. 260, Jannuary 1999.

De Gelder B. & Vroomen J., The Perception of Emotions by Ear and by Eye, *Cognition and Emotion*, 14, 2000.

De Gelder B., Vroomen J., De Jong S. J., Masthoff E. D., Trompenaars F. J. & Hodiamont P., Multisensory Integration of Emotional Faces and Voices in Schizophrenics, *Schizophrenia Research*, Vol. 72, No. 2, Jannuary 2005.

Demattè M. L., Osterbauer R. & Spence C., Olfactory cues Modulate Facial Attractiveness, *Chemical Senses*, Vol. 32, No. 6, July 2007.

De Meo R., Murray M. M., Clarke S. & Matusz P. J., Top-down Control and Early Multisensory Processes: Chicken vs. Egg, *Frontiers in integrative neuroscience*, Vol. 9, No. 17, March 2015.

Desjardins R. N., Rogers J. & Werker J. F., An Exploration of Why Preschoolers Perform Differently than Do Adults in Audiovisual Speech Perception Tasks, *Journal of Experimental Child Psychology*, Vol. 66, No. 1, July 1997.

Desjardins R. N. & Werker J. W., Is the Integration of Heard and Seen Speech Mandatory for Infants, *Develpmental Psychobiology*, Vol. 45, No. 4, December 2005.

Dick A. S., Solodkin A. & Small S. L., Neural Development of Networks for Audiovisual Speech Comprehension, *Brain and Language*, Vol. 114, No. 2, August 2010.

Doi H. & Shinohara K., Unconscious Presentation of Fearful Face Modulates Electrophysiological Responses to Emotional Prosody, *Cerebral Cortex*, Vol. 25, No. 3, March 2015.

Donohue S. E., Woldorff M. G. & Mitroff S. R., Video Game Players Show More Precise Multisensory Temporal Processing Abilities, *Attention, Perception, & Psychophysics*, Vol. 72, No. 4, May 2010.

Downar J., Grawley A. P., Mikulis D. J. & Davis K. D., A Multimodal Cortical Network for the Detection of Changes in the Sensory Environment, *Nature Neuroscience*, Vol. 3, March 2000.

Driver J. & Noesselt T., Multisensory Interplay Reveals Crossmodal Influences on "Sensory-Specific" Brain Regions, *Neuron*, Vol. 57, No. 1, January 2008.

Emmorey K., Allen J. S., Bruss J., Schenker N. & Damasio H., A Morphometric Analysis of Auditory Brain Regions in Congenitally Deaf Adults, *Proceedings of the National Academy of Sciences U. S. A.*, Vol. 100. No. 17, August 2003.

Epperson C. N., Amin Z., Ruparel K., Gur R. & Loughead J., Interactive Effects of Estrogen and Serotonin on Brainactivation during Working Memory and Affective Processing in Menopausal Women, *Psychoneuroendocrinology*, Vol. 37, No. 3, August 2012.

Ernst M. O. & Bülthoff H. H., Merging the Senses into a Robust Percept, *Trends in Cognitive Sciences*, Vol. 8, No. 4, April 2004.

Escoffier N., Sheng D. Y. J. & Schirmer A., Unattended Musical Beats Enhance Visual Processing, *Acta Psychologica*, Vol. 135, No. 1, September 2010.

Falchier A., Clavagnier S., Barone P. & Kennedy H., Anatomical Evidence of Multimodal Integration in Primate Striate Cortex. *Journal of Neuroscience*, Vol. 22, No. 13, July 2002.

Fan Y. T., Decety J., Yang C. Y., Liu J. L. & Cheng Y., Unbroken Mirror Neurons in Autism Spectrum Disorders, Journal of Child Psychology and Psychiatry, Vol. 51. No. 9, September 2010.

Farb N. A., Segal Z. V. & Anderson A. K., Attentional Modulation of Primary Interoceptive and Exteroceptive Cortices, *Cerebral Cortex*, Vol. 23, No. 1, January 2013.

Finney E. M., Clementz B. A., Hickok G. & Dobkins K. R., Visual Stimuli Activate Auditory Cortex in Deaf Subjects: Evidence from MEG, *Neuroreport*, Vol. 14, No. 11, August 2003.

Finney E. M. , Fine I. & Dobkins K. R. , Visual Stimuli Activate Auditory Cortex in the Deaf, *Nature Neuroscience*, Vol. 4, No. 12, December 2001.

Frassinetti F. , Bolognini N. & Ladavas E. , Enhancement of Visual Perception by Crossmodal Visuo-auditory Interaction, *Experimental Brain Research*, Vol. 147, No. 3, December 2002.

Fort A. , Delpuech C. , Pernier J. & Giard M. H. , Dynamics of Cortico-subcortical Crossmodal Operations Involved in Audio-visual Object Detection in Humans, *Cerebral Cortex*, Vol. 12, No. 10, October 2002.

Foxe J. J. & Molholm S. , Ten Years at the Multisensory Forum: Musings on the Evolution of a Field, *Brain Topography*, Vol. 21. No. 3, May 2009.

Foxe J. J. , Morocz I. A. , Murray M. M. , Higgins B. A. , Javitt D. C. & Schroeder C. E. , Multisensory Auditory-somatosensory Interactions in Early Cortical Processing Revealed by High-density Electrical Mapping, *Cognitive Brain Research*, Vol. 10, No. 1, September 2000.

Friston K. , The Free-energy Principle: A Unified Brain Theory, *Nature Reviews Neuroscience*, Vol. 11, No. 2, January 2010.

Fujioka T. , Trainor L. J. , Large E. W. & Ross B. , Beta and Gamma Rhythms in Human Auditory Cortex during Musical Beat Processing, *Ann N Y Acad Sci*, July 2009.

García-Larrea L. , Lukaszewicz A. C. & Mauguiére F. , Revisiting the Oddball Paradigm. Non-target Vs Neutral Stimuli and the Evaluation of ERP Attentionaleffects, *Neuropsychologia*, Vol. 30, No. 8, August 1992.

Gergely G. , The Object of Desire: "Nearly, but Clearly Not, Like Me": Contingency Preference in Normal Children Versus Children with Au-

tism, *Bulletin of the Menninger Clinic*, Vol. 65, No. 3, 2001.

Gergely G. & Watson J. S., Early Socio-emotional Development: Contingency Perception and Social-biofeedback Model, In *Early social cognition: Understanding others in the first months of life* (ed. P. Rochat), 1999, pp. 101–136. Lawrence Erlbaum Associates, Hillsdale, NJ.

Guest S., Catmur C., Lloyd D. & Spence C., Audiotactile Interactions in Roughness Perception, *Experimental Brain Research*, Vol. 146, No. 2, September 2002.

Ghazanfar A. A., Maier J. X., Hoffman K. L. & Logothetis N. K., Multisensory Integration of Dynamic Faces and Voices in Rhesus Monkey Auditory Cortex, *Journal of Neuroscience*, Vol. 25, No. 20, May 2005.

Ghazanfar A. A. & Schroeder C. E., Is Neocortex Essentially Multisensory, *Trends in Cognitive Sciences*, Vol. 10, No. 6, June 2006.

Giard M. H. & Peronnet F., Auditory-visual Integration during Multimodal Object Recognition in Humans: A Behavioral and Electrophysiological Study, *Journal of Cognitive Neuroscience*, Vol. 11, No. 5, September 1999.

Giary M. & Ulrich R., Motor Coactivation Revealed by Response Force in Divided and Focused Attention, *Journal of Experimental Psychology: Human Perception and Performance*, Vol. 19, No. 6, December 1993.

Gibson E. J., *Principles of perceptual learning and development*. New York: Appleton, 1969.

Goldberg M. E. & Wurtz R. H., Activity of Superiorcolliculus in Behaving Monkey: II. Effects of Attentionin Neural Responses, *Journal of Neurophysiology*, Vol. 35, No. 4, July 1972.

Grahn J. A. & Rowe J. B. , Finding and Feeling the Musical Beat: Striatal Dissociations between Detection and Prediction of Regularity, *Cerebral Cortex*, Vol. 23, No. 4, April 2012.

Groh J. M. & Sparks D. L. , Saccades to Somatosensory Targets. I. Behavioral Characteristics, *Journal of Neurophysiology*, Vol. 75, No. 1, January 1996.

Grossmann T. , Striano T. & Friederici A. D. , Crossmodal Integration of Emotional Information from Face and Voice in the Infant Brain, *Developmental Science*, Vol. 9, No. 1 - 3, May 2006.

Hamilton R. H. , Shenton J. T. & Coslett H. B. , An Acquired Deficit of Audiovisual Speech Processing, *Brain and Language*, Vol. 98, No. 1, July 2006.

Hairston W. D. , Burdette J. H. , Flowers D. L. , Wood F. B. & Wallace M. T. , Altered Temporal Profile of Visual-auditory Multisensory Interactions in Dyslexia, *Experimental Brain Research*, Vol. 166, No. 3, October 2005.

Harrar V. , Tammam J. , Pérez-Bellido A. , Pitt A. , Stein J. & Spence C. , Multisensory Integration and Attention in Developmental Dyslexia, *Current Biology*, Vol. 24, No. 5, March 2014.

Hein G. & Knight R. T. , Superior Temporal Sulcus—It's My Area: Or is It, *Journal of Cognitive Neuroscience*, Vol. 20, No. 12, December 2008.

Heslenfeld D. , Kenemans J. L. Kok A. & Molenaar P. C. M. , Feature Processing and Attention in the Human Visual System: An Overview, *Biological Psychology*, Vol. 45, No. 1 - 3, March 1997.

Hillyard S. A. , Hink R. F. , Schwent V. L. & Picton T. W. , Electrical Signs of Selective Attention in the Human Brain, *Science*,

Vol. 182, No. 4108, October 1973.

Iversen J. R., Repp B. H. & Patel A. D., Top-down Control of Rhythm Perception Modulates Early Auditory Responses, *Ann N Y Acad Sci*, July 2009, No. 1169.

Jean-Pierre B., Franziska D. & Ernst M. O., Vision and Touch are Automatically Integrated for the Perception of Sequences of Events, *Journal of Vision*, Vol. 6, No. 5, Apr 2006.

Jessen S. & Kotz S. A., The Temporal Dynamics of Processing Emotions from Vocal, Facial, and Bodily Expressions, *Neuroimage*, Vol. 58, No. 2, September 2011.

Jones M. R., Time, Our Lost Dimension: Toward a New Theory of Perception, Attention, and Memory, *Psychological Review*, Vol. 83, No. 5, September 1976.

Jones M. R. & Boltz M., Dynamic Attending and Responses to Time, *Psychological Review*, Vol. 96, No. 3, July 1989.

Jones C., Happé F., Baird G., et al, Auditory Discrimination and Auditory Sensory Behaviours in Autism Spectrum Disorders, *Neuropsychologia*, Vol. 47, No. 13, November 2009.

Kayser C. & Logothetis N. K., Do Early Sensory Cortices Integrate Crossmodal Information, *Brain Struct Funct*, September 2007, No. 212.

Kayser C., Petkov C. I. & Logothetis N. K., Visual Modulation of Neurons in Auditory Cortex, *Cereb Cortex*, Vol. 18, No. 7, July 2008.

Kenemans J. L., Kok A. & Smulders F. T., Event-related Potentials to Conjunctions of Spatial Frequency and Orientation as a Function of Stimulus Parameters and Response Requirements, *Electroencephalography & Clinical Neurophysiology*, Vol. 28, No. 88, February 1993.

Kientz M. A. & Dunn W., A Comparison of the Performance of Children with and without Autism on the Sensory Profile, *American Journal of Occupational Therapy*, Vol. 51, No. 7, August 1997.

Klasen M., Chen Y. H. & Mathiak K., Multisensory Emotions: Perception, Combination and Underlying Neuralprocesses, *Reviews in the Neurosciences*, Vol. 23, No. 4, 2012.

Klasen M., Kenworthy C. A., Mathiak K. A., Kircher T. T. J. & Mathiak K., Supramodal Representation of Emotions, *Journal of Neuroscience*, Vol. 31, No. 38, September 2011.

Knig Klasen M., Kreifelts B., Chen Y. H., Seubert J. & Mathiak K., Neural Processing of Emotion in Multimodal Settings, *Frontiers in Human Neuroscience*, Vol. 8, No. 8, October 2014.

Koelewijn T., Bronkhorst A. & Theeuwes J., Attention and the Multiple Stages of Multisensory Integration: A Review of Audiovisual Studies, *Acta Psychologica*, Vol. 134, No. 3, July 2010.

Kokinous J., Tavano A., Kotz S. A. & Schroeger E., Perceptual Integration of Faces and Voices Depends on the Interaction of Emotional Content and Spatial Frequency, *Biological Psychology*, No. 123, February 2017.

Koppen C. & Spence C., Audiovisual Asynchrony Modulates the Colavita Visual Dominance Effect, *Brain Research*, No. 1186, December 2007.

Kreifelts B., Ethofer T., Grodd W., Erb M. & Wildgruber D., Audiovisual Integration of Emotional Signals in Voice and Face: An Event-related FMRI Study, *Neuroimage*, Vol. 37, No. 4, November 2007.

Kreifelts B., Ethofer T., Huberle E., Grodd W. & Wildgruber D., Association of Trait Emotional Intelligence and Individual FMRI-activation Patterns during the Perception of Social Signals from Voice and Face,

Human Brain Mapping, Vol. 31, No. 7, July 2010.

Kuhl P. & Meltzoff A., The Bimodal Perception of Speech in Infancy, *Science*, Vol. 218, No. 4577, December 1982.

Kuhl P. K. & Meltzoff A. N., Speech as an Intermodal Object of Perception. In A. Yonas (Ed.), *Perceptual development in infancy. The Minnesota Symposia on Child Psychology*. Hillsdale, NJ: Erlbaum, 1988.

Kuhl P. K. & Meltzoff A. N., The bimodal perception of speech in infancy, *Science*, 1982.

Kushnerenko E., Teinonen T., Volein A. & Csibra G., Electrophysiological Evidence of Illusory Audiovisual Speech Percept in Human Infants, *Proceedings of the National Academy of Sciences U.S.A.*, Vol. 105, No. 32, August 2008.

LaBerge D., *Attentional processing: The brain's artof mindfulness*. Cambridge: Harvard University Press. 1995.

Lakatos P., Chen C. M., O'Connell M. N., Mills A. & Schroeder C. E., Neuronal Oscillations and Multisensory Interaction in Primary Auditory Cortex, *Neuron*, Vol. 53, No. 2, January 2007.

Large E. W. & Jones M. R., The Dynamics of Attending: How People Track Time Varying Events, *Psychological Review*, Vol. 106, No. 1, January 1999.

Laurienti P. J., Burdette J. H., Maldjian J. A. & Wallace M. T., Enhanced Multisensory Integration in Older Adults, *Neurobiology of Aging*, Vol. 27, No. 8, August 2006.

Laurienti P. J., Kraft R. A., Maldjian J. A., Burdette J. H. & Wallace M. T., Semantic Congruence is a Critical Factor in Multisensory Behavioral Performance, *Experimental Brain Research*, Vol. 158,

No. 4, October 2004.

Lee H. J., Tru E., Mamou G., Sappey-Marinier D. & Giraud A. L., Visual Speech Circuits in Profound Acquired Deafness: A Possible Role for Latent Multimodal Connectivity, *Brain*, Vol. 130, No. 11, November 2007.

Leekam S. R., Nieto C., Libby S. J., Wing L. & Gould J., Describing the Sensory Abnormalities of Children and Adults with Autism, *Journal of Autism and Developmental Disorders*, Vol. 37, No. 5, May 2007.

Lewis J. W. & Van Essen D. C., Corticocortical Connections of Visual, Sensorimotor, and Multimodal Processing Areas in the Parietal Lobe of the Macaque Monkey, *Journal of Comparative Neurology*, Vol. 428, No. 1, December 2000.

Lewkowicz D. J., The Development of Intersensory Temporal Perception: An Epigenetic Systems/limitations View, *Psychological Bulletin*, Vol. 126, No. 2, March 2000.

Lewkowicz D. J. & Ghazanfar A. A., The Decline of Cross-species Intersensory Perception in Human Infants, *Proceedings of the National Academy Sciences USA*, No. 10, 2006.

Lewkowicz D. J., Leo I. & Simion F., Intersensory Perception at Birth: Newborns Match Nonhuman Primate Faces and Voices, *Infancy*, No. 15, January 2010.

Lewkowicz D. J. & Turkewitz G., Intersensory Interaction in Newborns: Modification of Visual Preferences Following Exposure to Sound, *Child Development*, No. 52, September 1981.

Linden J. F., Grunewald A. & Andersen R. A., Responses to Auditory Stimuli in Macaque Lateral Intraparietal Area II. Behavioral Modulation,

Journal of Neurophysiology, Vol. 82, No. 1, July 1999.

Liu P., Rigoulot S. & Pell M. D., Culture Modulates the Brain Response to Human Expressions of Emotion: Electrophysiological Evidence, *Neuropsychologia*, No. 67, Jannuary 2015.

Lucas S. A., Auditory Discrimination and Speech Production in the Blind Child, *International Journal of Rehabilitation Research*, No. 7, 1984.

MacKain K., Studdert-Kennedy M., Spieker S. & Stern D., Infant Intermodal Speech Perception is a Left-hemisphere Function, *Science*, Vol. 219, No. 4590, March 1983.

MacSweeney M., Calvert G. A., Campbell R., et al., Speechreading Circuits in People Born Deaf, *Neuropsychologia*, Vol. 40, No. 7, 2002.

Magnée M. J., De Gelder B., Van Engeland H. & Kemner C., Audiovisual Speech Integration in Pervasive Developmental Disorder: Evidence from Event-related Potentials, *Journal of Child Psychology and Psychiatry*, Vol. 49, No. 9, September 2008.

Mangun G., NeuralMechanisms of Visual Selective Attention, *Psychophysiology*, Vol. 32, No. 1, January 1995.

Martuzzi R., Murray M. M., Michel C. M., Thiran J. P., Maeder P. P., Clarke S., et al, Multisensory Interactions within Human Primary Cortices Revealed by BOLD Dynamics, *Cerebral Cortex*, Vol. 17, No. 7, August 2007.

McDonald J. J., Teder-Sälejärvi W. A. & Hillyard S. A., Involuntary Orienting to Sound Improves Visual Perception, *Nature*, Vol. 407, No. 6806, October 2000.

McGurk H. & MacDonald J., Hearing Lips and Seeing Voices, *Nature*,

Vol. 264, No. 5588, December 1976.

Ménard L., Dupont S., Baum S. R. & Aubin J., Production and Perception of French Vowels by Congenitally Blind Adults and Sighted Adults, *Journal of the Acoustical Society of America*, Vol. 126, No. 3, September 2009.

Meredith M. A., Nemitz J. W. & Stein B. E., Determinants of Multisensory Integration in Superior Colliculus Neurons. I. Temporal Factors, *The Journal of Neuroscience*, Vol. 7, No. 10, 1987.

Meredith M. A. & Stein B. E., Visual, Auditory, and Somatosensory Convergence on Cells in Superiorcolliculus Results in Multisensory Integration, *Journalof Neurophysiology*, Vol. 56, No. 3, September 1986.

Meredith M. A. & Stein B. E., Spatial Determinants of Multisensory Integration in Cat Superior Colliculus Neurons, *Journal of Neurophysiology*, Vol. 75, No. 5, May 1996.

Meredith M. A., On the Neuronal Basis for Multisensory Convergence: A Brief Overview, *Cognitive Brain Research*, Vol. 14, No. 1, June 2002.

Mileva M., Tompkinson J., Watt D. & Burton A. M., Audiovisual Integration in Social Evaluation, *Journal of Experimental Psychology: Human Perceptionand Performance*, Vol. 44, No. 1, January 2018.

Miller J., Divided Attention: Evidence for Coactivation with Redundant Signals, *Cognitive psychology*, Vol. 14, No. 2, April 1982.

Miller J., Timecourse of Coactivation in Bimodal Divided Attention, *Perception & Psychophysics*, Vol. 40, No. 5, November 1986.

Miller L. M. & D'esposito M., Perceptual Fusion and Stimulus Coincidence in the Cross-modal Integration of Speech, *The Journal of Neuro-

science, Vol. 25, No. 25, June 2005.

Mishra J. & Gazzaley A., Attention Distributed across Sensory Modalities Enhances Perception Performance, *The journal of neuroscience*, Vol. 32, No. 35, August 2012.

Mishra J., Martinez A., Sejnowski T. J. & Hillyard S. A., Early Cross-modal Interactions in Auditory and Visual Cortex Underlie a Sound-induced Visual Illusion, *Journal of Neuroscience*, Vol. 27, No. 15, April 2007.

Mittag M., Alho K., Takegata R., Makkonen T. & Kujala T., Audiovisual Attention Boosts Letter-speech Sound Integration, *Psychophysiology*, Vol. 50, No. 10, October 2013.

Mohammed T., Campbell R., MacSweeney M., Milne E., Hansen P. & Coleman M., Speechreading Skill and Visual Movement Sensitivity are Related in Deaf Speechreaders, *Perception*, Vol. 34, No. 2, 2005.

Molholm S., Ritter W., Murray M. M., Javitt D. C., Schroeder C. E. & Foxe J. J., Multisensory Auditory-visual Interactions during Early Sensory Processing in Humans: A High-density Electrical Mapping Study, *Cognitive Brain Research*, Vol. 14, No. 1, June 2002.

Morrongiello B. A., Fenwick K. D. & Chance G., Cross-modal Learning in Newborn Infants: Inferences about Properties of Auditory-visual Events, *Infant Behavior and Development*, No. 21, 1998.

Muchnik C., Efrati M., Nemeth E., Malin M. & Hildesheimer M., Central Auditory Skills in Blind and Sighted Subjects, *Scandinavian Journal of Audiology*, Vol. 20, No. 1, 1991.

Muller V. I., Cieslik E. C., Turetsky B. I. & Eickhoff S. B., Crossmodal Interactions in Audiovisual Emotion Processing, *Neuroimage*,

Vol. 60, No. 1, 2012.

Noesselt T., Rieger J. W., Schoenfeld M. A., Kanowski M., Hinrichs H., Heinze H. J. & Driver J., Audiovisual Temporal Correspondence Modulates Human Multisensory Superior Temporal Sulcus Plus Primary Sensory Cortices, *The Journal of Neuroscience*, Vol. 27, No. 42, October 2007.

Nozaradan S., Peretz I., Missal M. & Mouraux A., Tagging Theneuronal Entrainment to Beat and Meter, *Journal of Neuroscience*, Vol. 31, No. 28, July 2011.

Oberman L. M. & Ramachandran V. S., The Simulating Social Mind: The Role of the Mirror Neuron System and Simulation in the Social and Communicative Deficits of Autism Spectrum Disorders, *Psychological Bulletin*, Vol. 133, No. 2, March 2007.

Oberman L. S. & Ramachandran V. S., Preliminary Evidence for Deficits in Multisensory Integration in Autism Spectrum Disorders: The Mirror Neuron Hypothesis, *Social Neuroscience*, Vol. 3, No. 3, 2008.

Odegaard E. C., Arieh Y. & Marks L., Cross-modal Enhancemnt of Perceived Brightness: Sensory Interaction Versus Response Bias, *Perception & Psychophysics*, Vol. 65, No. 1, February 2003.

Olson I. R., Gatenby J. C. & Gore J. C., A Comparison of Bound and Unbound Audio-visual Information Processing in the Human Cerebral Cortex, *Cognitive Brain Research*, Vol. 14, No. 1, June 2002.

O'Neill M. & Jones R. S. P., Sensory-perceptual Abnormalities in Autism: A Case for More Research, *Journal of Autism and Developmental Disorders*, Vol. 27, No. 3, June 1997.

Park J. Y., Gu B. M., Kang D. H., Shin Y. W., Choi C. H., Lee J. M. & Kwon J. S., Integration of Cross-modal Emotional Information in the Human Brain: AnfMRI Study, *Cortex*, Vol. 46, No. 2, February 2010.

Pasqualotto A., Dumitru M. L. & Myachykov A., Editorial: Multisensory Integration: Brain, Body, and World, *Frontiers in Psychology*, Vol. 6, January 2016.

Patterson M. L. & Werker J. F., Matching Phonetic Information in Lips and Voice is Robust in 4. 5-month-old Infants, *Infant Behavior and Development*, No. 22, December 1999.

Patterson M. L. & Werker J. F., Two-month-old Infants Match Phonetic Information in Lips and Voice, *Developmental Science*, Vol. 6, No. 2, 2003.

Pavani F., Spence C. & Driver J., Visual Capture of Touch: Out-of-the-body Experiences with Rubber Gloves, *Psychological Science*, Vol. 11, No. 5, September 2000.

Paulmann S., Jessen S. & Kotz S. A., Investigating the Multimodal Nature of Human Communication Insights from ERPs, *Journal of Psychophysiology*, Vol. 23, No. 2, 2009.

Penhune V. B., Cismaru R., Dorsaint-Pierre R., Petitto L. A. & Zatorre R. J., The Morphometry of Auditory Cortex in the Congenitally Deaf Measured Using MRI, *Neuroimage*, Vol. 20. No. 2, October 2003.

Piaget J., *The origins of intelligence in children*. New York: International Universities Press, 1952.

Poliakoff E., Ashworth S., Lowe C. & Spence C., Vision and Touch in Ageing: Crossmodal Selective Attention and Visuotactile Spatial Interactions, *Neuropsychologia*, Vol. 44, No. 4, February 2006.

Pons F., Lewkowicz D. J., Soto-Faraco S. & Sebastián-Gallés N., Narrowing of Intersensory Speech Perception in Infancy, *Proceedings of the National Academy of Sciences USA*, No. 106, 2009.

Pourtois G., De Gelder B., Vroomen J., Rossion B. & Crommelinck M., The Time-course of Intermodalbinding between Seeing and Hearing Affective Information, *Neuroreport*, Vol. 11, No. 6, April 2000.

Proverbio A. M. & De Benedetto F., Auditory Enhancement of Visual Memory Encoding is Driven by Emotional Content of the Auditory Material and Mediated by Superior Frontal Cortex, *Biological Psychology*, No. 132, February 2018.

Raab D. H., Statistical Facilitation of Simple Reaction Times, *Transactions of the New York Academy of Sciences*, Vol. 24, March 1962.

Raymond V. E., Boxtel J. J. A. V., Parker A. L. & David A., Multisensory Congruency as a Mechanism for Attentional Control over Perceptual Selection, *Journal of Neuroscience the Official Journal of the Society for Neuroscience*, Vol. 29, No. 37, September 2009.

Rhodes S. M. & Donaldson D. I., Association and not Semantic Relationships Elicit the N400 Effect: Electrophysiological Evidence from an Explicit Language Comprehension Task, *Psychophysiology*, Vol. 45, No. 1, Jannuary 2008.

Rosenblum L. D., Schmuckler M. A. & Johnson J. A., The McGurk Effect in Infants, *Perception and Psychophysics*, Vol. 59, No. 3, April 1997.

Ritter W., Simson R. & Vaughan H. Effects of theAmount of Atimulus Information Processed on Negative Event-related Potentials, *Electroencephalography & Clinical Neurophysiology*, Vol. 28, No. 69, March 1988.

Rizzolatti G. & Craighero L., The Mirror Neuron System, *Annual Review* of Neuroscience, No. 27, 2004.

Rockland K. S. & Ojima H., Multisensory Convergence in Calcarine Visual Areas in Macaque Monkey, Iternational Journal of Psychophysiology, Vol. 50, No. 1, October 2003.

Romei V., Murray M. M., Cappe C. & Thut G., Preperceptual and Stimulus-selective Enhancement of Low-level Human Visual Cortex Excitability by Sounds, Current Biology, Vol. 19, No. 21, November 2009.

Romei V., Murray M. M., Cappe C. & Thut G., The Contributions of Sensory Dominance and Attentional Bias to Cross-modal Enhancement of Visual Cortex Excitability, Journal of Cognitive Neuroscience, Vol. 25. No. 7, July 2013.

Romei V., Murray M. M., Merabet L. B. & Thut G., Occipital Transcranial Magnetic Stimulation Has Opposing Effects on Visual and Auditory Stimulus Detection: Implications for Multisensory Interactions, The Journal of neuroscience, Vol. 27, No. 43, November 2007.

Romei V., Murray M. M., Merabet L. B. & Thut G., Occipital Transcranial Magnetic Stimulation Has Opposing Effects on Visual and Auditory Stimulus Detection: Implications for Multisensory Interactions, The Journal of neuroscience, Vol. 27, No. 43, November 2007.

Ross L. A., Saint-Amour D., Leavitt V. M., Javitt D. C. & Foxe J. J., Do You See What I am Saying? Exploring Visual Enhancement of Speech Comprehension in Noisy Environments, Cerebral Cortex, Vol. 17, No. 5, May 2007.

Ross L. A., Saint-Amour D., Leavitt V. M., Molholm S., Javitt D. C. & Foxe J. J., Impaired Multisensory Processing in Schizophrenia: Deficits in the Visual Enhancement of Speech Comprehension under

Noisy Environmental Conditions, *Schizophrenia Research*, Vol. 97, No. 1 – 3, December 2008.

Rouger J., Fraysse B., Deguine O. & Barone P., McGurk Effects in Cochlear-implanted Deaf Subjects, *Brain Research*, No. 1188, January 2008.

Rouger J., Lagleyre S., Fraysse B., Deneve S., Deguine O. & Barone P., Evidence that Cochlearimplanted Deaf Patients are Better Multisensory Integrators, *Proceedings of the National Academy of Sciences USA*, Vol. 104, No. 17, April 2007.

Rowland B. A. & Stein B. E., A Model of the Temporal Dynamics of Multisensory Enhancement, *Neuroscience & Biobehavioral Reviews*, No. 41, April 2014.

Sai F. Z., The Role of the Mother's Voice in Developing Mother's Face Preference: Evidence for Intermodal Perception at Birth, *Infant and Child Development*, No. 14, 2005.

Saint-Amour D., De Sanctis P., Molholm S., Ritter W. & Foxe J. J., Seeing Voices: High-density Electrical Mapping and Source-analysis of the Multisensory Mismatch Negativity Evoked during the McGurk Illusion, *Neuropsychologia*, Vol. 45, No. 3, February 2007.

Santangelo V. & Spence C., Multisensory Cues Capture Spatial Attention Regardless of Perceptual Load, *Journal of Experimental Psychology: Human Perception and Performance*, Vol. 33, No. 6, December 2007.

Santangelo V., VanDer Lubbe R. H., Belardinelli M. O. & Postma A., Multisensory Integration Affects ERP Components Elicited by Exogenous Cues, *Experimental Brain Research*, Vol. 185, No. 2, February 2008.

Sarko D. K., Nidiffer A. R., Powers I. I. I. A. R., Ghose D. &

Wallace M. T., "*Spatial and Temporal Features of Multisensory Processes*," in *The Neural Basis of Multisensory Processes*, ed M. M. Murray and M. T. Wallace (Boca Raton, FL: CRC Press), 2012.

Schelenz P. D., Klasen M., Reese B., Regenbogen C., Wolf D., Kato Y. & Mathiak K., Multisensoryintegration of Dynamic Emotional Faces and Voices: Method for Simultaneous EEG-fMRI Measurements, *Frontiers in Human Neuroscience*, Vol. 7, No. 1, 2013.

Schroeder C. E., Lindsley R. W., Specht C., Marcovici A., Smiley J. F. & Javitt D. C., Somatosensory Input to Auditory Association Cortex in the Macaque Monkey, *Journal of Neurophysiology*, Vol. 85, No. 3, March 2001.

Schorr E. A., Fox N. A., Van Wassenhove V. & Knudsen E. I., Auditory-visual Fusion in Speech Perception in Children with Cochlear Implants, *Proceedings of the National Academy of Sciences USA*, Vol. 102, No. 51, December 2005.

Sekiyama K. & Tohkura Y., McGurk Effect in Non-English Listeners: Few Visual Effects for Japanese Subjects Hearing Japanese Syllables of High Auditory Intelligibility, *Journal of the Acoustical Society of America*, Vol. 90, No. 4, October 1991.

Senkowski D., Saint-Amour D., Gruber T. & Foxe J. J., Look Whos Talking: The Deployment of Visuo-spatial Attention during Multisensory Speech Processing under Noisy Environmental Conditions, *Neuroimage*, Vol. 43, No. 2, November 2008.

Senkowski D., Talsma D., Grigutsch M., Herrmann C. S. & Woldorff M. G., Good Times for Multisensory Integration: Effects of the Precision of Temporal Synchrony as Revealed by Gamma-band Oscillations, *Neuropsychologia*, Vol. 45, No. 3, February 2007.

Sekuler R. , Sekuler A. B. & Lau R. , Sound Alters Visual Motion Perception, *Nature*, Vol. 385, No. 6614, January 1997.

Shams L. , Kamitani Y. & Shimojo S. , What You See is What You Hear, *Nature*, Vol. 408, No. 6814, December 2000.

Shams L. , Kamitani Y. , Thompson S. & Shimojo S. , Sound Alters Visual Evoked Potentials in Humans, *Neuroreport*, Vol. 12, No. 17, December 2001.

Shams L. , Iwaki S. , Chawla A. & Bhattacharya J. , Early Modulation of Visual Cortex by Sound: An MEG Study. *Neuroscience Letters*, Vol. 378, No. 2, April 2005.

Shimojo S. & Shams L. , Sensory Modalities are Not Separate Modalities: Plasticity and Interactions, *CurrentOpinion in Neurobiology*, Vol. 11, No. 4, September 2001.

Slutsky D. A. & Recanzone G. H. , Temporal and Spatial Dependency of the Ventriloquism Effect, *Neuroreport*, Vol. 12, No. 1, January 2001.

Smith E. G. & Bennetto L. , Audiovisual Speech Integration and Lipreading in Autism, *Journal of Child Psychology and Psychiatry*, Vol. 48, No. 8, August 2007.

Small D. M. & Prescott J. Odor/taste Integration and the Perception of Flavor, *Experimental Brain Research*, Vol. 166, No. 3, October 2005.

Snowling M. J. , The Development of Grapheme-phoneme Correspondence in Normal and Dyslexic Readers, *Journal of Experimental Child Psychology*, Vol. 29, No. 2, April 1980.

Soto-Faraco S. , Lyons J. , Gazzaniga M. , Spence C. & Kingstone A. , The Ventriloquist in Motion: Illusory Capture of Dynamic Information across Sensory Modalities, *Brain Research. Cognitive Brain Research*,

Vol. 14, No. 1, June 2002.

Spence C., Audiovisual Multisensory Integration, *Acoustical Science and Technology*, Vol. 28, No. 2, March 2007.

Spence C. & Driver J., Crossmodal Space and Crossmodal Attention, Oxford, New York, U.S.A.: Oxford University Press, 2004.

Spence C. & Squire S., Multisensory Integration: Maintaining the Perception of Synchrony, *Current Biology*, Vol. 13, No. 13, August 2003.

Spierer L., Manuel A. L., Bueti D. & Murray M. M., Contributions of Pitch and Bandwidth to Sound-induced Enhancement of Visual Cortex Excitability in Humans, *Cortex*, Vol. 49, No. 10, January 2013.

Stanford T. R. & Stein B. E., Superadditivity in Multisensory Integration: Putting the Computation in Context, *Neuroreport*, Vol. 18, No. 8, May 2007.

Stein B. E., London N., Wilkinson L. K. & Price D. D., Enhancement of Perceived Visual Intensity by Auditory Stimuli: A Psychophysical Analysis, *Journal of Cognitive Neuroscience*, No. 8, November 1996.

Stein B. E. & Meredith M. A., *The merging of thesenses*. Cambridge: MIT Press. 1993.

Stein B. E. & Stanford T. R., Multisensory Integration: Current Issues from the Perspective of the Single Neuron, *Nature Reviews Neuroscience*, Vol. 9, No. 4, April 2008.

Stein B. E., Stanford T. R., Ramachandran R., Jr Perrault T. J. & Rowland B. A., Challenges in Quantifying Multisensory Integration: Alternative Criteria, Models, Andinverse Effectiveness, *Experimental Brain Research*, Vol. 198, No. 2 – 3, September 2009.

Streri A., Tactile Discrimination of Shape and Intermodal Transfer in 2-to 3-month – old Infants, *British Journal of Developmental Psychology*, No. 5, 1987.

Streri A. & Gentaz E., Crossmodal Recognition of Shape from Hand to Eyes in Human Newborns, *Somatosensory and Motor Research*, No. 20, 2003.

Steve G., Caroline C., Donna L. & Charles S., Audiotactile Interactions in Roughness Perception, *Experimental Brain Research*, Vol. 146, No. 2, September 2002.

Stevenson R. A., Altieri N. A., Kim S., Pisoni D. B. & James T. W., Neural Processing of Asynchronous Audiovisual Speech Perception, *Neuroimage*, Vol. 49, No. 4, Februaty 2010.

Stevenson R. A., Ghose D., Fister J. K., Sarko D. K., Altieri N. A., Nidiffer A. R. ...& Wallace M. T., Identifying and Quantifying Multisensory Integration: A Tutorial Review, *Brain Topography*, Vol. 27, No. 6, April 2014.

Su Y. H., Content Congruency and Its Interplay with Temporal Synchrony Modulate Integration between Rhythmic Audiovisual Streams, *Frontiers in Integrative Neuroscience*, No. 8, February 2014.

Talsma D., Predictive Coding and Multisensory Integration: An Attentional Account of the Multisensory Mind. *Frontiers in Integrative Neuroscience*, Vol. 26, No. 6, March 2015.

Talsma D., Doty T. J. & Woldorff M. G., Selective Attention and Audiovisual Integration: Is Attending to Both Modalities A Prerequisite for Early Integration, *Cerebral Cortex*, Vol. 17, No. 3, March 2007.

Talsma D. & Woldorff M. G., Selective Attention and Multisensory Integration: Multiple Phases of Effects on the Evoked Brain Activity, *Journal of*

Cognitive Neuroscience, Vol. 17, No. 7, July 2005.

Teder-Salejarvi W. A., McDonald J. J., Di Russo F. & Hillyard S. A., An Analysis of Audio-visual Crossmodal Integration by Means of Event-related Potential (ERP) Recordings, *Cognitive Brain Research*, Vol. 14, No. 1, January 2002.

Teder-Sälejärvi W., Russo F. D., McDonald J. J. & Hillyard S., Effects of Spatial Congruity on Audio-visual Multimodal Integration, *Journal of Cognitive Neuroscience*, Vol. 17, No. 9, September 2005.

Ten Oever S., Sack A. T., Wheat K. L., Bien N. & Van Atteveldt N., Audio-visual onset Differences are Used to Determine Syllable Identity for Ambiguous Audio-visual Stimulus Pairs, *Frontiers in Psychology*, No. 4, June 2013.

VanDer Burg E., Olivers C. N., Bronkhorst A. W. & Theeuwes J., Audiovisual Events Capture Attention: Evidence from Temporal Order Judgments, *Journal of Vision*, Vol. 8, No. 5, May 2008.

VanDer Burg E., Olivers C. N., Bronkhorst A. W. & Theeuwes J., Poke and Pop: Tactile-visual Synchrony Increases Visual Saliency, *Neuroscience Letters*, Vol. 450, No. 1, January 2009.

VanDer Stelt O., Kok A., Smulders F. T. Y., Snel J. & Gunning B., Cerebral Event-related Potentials Associated with Selective Attention to Color: Developmental Changes from Childhood to Adulthood, *Psychophysiology*, Vol. 35, No. 3, May 1998.

Van Ee R., Van Boxtel J. J., Parker A. L. & Alais D., Multisensory Congruency as a Mechanism for Attentional Control over Perceptual Selection, *The Journal of Neuroscience*, Vol. 29, No. 37, September 2009.

Vatakis A. & Spence C., Crossmodal Binding: Evaluating the "Unity

Assumption" Using Audiovisual Speech Stimuli, *Percept. Psychophys*, Vol. 69, No. 5, July 2007.

Vidal J., Giard M. H., Roux S., Barthelemy C. & Bruneau N., Cross-modal Processing of Auditory-visual Stimuli in a No-task Paradigm: A Topographic Event-related Potential Study, *Clinical Neurophysiology*, Vol. 119, No. 4, April 2008.

Vogel E. K. & Luck S. J., The Visual N1 Component as an Index of a Discrimination Process, *Psychophysiology*, No. 37, March 2000.

Vroomen J. &De Gelder B., Sound Enhances Visual Perception: Cross-modal Effects of Auditory Organization on Vision, *Journal of Experimental Psychology: Human Perception and Performance*, Vol. 26, No. 5, October 2000.

Vroomen J., Bertelson P. &De Gelder B., Directing Spatial Attention towards the Illusory Location of a Ventriloquized Sound, *ActaPsychologica*, Vol. 108, No. 1, June 2001.

Vroomen J., Bertelson P. &De Gelder B., The Ventriloquist Effect does not Depend on the Direction of Automatic Visual Attention, *Perception & Psychophysics*, Vol. 63, No. 4, May 2001.

Welch R. B. & Warren D. H., Immediate Perceptual Response to Intersensory Discrepancy, *Psychological Bulletin*, Vol. 88, No. 3, November 1980.

Walla P., Olfaction and Its Dynamic Influence on Word and Face Processing: Cross-modal Integration, *Progress in Neurobiology*, Vol. 84, No. 2, February 2008.

Wallace M. T., Meredith M. A. & Stein B. E., Multisensory Integration in the Superior Colliculusof the Alert Cat, *Journal of Neurophysiology*, Vol. 80, No. 2, August 1998.

Wallace M. T. & Stein B. E., Development of Multisensory Neurons and Multisensory Integration Incat Superior Colliculus, *Journal of Neuroscience*, Vol. 17, April 1997.

Wallace M. T. & Stein B. E., Sensory and Multisensory Responses in the Newborn Monkeysuperior Colliculus, *Journal of Neuroscience*, Vol. 21, No. 22, November 2001.

Watanabe K. & Shimojo S., Attentional Modulation in Perception of Visual Motion Events, *Perception*, Vol. 27, No. 9, 1998.

Watanabe K. & Shimojo S., When Sound Affects Vision: Effects of Auditory Grouping on Visual Motion Perception, *Psychological Science*, Vol. 12, No. 2, March 2001.

Welch R. B. & Warren D. H., Immediate Perceptual Response to Intersensory Discrepancy, *Psychological Bulletin*, Vol. 88, No. 3, November 1980.

White T. L. & Prescott J., Chemosensory Cross-modal Stroop Effects: Congruent Odors Facilitate Taste Identification, *Chemical Senses*, Vol. 32, No. 4, May 2007.

Williams J. H., Massaro D. W., Peel N. J., Bossele A. & Suddendorf T., Visual-auditory Integration during Speech Imitation in Autism, *Research in Developmental Disabilities*, Vol. 25, No. 6, December 2004.

Wilschut A., Theeuwes J. & Olivers C. N., The Time Course of Attention: Selection is Transient, *PLoS One*, Vol. 6, No. 11, 2011.

Wright T. M., Pelphrey K. A., Allison T., McKeown M. J. & McCarthy G., Polysensory Interactions along Lateral Temporal Regions Evoked by Audiovisual Speech, *Cerebral Cortex*, Vol. 13, No. 10, Octtober 2003.

Yang W., Yang J., Gao Y., Tang X., Ren Y., Takahashi S., et al.,

Effects of SoundFrequency on Audiovisual Integration: An EventRelated Potential Study, *PLoS ONE*, Vol. 10, No. 9, September 2015.

Yeh P. W., Geangu E. & Reid V., Coherent Emotionalperception from Body Expressions and the Voice, *Neuropsychologia*, No. 91, October 2016.

Zampini M., Guest S., Shore D. I. & Spence C., Audio-visual Simultaneity Judgments, *Perception & Psychophysics*, Vol. 67, No. 3, April 2005.